There She Goes

There She Goes

FEMINIST FILMMAKING AND BEYOND

edited by CORINN COLUMPAR *and* SOPHIE MAYER

wayne state university press
detroit

13 12 11 10 09   5 4 3 2 1

Library of Congress Cataloging-in-Publication Data

There she goes : feminist filmmaking and beyond / edited by Corinn Columpar and Sophie Mayer.
p. cm. — (Contemporary approaches to film and television)
Includes bibliographical references and index.
ISBN 978-0-8143-3390-7 (pbk. : alk. paper)
1. Women motion picture producers and directors. 2. Motion pictures--Production and direction.
3. Feminism and motion pictures. 4. Feminist films—History and criticism. 5. Women in the
motion picture industry. 6. Women in motion pictures. I. Columpar, Corinn, 1970–
II. Mayer, Sophie, 1978–
PN1995.9.W6T42 2009
791.43082—dc22
2009010794

Typeset by Maya Rhodes
Composed in Adobe Garamond

FOR OUR MOTHERS

• • •

Contents

Acknowledgments

For institutional and intellectual support: the Cinema Studies Institute, Innis College, and the Department of English at University of Toronto; the Screen Media and Cultures Programme and Faculty of Modern and Medieval Languages at University of Cambridge; the Andrew W. Mellon Foundation (postdoctoral fund); and the Society for Cinema and Media Studies.

For generously agreeing to share their images: Maysam Makhmalbaf and Makhmalbaf Film House, Miranda July, Sally Potter and Adventure Pictures, Janie Geiser, Michelle Citron, Agnès Varda and Ciné-Tamaris, Killer Films and Strand Releasing, Tracey Moffatt and Women Make Movies, and Leslie Thornton.

For their valuable contributions to the publication process: all at Wayne State University Press, especially Barry Keith Grant, Annie Martin, Carrie Downes Teefey, Maya Rhodes, and Renae Morehead.

For their enterprise and enthusiasm: our contributors.

For ongoing encouragement: SF Said and Frederick Bartolovic.

Introduction

Corinn Columpar and Sophie Mayer

Looking at *Time Out London*'s film schedule for the weekend that we finalized this introduction, it seemed like our work had already been done. Due recognition was being accorded to the full spectrum of women's moving image work. On Saturday, January 12, 2008, New York underground art film *Variety* (Bette Gordon, 1982) screened at the Institute of Contemporary Arts, and it was followed by *Sex Positive,* a night of women's experimental short films and performance celebrating punk, pro-sex feminist Kathy Acker, organized by Club des Femmes.[1] On Sunday, the thirteenth, the British Film Institute, in a resonant coincidence, screened the silent feature *A Fool There Was* (Frank Powell, 1915), Theda Bara's definitional first screen outing as a "vamp" who enjoyed sexual power over men. Yet such events remain the exception rather than the rule, and women's involvement in cinema, from its earliest days to the cutting edge of the present, is rarely conceived as a continuous narrative. While *There She Goes: Feminist Filmmaking and Beyond* does not seek to offer a historiographical continuum, it stages systematically that which was sheer chance in the weekend described: contiguities across eras, genres, and oeuvres that place women at the center of moving image–making. In so doing it responds to two imperatives that also fuel contemporary screenings and, moreover, criticism of work like *A Fool There Was.*

The first imperative is that of remembering and thereby preserving work in danger of erasure. Kira Cochrane, writing in *The Guardian* about Bara, ended her article with a powerful and provocative analogy between the eradication of female cinematic pioneers and the loss of silent film: "Watching *A Fool There Was*—seeing just how magnetic Bara was in motion—makes you realise how ill-served those early silent stars have been. Around 80%, or even

1

90%, of silent films have now been lost, partly through neglect, partly due to the recycling of nitrate film, and partly because nitrate is more flammable than a matchstick. Only four of Bara's films survive, after a Fox storage facility exploded in 1937."[2] Yet it is not only women's output from the silent past that, like combustible and neglected silver nitrate, has been neglected and risks being lost; much of the more contemporary cinematic and para-cinematic work by women, particularly in time-based or site-specific genres such as installation or performance art, is likewise at risk.

The second imperative at issue is that of developing analytical tools and research agendas for work that challenges the classical paradigm deconstructed and, paradoxically enough, made normative by apparatus theory. In her contribution to a special issue of *Signs* from 2004, wherein a host of feminist film scholars assessed the state of the field, Patrice Petro notes the increasing frequency with which contemporary academics are turning their attention to figures like Bara and, more generally, early cinema. In an effort to explain this trend she not only points to the tremendous amount of "historical recovery and retrieval" that remains to be done when it comes to women's contributions to the film industry prior to its consolidation and standardization but also suggests that "early cinema affords insights into our own global media culture, that the early years of the twentieth century are remarkably prescient of our own modernity, and that the focus on women as producers, consumers, and historical agents allows for a more complex and expansive understanding of where we have been and where we are today."[3] In other words, insofar as the past of early cinema and the present of "convergence culture" approximate each other, they serve as sites for a productive cross-fertilization.[4] Just as a diversity of inclusive practices was able to flourish prior to the vertical integration of the American film industry, a number of new possibilities for feminist modes of production, distribution, exhibition, and spectatorship within and across platforms have prevailed amid the horizontal integration of global media industries.

While not a project dedicated to women film pioneers per se, *There She Goes* is nonetheless an act of recovery and retrieval since it foregrounds these new possibilities as well as their antecedents, be they of the preclassical or classical era. Indeed, the agenda of this volume is to examine the flows within and through feminist film culture by both foregrounding contemporary figures that embody the polymorphous potential of the present and revisiting, in order to re-vision, the past through a newly ground lens. The result is a collection of essays that draws attention to practices, texts, and producers whose interstitial nature makes them difficult to recognize in a discursive field conditioned by disciplinary divisions. Following in the footsteps of the filmmakers whose work it features, *There She Goes* seeks to make trouble not only in the archives but also at the boundaries—be they drawn around artistic, industrial, political, or critical practices.

A Gigantic Plan

When Rachel Kushner asked Miranda July what kind of project she intended to tackle in the wake of the success of her first feature-length film, *Me and You and Everyone We Know* (2005), July replied, with characteristic whimsy and sharp insight, "I have a gigantic plan, Rachel, and it involves performance, and fiction, and radio, and the www, and TV and features that are both 'conventional' and totally not. And when I'm done with my plan, when I'm very old, hopefully there will be a little more space for people living with profound doubt to tell their stories in all different mediums. Also Hollywood won't be so sexist."[5] Locating her work as a commercial filmmaker within a much larger field of cultural production and social change, July functions as an exemplar of a contemporary film culture wherein people and products are moving with increasing frequency among venues (gallery, theater, festival, and online), materials (celluloid and digital video), locales (including those in both the "First" and "Third" Worlds), modes of production (studio-financed and "independent," auteurist and collaborative), and artistic roles (actor, director, producer, and writer). A number of contemporary scholars have begun to investigate such flows within the context of studies dedicated to alternate industrial practices that have taken shape in creative response to Hollywood's continued domination of the global film market. Yet what is often occluded in these studies are the extensive contributions, both past and present, that women have made to such practices while struggling for access to cinematic means of production and integrating film into a broader program of aesthetic and political representation. In other words, what remains to be explored is the extent to which a number of material and ideological factors, including the sexism of Hollywood identified so baldly by July, has compelled women to engage in a particular mode of cultural production: one characterized by active and ongoing negotiation with and between a diverse range of artistic, political, and commercial paradigms.

There She Goes seeks to redress this lacuna by examining women's work at the interstices—be it between different branches of the film industry, modes of filmmaking, national or transnational contexts, exhibition media, or varieties of visual representation—in order to assess the fruits that such syncretic labors yield. In the process it contextualizes traditional screen cinema within a larger field of artistic production, which includes still photography, music videos, installation art, digital media, performance art, and dance. Moreover, it pays particular attention to a variety of contextual factors that shape such work, from the conditions of its production and circulation to its engagement with various social movements and critical traditions, including, but not limited to, feminism. The result is a body of critical work that is far more responsive to the vicissitudes and achievements of feminist cultural production than those studies that take the conventions of classical cinema and auteurist criticism as normative. In short, *There She Goes* announces a new appraisal of filmmaking that is tied to and celebratory of feminist notions of fluidity and reinvention, as well as their intellectual and affective potential for filmmakers and filmgoers alike.

Activ(ist) Viewing

In 2006, *Camera Obscura* followed in the footsteps of *Signs* by compiling an "Archive for the Future." The editors asked feminist scholars and practitioners to contribute reflections on the events, debates, and issues associated with the journal's past thirty years and, moreover, to connect imaginatively the theories and strategies represented by *Camera Obscura*'s continued existence to a feminist future. Among the contributions, Yvonne Rainer's stands out for its political urgency. Exploring "Mulvey's Legacy," Rainer exposits not the filmmaking practice that Laura Mulvey pioneered but rather feminist activism against threats to abortion rights. In doing so, Rainer extracts Mulvey's "Visual Pleasure and Narrative Cinema," along with its "Afterthoughts," from the rarefied atmosphere of theoretical introspection in which it is too often located and places it in a charged history.[6] She explicitly yokes Mulvey's reading of cinesemiotic violence against women on screen with a sociopolitical context of lived violence.

"Mulvey's Legacy" figures three ways in Rainer's article: as "a cri de coeur that was echoed in protests on both sides of the Atlantic," creating a community of feminist artists, thinkers, and activists that took to the street as well as the cinema and academy; as a utopian formulation instigated by that community in order to find alternate strategies with which to mobilize media-makers to resist hegemonic cultural representations; and as a challenge to a new generation of feminists to activate a similar triangulation of theory, practice, and activism.[7] In conclusion, Rainer states that she has "a yearning for the electrifying fervor—specifically feminist or not—of films made by directors working in those decades. . . . Whether or not these film/videomakers were influenced directly by Mulvey's essay is moot; its effects had already entered the charged air we breathed. The air I now breathe feels weighted with expectancy. I continue to be buoyed by that history, a history that feels about to erupt again. How did it happen then? What is to be done now?"[8]

There She Goes is formulated as a timely answer to Rainer's challenge and her questions, demonstrating a flow between accounts of "that moment" and studies of emergent practices. As with the filmmakers Rainer cites, Mulvey's essay is an influence throughout the book, but not a citation necessary to prove once again the validity and urgency of a feminist film theory. We take that point as given, and take as given as well the existence of multiple feminisms, both in the sense of theoretical approaches (psychoanalytic, new historicist, materialist) and intersectional alliances that allow for the critical interrogation of gender in congruence with other determinants of social power and position, including race and class. What is perhaps less given, and thus worth stating, are the dual threads that connect *There She Goes* to Rainer's challenge.

The first of these is the recognition of a need to imbricate historical investigation and documentation ("How did it happen then?") and futurological precepts or manifesta ("What is to be done now?"). Only Alison Hoffman's essay on Miranda July and affective communities names the moment of this book as post-9/11, yet all the essays respond rebelliously to those phenomena that Susan Faludi amply demonstrates to be commonplace in this era: the flagrant demonization of feminism, the severe curtailment of women's presence in the public sphere, the revivification of "sex-coded rescue language" in popular culture, and the steadfast refusal to grant issues of gender equity any political or social priority.[9] In short, in paying attention to the liberatory potential of specific counter-histories and strategies, the volume as a whole responds to what Rainer calls "the current ineptitudes and protofascist proclivities of [George W.] Bush and company."[10] In so doing it dovetails with the spate of recent work on the historical archive, politicizing the question of whose perspective gets remembered, documented, or memorialized, particularly in an era organized by cinematicity.

That organizing principle, which informs much of the work featured in this volume, from the remediation of silent cinema in Janie Geiser's work to digital archiving in Sally Potter's, entwines the second thread, which is the question of the spectator as agent, ably explored through spectatorship studies by Jackie Stacey and others. Rainer's move from Mulvey to marching suggests, however, that both feminist film theory and the films that responded to it motivated not only spectatorial agency in reformulating representation but also *political* agency by women equipped with a radical understanding of the intersections of representation and lived experience, particularly in its affective dimensions. Many of the texts examined in this volume express this sense of agency through the filmmaker's presence as an on-screen subject engaged in the politicization of herself, her work, and her spectators. Indeed, over half of the practitioners discussed position themselves reflexively as screen subjects: Sadie Benning, Michelle Citron, Maya Deren, Miranda July, Tracey Moffatt, Sally Potter, Cindy Sherman, Leslie Thornton, and Agnès Varda. By gathering emergent scholars who are interrogating the *auteure* as political agent, *There She Goes* strives to create the kind of affective feminist community that Rainer hopes will "erupt again."

Programming the Virtual Feminist Cinematheque

Based on the self-reflective projects initiated by both *Signs* and *Camera Obscura*, it would seem that feminist film scholarship is at a crossroads. Rainer's rereading notwithstanding, Mulvey's "Visual Pleasure" is typically regarded, especially by contemporary students encountering it for the first time, as a doctrinaire artifact of a bygone era. With its hermetic logic, its immaterial spectator, and its tight-lipped refusal of pleasure, it is utterly out of step with our current cultural climate. Yet it is still offered up in many contexts as the summation (and the summit?) of feminist film theory, as if nothing else had come in its wake. Of course, those of us working in the field know this is not the case; feminist film scholarship continues to take shape in concert with a plurality of methodological approaches: not only psychoanalysis, but also phenomenology, historical materialism, and cognitivism, among others. This proliferation of new film feminisms gestures to the need felt by so many in the field at this particular juncture to speak to where we are going and where we have been. While this volume does not propose to answer those directional questions definitively, it nonetheless signals a decisive shift, seemingly the same shift to which *Signs* and *Camera Obscura* were in part responding.

Like film theory at large, feminist film theory is being transformed by a return of the repressed, as many of the things that apparatus theory systematically sidelined—emotion, sensation, corporeality, and pleasure—are coming to the fore. While an attention to such matters could be regarded with suspicion as a turn toward the personal and idiosyncratic and thus away from the social and systemic, the essays in this volume suggest otherwise. Indeed, they collectively think through the politics of the palpable, retaining an investment in past paradigms, while nonetheless shoring up Griselda Pollock's contention that "*feminist* itself marks the virtual as a perceptual becoming of what is not yet actual. It is a *poïesis* of the future, not a simple programme of corrective demands."[11] For Pollock that poiesis takes shape in the concept of a virtual feminist museum, that is, "a research laboratory . . . daring to plot networks and transformative interactions between the images differently framed by feminist analysis and theory."[12] Insofar as its contents are inimical to both patriarchy and capitalism, the exhibition she mounts textually in *Encounters in the Virtual Feminist Museum* could never be housed within the museum; thus it is not virtual in the sense of cybernetic, but rather phantasmatic. It is in the spirit of Pollock's alternate institution that *There She Goes* proceeds: hence its status as a virtual feminist cinematheque programmed by two "aca-fans" for whom pleasure and critique are absolutely intertwined.[13]

The virtual cinematheque is, of course, unlimited, but the codex form is not. The program on offer here is constrained by the pragmatics of publication, from the unpredictable diffusion of a call for papers to the physical size of the volume. That it has achieved coherence is in great part due to the scholars included, who are deeply attuned to currents in contemporary thought and practice. That it is also, however, incomplete (and always would have to be) is the source of an editorial quandary. In particular, *There She Goes* offers limited recognition of the work of rising women directors from the Global South, such as Lucrecia Martel and Fanta Régina Nacro, and of women filmmakers of color in settler societies (Tracey Moffatt excepted); it only addresses the place of feminist pornography in the cinematheque in passing (specifically, in Kay Armatage's account of her programming choices for the Toronto International Film Festival); and, finally, it does not take up issues around the relationship between various film feminisms and transgender and transsexual filmmakers and theorists, nor does it address the migration of many U.S. women directors to serial (postfeminist?) television. In short, *There She Goes* offers one program within a contestatory, expansive, inclusive, and ongoing noninstitutional organizational principle that invites other curators to take up the challenge. As Michelle Citron creates work for "viewsers" (interactive viewer/users), so *There She Goes* contains within it the call for an active audience looking to go beyond the book's limits. While we gesture overtly to feminist futures, we do not account for all of them.

In curating a virtual season, we thus propose not a canon but a series of connectivities and flows between artists and texts, echoing the work done by the subjects included. Many of the films, videos, installations, and performances we feature are explicitly engaged in critical negotiations with the archive that are always focused on recovering and propelling feminist film into the future. In this sense, the artists similarly slip the boundary between fan and critic, as well as between spectator, producer, and programmer. While this mobility is patently true of many avant-garde practitioners, such as Jonas Mekas, it is—to use Melinda Barlow's phrase—"gender-poignant" due to the erasure of women's work, which often begins with their economic struggles to produce a substantial oeuvre. This erasure is redoubled by current critiques of auteurism, which proscribe the inscription of subjectivity and enunciation. *There She Goes* seeks to redress this excision without recourse to either the *politique des auteurs,* which positions the director as sole author of meaning, or auteur criticism's frequent insistence on biographical interpretation. Rather, we posit implicitly the idea of the *auteure* as a node, an agent participating in a poetics of exchange through cinematic labor of all kinds.[14] Auteurism is redefined through giving due consideration to the full extent of the work of the feminist *auteure:* foregrounding (feminized) labor excluded from the auteurial focus on filmmaking, such as curation, distribution, archiving, and programming. Engaged with the virtual feminist cinematheque, this labor always extends in a feminist gesture collaboratively, collectively, and connectively beyond the *auteure's* oeuvre.

Somehow the Vital Connection Is Made

There She Goes proceeds through connection: the book consists of seven sections, each containing two chapters paired for their specific resonances. While each pair addresses feminist filmmaking and what lies beyond it, each also responds to a particular kind of flow and connectivity. The first three sections explore this at the level of curation and exhibition, while the subsequent four consider local connections such as those between the film and the audience or between works within an oeuvre, down to those occurring on the surface of the film. Yet even across this midpoint divide in the book, there are connections: the latter sections conjoin their local concerns with an investigation of global networks, while the first three contain considerations of intimate exchanges as well as public ones.

Comprising "Continuities" are two essays that work together to trace a line of tactile descent from the experimental "body art" work of feminist artists in the 1970s through contemporary multimedia work that employs digital technologies for their horizon of politically productive possibilities: the capacity for interactivity and connectivity, the opportunity to re-member the past and re-vision the future. In "The Persistence of (Political) Feelings and Hand-Touch Sensibilities: Miranda July's Feminist Multimedia-Making" Alison Hoffman contextualizes July's varied body of work, which includes websites and video chain letters as well as a feature length film, within a larger history of feminist cultural production that extends back to the collaborative and interstitial art praxis of those women, like Carolee Schneemann and Yoko Ono, affiliated with Fluxus. In so doing, she locates July's work in a feminist tradition that links affect to politics and individual vulnerability to collective agency. As such, it emerges as the kind of productive response to the post-9/11 moment that Judith Butler has recently called for, a timely rejoinder to Rainer's assessment of utopia in her film *Privilege* (1990): "the harder it is to imagine, the more necessary it becomes." While Hoffman's article acknowledges the flows connecting second- and third-wave feminists, Sophie Mayer's "The Archivist Tango: Sally Potter Collects Herself" takes as its subject a filmmaker whose lengthy career defies such periodization. Informed by the impulse animating Potter's recent efforts to amass materials related to her films in an online interactive archive, Mayer's essay casts a retrospective glance across Potter's body of work in order to suggest that her entire career has been marked by a desire to refashion the archive along feminist lines through an emphasis on the place of performance, identified as ephemeral and affective, therein. The result is an archive in its own right, one wherein Mayer catalogs those gestures of resistance, both fleeting and enduring, corporeal and discursive, that lend Potter's work its charge.

Much like Potter, the two artists examined in "Interactions" are also engaged in work that is grounded in film yet opens out onto other forms: with her installation *The Spider's Wheels* (2006) Janie Geiser creates an interactive environment organized around the exploits of a hypothetical silent screen heroine, while Michelle Citron constructs database narratives with her recent series of CD-ROMs. Of primary concern to the essays in this section is the extent to which these works transform the spectatorial experience by allowing the viewer to negotiate actively her movement, be it through a multidimensional space (Geiser) or a multistrand narrative (Citron). In "Toward a Feminist Coney Island of the Avant-Garde: Janie Geiser Recasts the Cinema of Attractions," Melinda Barlow produces a richly evocative description of *The Spider's Wheels* as well as the multiple traditions on which it draws, including serial films from the teens, video installation art, and the cinema of attractions. In so doing she captures with tantalizing precision the myriad effects Geiser's work induces, ranging from the visceral to the ideological, the immediate to the lingering. Reflecting critically on her own work, Michelle Citron likewise foregrounds the experience of her viewers, whom she recasts as "viewsers" in light of their (inter)activity. Unlike so much new media scholarship, which forecasts into an elusive future, Citron's "Slipping the Borders/Shifting the Fragments: A Working Paper" is of the here and now, providing a glimpse into the critical and creative process to which CD-ROM technology gets pressed in the service of Citron's career-long agenda: the interrogation of narration, the experimentation with form, and the imbrication of the social and the psychological.

Given their subject matter, all four of the essays already introduced point beyond purely textual considerations to nontraditional models of circulation and exhibition. The two contributions in "Networks," however, take up such concerns explicitly by highlighting the efforts of women to create an infrastructure that supports women's filmmaking. First, Theresa L. Geller discusses Maya Deren's pioneering efforts in this vein in "'Each Film Was Built as a Chamber and Became a Corridor': Maya Deren's Film Aesthetics as Feminist Praxis." Employing a historiographical approach informed by Teresa de Lauretis's redefinition of the aesthetic, Geller argues that Deren's efforts in the 1950s to establish an independent film system, particularly through the Creative Film Foundation, constitute an extension of her filmmaking activities in the 1940s. Indeed, undergirding both initiatives is an overriding concern with the relations between the private and public spheres, a concern that only gained more urgency in the postwar era when women's domestication became a national priority in the United States. Concluding her essay with a nod toward Deren's enduring legacy, particularly in the founding of Circles Women in Distribution, Geller sets the scene perfectly for Kay Armatage's "Material Effects: Fashions in Feminist Programming," which begins with a first-hand account of a related phenomenon: the Women's Film Week at the 1972 Edinburgh International Film Festival. From there, Armatage constructs a genealogy of her own development as a programmer for the Toronto International Film Festival that is at turns anecdotal and analytical. The result is a fascinating account of feminist film culture from an insider's vantage, which lays bare the stakes involved in a job that entails a series of activities charged with political potential: cultivating niche audiences, championing underdog films, and framing popular discussions of culture and ideology at large.

The conversations made possible by film festivals are the focus of the following section, appositely titled "Dialogues." Through two essays focusing on a form long imbricated with feminist theory and practice—documentary—Mayer and Virginia Bonner draw attention to spectatorial engagement both as it is posited and shaped by the films of Kim Longinotto and Agnès Varda, and as it occurs in real viewing situations. In "Shooting for Change: An Interview with Kim Longinotto," the British director draws parallels between her working practice of sharing filmmaking credit with a local codirector to the situation in which she is filming and the kind of collaborative communities that she documents, as well as the kind of spectatorial connection that her films seek. Focusing her projects on questions of social change, particularly in Iran and Africa, Longinotto asserts the importance and formal

10

rigor of witnessing as a tool for social transformation. While her films are not campaigning, their strategic use of character and situation, she suggests, can form a bond between subject and viewer that creates the circumstances for joint political action. In "The Gleaners and 'Us': The Radical Modesty of Agnès Varda's *Les Glaneurs et la glaneuse*," Bonner titles this documentary practice "shooting in the second person," arguing that Varda—politicized but, like Longinotto, not polemical—interpellates the viewer through both verbal and visual address as "tu." This, she argues, places the middle-class viewers, whom she has observed at many screenings, in the position of the working poor gleaners who are the most prominent subjects of Varda's digital camera. Shooting herself—both in the sense of handling the camera and turning it on her own body—Varda practices a "radical modesty" by aligning herself with the gleaners, posing wittily as both gleaner and gleaned object in shots that raise questions about representations of the aging, laboring female body.

"Tableaux" features articles by Corinn Columpar and Michelle Meagher on two artists who take a stand before the camera as well as behind it: respectively, Tracey Moffatt and Cindy Sherman, both of whom defy conventions of photographic realism and subvert dominant cultural narratives with their work in, and between, photography and film. Responsive to these projects, the two essays are explicitly concerned with the way in which critical discourses position, and indeed gender, the relation between feature film and gallery photography. As Meagher's essay title, "Final Girls: Appropriation, Identification, and Fluidity in Cindy Sherman's *Office Killer*," suggests, she reads Sherman's neglected feature *Office Killer* (1997) through Carol Clover's feminist re-visioning of the slasher genre, connecting the genre's tropes, such as the "terrible place" and the "final girl," to Sherman's representational investigations of gender and cinema in her photographic oeuvre. Identifying Sherman with *Office Killer*'s "final girl" (who is also the monster/slasher), Meagher posits Clover's fluid identification, in which attacker and victim are "expressions of the same viewer," as a productive and profound thesis for understanding Sherman's feminist (r)use of the postmodernist pose.[15] An equally profound play with the embodied and gestural potential of the pose as it links the photographic and cinematic is at the heart of Columpar's "At the Limits of Visual Representation: Tracey Moffatt's Still and Moving Images." Arguing that the Australian artist pushes the limits of visual representation through precise deformations of narrative expectations that are as much racial and gendered as temporal and spatial, Columpar dis/articulates Moffatt's work as a radical refusal of suture. A reading of Moffatt's least conventional film, *beDevil* (1993), at the close level of the gesture and the speech act argues for both the film's vital place in Moffatt's oeuvre and its exemplary strategies of postcolonial enunciation.

Contestatory enunciation thematizes "Becomings," a section focused on the phenomenon of adolescent filmmakers' feminist resistance in two senses. First, Samira Makhmalbaf and Sadie Benning are the daughters of radical filmmakers (Mohsen Makhmalbaf and James Benning, respectively) who have both inherited and challenged their fathers' political and aesthetic models. Second, as SF Said and Chloé Hope Johnson explore, both filmmakers locate their aesthetic and activist compulsions not only within the national and cultural politics that shaped their fathers' filmmaking but within the politics of adolescence, gender, and sexuality as well. "'This Girl Behaves against It': An Interview with Samira Makhmalbaf" takes its title from Makhmalbaf's characterization of the protagonist of her film made in wartime Afghanistan, *At Five in the Afternoon* (2003). Makhmalbaf's eloquent answers, recorded at Cannes in 2003, a moment of hope for change within Iran, focus on her collaborative engagement with the subjects and performers of her films, often young women like herself, and the connection between access to self-expression for marginalized voices and the potential to generate political change, particularly via the media. Sadie Benning's project, which began by appropriating a Fisher Price camera as a tool for radical investigation of the cinematic presentation of the self, shares this dynamic connection between self-expression and activism with Makhmalbaf's work. As Johnson argues in "Becoming-Grrrl: The Voice and Videos of Sadie Benning," Benning has not only used many media (video, film, and live music) but has done so to represent and replicate a multiple sense of self as a resistant response to dominant culture's insistence on coherence. Johnson draws together recent feminist readings of Gilles Deleuze and Félix Guattari's "becoming-woman" to develop the figure of the "becoming-grrrl," for whom adolescence is a place of resistance engaging liminalities between child and adult, public and private, mediated and live. Johnson celebrates Benning's remediations and intertextual citations of pop culture as a subversion of corporate media's (hetero)normativity and thus an insistently politicized statement of a queer adolescent desire.

The politics of desire pulse through the book's final section, "Surfacings." Homay King and Elizabeth Watkins carefully peel back layers of image and sound to address alternative mobilizations of conventional images of femininity and the supposed conundrum of female desire. King's "Translating Orientalism: Leslie Thornton's *Adynata*" explores the way in which the film title's statement of the impossibility of speech is formally subverted through a complex layering of found sound and images whose surprising conjunctions and disjunctions query viewer expectations about an Orientalized femininity that circulates widely throughout the West. King's carefully contextualized reading historicizes Thornton's deliberate play with connections between images of Eastern women and signification itself. Rather than reading the film as three-dimensional narrative space, King focuses on the film's negotiations with materiality, drawing together the textual and the textural to conceive of the film as *fabric*. In the process she sites Thornton's historical interventions in the warp and weft, rather than just the images, of the film's tapestry, and thereby emphasizes the fugitive, indeed fluid, nature of meaning. In "Color and Fluids: The (In)Visibility of *The Portrait of a Lady*" Watkins follows a thread of materiality through Jane Campion's *The Portrait of a Lady* (1996), arguing for the film's use of fluids as a distinctive modeling of female subjectivity. As against Mary Ann Doane's "thematic of fluids," Watkins investigates Luce Irigaray's insistence on the irreducible bodiliness of fluidity to motivate a thorough reading of fluids at all levels of film form. Rather than profilmic fluids, Watkins foregrounds the actual fluids of film processing and the formal choices in lighting and sound that affect their manifestation in the print. Watkins draws out this chemical effect to reveal its representation of character affect as both feminine and feminist in its conjuration of protagonist Isabel's embodied perception.

"Gorgeously Imagined Riches"

Explicitly linking fluidity with the material over and beyond the metaphorical or metaphysical and thereby offering up new horizons of critical possibility, Watkins's essay is a fitting conclusion to *There She Goes*. In *Portrait* both Isabel and her step-daughter, Pansy, measure themselves against the "portrait of a lady" that remains the standard of female representation in Euro-Western art and culture. Yet what Campion uncovers with her version of this scenario and, more generally, with her re-vision of the canon is the act of emergence—the "becoming grrrl"—therein. Campion sums up the affective power of such images of resistant potential in her introduction to the 2008 Virago edition of Janet Frame's autobiography *An Angel at My Table*, whose cinematic adaptation brought Campion to international prominence. Writing of her adolescent first encounter with Frame's work, through the short story collection *Owls Do Cry*, Campion identifies exactly the "poetic, powerful, and fated" resonance that each essay in *There She Goes* sounds with its subject. "It was this inner world of gorgeously imagined riches that Janet affirmed in Daphne [a character in *Owls*], but also in me, and quite probably in all sensitive teenage girls. We had been given a voice, poetic, powerful and fated—a beautiful, mysterious song of the soul."[16] Critically connecting her own imaginary to Frame's celebration of adolescent femininity as pleasurable excess (rather than lack), Campion refuses the logic not only of psychoanalysis but also of a critical practice that isolates the *auteure* and further separates critic from filmmaker on the one hand and fan on the other. *There She Goes* puts forward the "aca-fan" and artist-curator as dynamic vectors whose "gigantic plan" combines a resistance to corporate and technological globalization with an embrace of its myriad flows, insisting on the importance of collaboration, connection, affect, networks, and boundary crossing for feminist filmmaking and beyond.

Notes

1. London-based moving image media feminist curators Club des Femmes "are a positive female space for the re-examination of ideas through art. In the age of the sound-bite, Club Des Femmes is a much-needed open platform for more radical contextualisation and forward-looking future vision: a chance to look beyond the mainstream." http://clubdesfemmes.blogspot.com.

2. Kira Cochrane, "If Looks Could Kill," *The Guardian,* January 10, 2008, http://film.guardian.co.uk/features/featurepages/0,,2238272,00.html.

3. Patrice Petro, "Reflections on Feminist Film Studies, Early and Late," *Signs: Journal of Women in Culture and Society* 30, no. 1 (2004): 1273, 1274.

4. In employing the term "convergence culture" here, we not only invoke the foundational work of media theorist Henry Jenkins but also acknowledge the extent to which this term has come to serve as shorthand for the enormous changes wrought by the digital revolution in conjunction with globalization. See Henry Jenkins, *Convergence Culture: Where Old and Media Collide* (New York: New York University Press, 2006).

5. Rachel Kushner, "Miranda July," *BOMB* 92 (Summer 2005), http://bomb-site.com/issues/92/articles/2739.

6. "Visual Pleasure and Narrative Cinema," *Screen* 16, no. 3 (1975): 6–18; "Afterthoughts on 'Visual Pleasure and Narrative Cinema' Inspired by *Duel in the Sun*," *Framework* 15/16/17 (Summer 1981): 12–15.

7. Yvonne Rainer, "Mulvey's Legacy," *Camera Obscura* 21, no. 3 (2006): 168.

8. Ibid., 169.

9. Susan Faludi, *The Terror Dream: Fear and Fantasy in Post-9/11 America* (New York: Metropolitan Books, 2007).

10. Rainer, "Mulvey's Legacy," 169.

11. Griselda Pollock, *Encounters in the Virtual Feminist Museum: Time, Space, and the Archive* (London: Routledge, 2007), 10.

12. Ibid., 11.

13. The term "aca-fan" was coined by Henry Jenkins to denote "a hybrid creature

which is part fan and part academic," in "Confessions of an Aca-Fan: The Official Weblog of Henry Jenkins," http://henryjenkins.org/aboutme.html.

14. For a thorough account of the feminist politics of the term *auteure,* see Corinn Columpar, "The Dancing Body: Sally Potter as Feminist Auteure" in *Women Filmmakers: Refocusing,* ed. Jacqueline Levitin, Judith Plessis, and Valerie Raoul (Vancouver: University of British Columbia Press, 2003). Potter's self-reflexive narration in *The Tango Lesson,* which foregrounds intersubjectivity and embodiment, prompts Columpar to name the filmmaker an *auteure* and thereby to mark the difference of her approach from that of male auteurs who are defined in terms of singularity and authority (108). We adopt this term here to reflect how all the filmmakers discussed pursue, in their own ways, Potter's dual aim in *Tango,* at once naming herself as a creative artist and representing the collaborative nature of the creative act.

15. Carol Clover, "Her Body, Himself: Gender in the Slasher Film," in *Screening Violence,* ed. Stephen Prince (New Brunswick, NJ: Rutgers University Press, 2000), 130.

16. Jane Campion, introduction to *An Angel at My Table,* by Janet Frame (London: Virago, 2008), ix.

Continuities

Alison Hoffman

Chapter 1

The Persistence of (Political) Feelings and Hand-Touch Sensibilities

Miranda July's Feminist Multimedia-Making

Recent alternative media practices by young feminist artists in the United States, exemplified by Miranda July's media texts, advance the commitment to coalitional politics and media practices forged by feminist filmmakers and artists during the 1960s and 1970s. Like the collaborative, conceptual, and instructional (film) art of Carolee Schneemann and Yoko Ono, July's various projects and films engage in and imagine the possibilities of feminist multimedia-making. Through a dialogic "hand-touch sensibility," July's work promotes an embodied form of spectatorship and interactivity by privileging and imaging female bodies and desires, citing their multiple vulnerabilities as sources of both political and personal agency. Tracing the sticky, hand-touch sensibilities of July's work to Schneemann's and Ono's underscores the aesthetic and ethical connections across the second and third waves of feminist multimedia-making. Yet even with these connections to past feminist texts, July's work is anything but derivative. With her sticky fingers on the pulse of the affective dimensions of contemporary digital media and its ability to bring people together in all sorts of productive (usually odd and sometimes perverse) interdependencies, July's work simultaneously updates the meaning of feminist embodied interactivity while commenting on the United States' current political fears of contamination and threats to our "homeland security," bodily and otherwise. July's work builds out from the strategies of past feminist artists attuned to the agency of female bodies and flesh laid bare, and in doing so it produces a bold new present and future for feminist art and media praxis.

Reverberating Feminist (Art) Histories and Desires

In 1975, at the height of the feminist art movement in the United States, the experimental artist and filmmaker Carolee Schneemann performed what is now the most widely reproduced and discussed of her body art pieces, *Interior Scroll*. At the *Women Here and Now* program held at a church in Long Island, Schneemann's performance condensed her art's political themes and formalist concerns and integrated the criticisms she had received in the art world since her involvement with Fluxus in the early 1960s. Entering the performance space covered in a sheet, wearing a kitschy apron underneath, Schneemann proceeded to disrobe. Standing tall on a table, becoming a sculpture in the flesh, she brushed strokes of dark paint onto her body and then began reading from her book *Cézanne, She Was a Great Painter* while striking "action poses." Dropping the book, Schneemann widened her legs, bent her knees, and then gingerly pulled a long scroll of text from her vagina. She read it aloud: "I met a happy man / a structuralist film maker—but don't call me that / it's something else I do—he said we are fond of you / you are charming but don't ask us / to look at your films we cannot / there are certain films we cannot look at / the personal clutter the persistence of feelings / the hand-touch sensibility." Fully self-exposed, vulnerable, and defiant of her critics' charges of "excess," Schneemann's performance interrogates how sexism functioned as the dominant organizing and structuring force in the art world and its discourse prior to and during the 1970s. In the words of performance theorist Jeanie Forte, "it seems as though [Schneemann's] vagina itself is reporting sexism."[1] Certainly, Schneemann's vaginal reportage speaks to the ways that "feminist consciousness allowed women artists to see how completely the representational circulation of the female body before 1970 had existed on the level of spectacle, metaphor, fetish, object, property, vessel, caricature, and symbol."[2] At the same time, Schneemann's performance reclaims the body of the female nude, granting her agency, corporeal action, and voice. Her body and voice, even in such a vulnerable state of exposure, produce an abundance of material and discursive meanings that challenge the idea that a woman's body is lacking in any way.

Schneemann's corporeal live performances, art pieces, and earlier films helped lay the groundwork for the feminist art movement to come: a movement that eschewed formalist dogmas and embraced cross-media production methods and practices. Once the feminist art movement was in full swing, Schneemann continued to use the specific, contextual materiality of her own body to critique the institutions of patriarchy, capitalism, racism, and war while imagining new ways of "speaking the female body differently."[3] Schneemann, like so many feminist artists during the 1970s, also penned lengthy communiqués that took the female body as the starting point for a radical transformation of social values and behaviors. She not only wanted to transform the competitive practices in the art world but also envisioned creating larger communities grounded in cooperation and equity.[4] This ethic of noncompetition and interdependence carried over into the production methods of many women artists and filmmakers working during the 1970s. For them, collaboration became a "political act and a creative first choice."[5] Throughout the first years of the decade, many of these women programmed feminist film festivals, "met in small groups, started newsletters, opened co-operative galleries, [and] published alternative art magazines in an astonishing outpouring of energy."[6]

Collaboration, an ethics of interdependence, embracing cross-media practices, speaking politics, engaging the female body and granting it full subjectivity, "the persistence of feelings, the hand-touch sensibility": these desires and tenets of the second-wave feminist art movement continue to be embraced by contemporary third-wave feminist artists and media-makers, though the rhetoric of postfeminism and vulgar "anti-essentialism" would often have us believe otherwise.[7] "Bad girl" art and riot grrrl media of the 1990s appropriated the desires, tenets, and theories of the second-wave artists, and complicated them by emphasizing issues of race and sexuality while experimenting with abjection and gender-queering. In the new millennium, contemporary feminist and queer artists/media-makers "possess a sharp generational self-reflexivity . . . traversing subcultural, academic, and high art references with remarkable ease and a keen sense of their historical precursors."[8]

As recently as 2003, for example, Emily Roysdon, artist and co-editor of the journal *LTTR (Lesbians to the Rescue)*, performed a differentiated reenactment of Schneemann's *Interior Scroll* at the Miss Lower East Side Beauty Pageant in New York, hosted by drag king Murray Hill. Stripping off a floral-print jumper and high heels, Roysdon unrolled her self-authored text, "Democracy, Invisibility, and the Dramatic Arts," from her vagina and recited it with authority, invoking Schneemann's bodily, poetic enunciation.[9] Roysdon's lovingly queered and updated reenactment of *Interior Scroll* exemplifies how feminist art and media of the past reverberates in present third-wave and queer work. This reverberating art and media is not simply derivative of work produced in the 1960s and 1970s; nor should it be read as a (teleo)logical point in the linear history of U.S. feminism. Instead, these reverberations between past and present feminist art and media open up the entirety of the work, allowing us to access historical (con)texts in new ways. Contemporary feminist and queer work is always changing the history of feminism's past, just as the (ever-fluctuating) work from the past imbues feminism's present—sometimes with the "shock of the new," as the reception of Roysdon's reenactment suggests.

Yet it is perhaps in the work of cross-media artist Miranda July that these reverberating feminist (art) histories and desires can be most intensely felt, heard, and seen. Creating a diversity of feminist art and media since the mid-1990s, July requires classification in a category as expansive and all-encompassing as "cross-media artist," since she has produced everything from sound art, experimental videos, multimedia performance art, and short stories to an award-winning independent feature film, along with developing a series of video chain letters and an international online web project. Moving across and between the riot grrrl/punk/indie scene, art and experimental film community, independent cinema milieu, and literary world, July's multimedia-making serves as a reminder of feminist art/media's indiscretion and fluidity. The limited categories of "performance artist," "experimental filmmaker," or "writer" cannot be used to designate the multitude of work July performs. Like the work of so many feminist multimedia-makers of the past and present, July's necessitates the use of conjunctions.

While July's work is informed by the second wave feminist art movement's key tenets and desires (and therefore enlivens and renews them), it also appropriates and alters them to address effectively/affectively our contemporary historical moment's sociopolitical issues. Responding to a contemporary U.S. culture and politics that largely teaches and privileges domination, violence, and suspicion, July's work activates the persistence of feelings and hand-touch sensibilities both to model and to build coalitions that locate agency in a shared openness and (bodily) vulnerability. The result is a progressive "commonality of feeling" rather than a strictly identity-based community.[10] Through an analysis of July's coalition-building media projects, Joanie 4 Jackie (1995–present) and Learning to Love You More (2003–present), and an exploration of the affective elements and structure of her film *Me and You and Everyone We Know* (2005), it becomes clear how her feminist media-making—like Schneemann's—"offers a chance to start to imagine a world in which that violence might be minimized, in which an inevitable interdependency becomes acknowledged as the basis for . . . political community."[11]

Collaboration/Compilation/Coalition

BODY SOUND TAPE PIECE
Make body sound tapes of different
people at different times.
Of the old, young, crying, longing,
excited, calm, doubtful, etc.
—Yoko Ono, Spring 1964

Like Carolee Schneemann, Yoko Ono aligned her (body) art and filmmaking with Fluxus and New Left politics throughout the 1960s, and then with feminism during the 1970s. Deeply involved with Fluxus, an art movement developed in New York during the late 1950s and early 1960s, Ono collaborated with many other artists (particularly George Maciunas and, of course, John Lennon) to produce "Fluxfilms," along with posters, sculptures, body art, and objects. Rejecting borders that separated the canonized arts in favor of celebrating the promiscuity of diverse art practices and objects, Fluxus called for a dynamic use of multimedia and insisted that it is everyday existence, not what one learns in art school or views at the museum, that makes up the site of art.[12] In her writings, Ono expressed the hope that her multimedia texts would evoke what she called the "world of stickiness," the interconnections and intertextualities that surface across and between artistic media. Humanist and certainly "touchy-feely," Ono's art also attempts to chip away at the boundaries that keep people from connecting with one another, boldly articulating human commonalities through descriptions of and experiments with the "sticky" human body: its functions, sounds, smells, and tastes. Ono's book of instructions and drawings, *Grapefruit,* published in 1964, reads almost like an absurdist children's book of games and activities meant to be performed by the reader. Written in the imperative mode, *Grapefruit's* instructional art projects, like "Body Sound Tape Piece," encourage the reader to make inter-subjective art, recording human bodies for non-narrative works that are meant to inspire unlikely, yet meaningful, human connections.

Miranda July's Joanie 4 Jackie series of video chain-letters and her online project Learning to Love You More operate similarly to "Body Sound Tape Piece," yet utilize new technologies, allowing their users to connect to one another and make their art public and easily accessible through free video distribution and a free Internet site. These projects take up the second wave's commitment to collaborative art and media-making practice between women, while expanding "collaboration" through the use of compilation and an emphasis on coalition. July places herself firmly within these coalitions, needing them to keep imagining and creating. In a particularly insightful interview with art historian Julia Bryan-Wilson, July characterizes her work as "always [having] to do with other people," and needing Joanie 4 Jackie to "help create a space for [her]self."[13] Significantly, in her feature film *Me and You and Everyone We Know,* one of the main characters, Christine (played by July), is an experimental video artist who at first self-defines as a "solo artist" who strictly "works alone." By the film's conclusion, however, Christine branches out and collaborates on a short video installation with an elderly Latino man and finds herself both a better artist and happier person for doing so. July emphasizes the desirability and necessity of collaboration at the level of production and encodes this into her films and other projects.

Beginning Joanie 4 Jackie (first called Big Miss Moviola) in 1995, at the height of her involvement in the riot grrrl scene, July conceptualized her video project as both a challenge and a promise to women and girls: make a short movie, send it to her, and it will be seen.[14] Run independently by July, "Joanie 4 Jackie is a free alternative distribution system for women movie-makers—all of them."[15] The project compiles women and girls' films and videos, links ten of them together, and then sends them back to the participants along with a contact information booklet. Correspondence between the moviemakers is highly encouraged; the participants are meant to give each other feedback and possibly initiate collaborative projects with one another. Wider audiences also have easy and cheap access to these women's video chain letters: each compilation can be purchased through the independent record label K Records for only ten dollars.

Another part of Joanie 4 Jackie's challenge is making the work of established women artists and filmmakers more universally available, especially to young women. July explained in a 1999 interview that she "want[s] the work of 'avant-garde' women film/video artists to be standard fare for teenage girls."[16] She asks, "Can you even imagine what the future would be like if millions of girls were not only trading fanzines and their own movies, but trading videotapes of the work of Eleanor Antin, Jenny Holzer, Sadie Benning, and Kristen Lucas? I am going to invent ways for them to see work that will change the way they view what is possible."[17] And she has held up her promise: the Joanie 4 Jackie chain letter often incorporates short films by established women film/video artists that are otherwise difficult to find or incredibly expensive to purchase. For many young women or girls interested in experimental filmmaking, Joanie 4 Jackie represents their only viable source of established women film/video artists' work. Amazingly, Joanie 4 Jackie's video chain letter has yet to be broken: in 2003 July passed on the management of the project to Bard College's film department, and it continues to grow.

July's ongoing web-based project with artist Harrell Fletcher, Learning to Love You More, continues this thread of compilation and coalition. July and Fletcher create instructions or "assignments" and list them on their site; anyone can then take up an individual or multiple assignments, perform them, and then post their work online. "Like a recipe, meditation practice, or familiar song, the prescriptive nature of these assignments is intended to guide people towards their own experience," Fletcher and July explain on the site. All of the assignments and completed projects can be viewed/heard/read on the site at any time by anyone. Some of these assignments include

> *2. Make a neighborhood field recording.*
>
> *3. Make a documentary about a small child.*
>
> *11. Photograph a scar and write about it.*
>
> *14. Write your life story in less than a day.*
>
> *22. Recreate a scene from Laura Lark's life story.*[18]
>
> *30. Take a picture of strangers holding hands.*
>
> *56. Make a portrait of your friend's desires.*

A multiplicity of compiled projects from "different people at different times—of the old, young, crying, longing, excited, calm, doubtful, etc.," Learning to Love You More seems to realize Ono's "Body Sound Tape Piece." Its participants become "collaborators for each other in consummate reciprocity," to quote phenomenologist Maurice Merleau-Ponty.[19] Writing their own histories, recording others' histories, sharing them, and then sometimes metaphorically slipping into the skin of other participants to carry out assignments of re-creation or reenactment, Learning to Love You More's participants express an openness to the assignments and each other.

A more explicit political ethos runs through Learning to Love You More as well: assignment 41 instructs participants to "work to defeat Bush and his administration's ideologies and practices of hate and destruction," and provides "documentation of actions that have practical application." This assignment also asks participants to start "thinking about what prevents [participants or those in their] community from becoming politically engaged." An earlier assignment, 34, provides instructions for political engagement: "Make a protest sign and publicly protest something that you deeply and sincerely feel needs to be changed."

Wildly different, the participants and their postings, when read together, resist any sort of stable reading; an argument cannot be made about what they come to articulate either ideologically or aesthetically. This may be precisely the point. It is *difference* that structures the site and makes up its contents, yet its participants and their postings come to be united in what bell hooks calls a "commonality of feeling."[20] The participants unite in their desire to learn how to love others more (or better or differently) and in fostering an open and noncompetitive (digital) space in which to do so. With the goal of completing the site's assignments and sharing them in a space that anticipates and privileges difference, Learning to Love You More's participants forge a coalition grounded in vulnerability and interdependence. Calling for both introspection and a "sticky" engagement with other people, often strangers, the assignments encourage the formation of new, random, and intimate relationships in a mediated world.

Hand-Touch Vulnerabilities

Just as Joanie 4 Jackie and Learning to Love You More cultivate coalitions of vulnerability and interdependence, the communities that populate July's films progressively expose their interdependencies and vulnerabilities in order to connect meaningfully. Composed of a large ensemble cast (of children, teenagers, and adults of many ages and races), July's feature *Me and You and Everyone We Know* situates its doubting and longing characters in an extensive web of connectivity.[21] While at first the individual characters' stories seem unrelated, they become increasingly intertwined narratively as the film progresses through July's idiosyncratic use of intercutting and close-ups. While increasing characters' connectedness is a standard narrative progression in most ensemble cast films, particularly American independent films (such as those of Robert Altman, P. T. Anderson, and Todd Solondz), July distinguishes her ensemble piece by narrowing in on her characters' flesh: their often wounded or desiring body parts.

Indeed, July's is a cinema of hands, hair, and feet, all longing to be touched or healed, longing *to* touch and heal another. Tenderly and subtly, July crafts *Me and You* using the hand-touch sensibility described in Schneemann's *Interior Scroll,* and with this she images and inspires vulnerabilities that are flooded with both affect and agency. July's onscreen affective vulnerabilities open up empathetic audiences to their own embodied, variegated vulnerabilities, challenging the film scholar to interpret such an affective encounter and the political desires it generates.

Judith Butler's recent work sheds light on this challenge. In her collection of essays on politics after 9/11, *Precarious Life,* Butler maps out a theory of vulnerability as agency that resonates with July's films. Butler argues that bodily vulnerability is precisely what all human beings have in common, and essentially, this shared vulnerability is what connects us socially and politically: "Each of us is constituted politically in part by virtue of the social vulnerability of our bodies—as a site of desire and physical vulnerability, as a site of publicity at once assertive and exposed. Loss and vulnerability seem to follow from our being socially constituted bodies, attached to others, at risk of losing those attachments, exposed to others, at risk of violence by virtue of that exposure."[22] By definition, Butler tells us, our shared vulnerability makes us "physically dependent on one another, physically vulnerable to one another."[23] Rather than building up defense systems to mask our vulnerability or will it away, we must "attend to it, even abide by it . . . for to foreclose that vulnerability, to banish it . . . is to eradicate one of the most important resources from which we must take our bearings and find our way."[24] Attending to our shared vulnerability becomes another way of imagining community, "one in which we are compelled to take stock of our interdependence."[25]

Cinema is the ideal site to flesh out the agency of vulnerability and interdependence, as we are neither simply active nor passive, but rather open to becoming what a film suggests we become, no matter how resistant we might be to it. In the process of that becoming, we impress and confer new meanings onto the film, and it too becomes transformed. When engaging a cinematic text, our eyes and ears both "touch" and are "touched by" the images and sounds coming from the screen and speakers. Vivian Sobchack calls this a "sensual cross-modal activity" that transforms us into "cinesthetic subjects," or viewers who *experience* the cinema through this co-constitutive encounter that is neither completely on- or off-screen, but is thoroughly mediated at and on the site of our bodies.[26] Similarly, media theorist Laura U. Marks, in her book *Touch: Sensuous Theory and Multisensory Media,* stresses the dialogical process of the cinematic experience, naming what happens between a spectator and film an "intercorporeal relationship."[27] Both the film's "body" and the spectator's body touch each other, yet some films nurture this intercorporeal relationship better than others. July's films not only nurture such an intercorporeal relationship but also display a marked consciousness about doing so. Loaded with sensual details, arresting images, and (literally) touching characters, July's films lay bare the shared vulnerability at stake in such intercorporeal relationships, cinematic or otherwise. The vulnerability of the bodies in July's films refract our vulnerability and agency as viewers and suggest that we become more vulnerable, using our shared (bodily) vulnerability to build connections with others.

Me and You and Everyone We Know establishes its theme of vulnerability, its hand-touch sensibility, and its dyadic structure of wounding/healing in its opening sequence, initiating an affective encounter with its viewers straight away. Christine (July), an experimental video artist, has her camera positioned on a photograph of a typical, and almost cheesy, romantic scene: two lovers, a man and a woman, stand together at a beach and stare at a sunset. In one hand Christine holds a microphone, and with her other hand she points her finger back and forth between the lovers, using her "finger cue" to channel the voices and feelings of the lovers. Speaking the parts for the man and the woman, Christine engages them in a moving ceremony of emotional intimacy characterized by earnest promises of love and devotion that begin: "If you really love me then let's make a vow." Intercut with Christine's visual and aural production of lasting love is a different couple, awkwardly negotiating the end of their marriage. Richard (John Hawkes), a Caucasian shoe salesman, and Pam (JoNell Kennedy), his African American soon-to-be ex-wife, bicker over what belongs to whom as he packs his things, reluctantly moving out of the home they had established together. Their two sons, teenaged Peter (Miles Thompson) and six-year-old Robby (Brandon Ratcliff), draw ASCII art on the computer in their room. Despondent and uneasy, Richard decides to perform a ceremony of his own to mark his emotional loss onto his physical body. Positioned before his boys' bedroom window, Richard douses his left hand with lighter fluid and sets it aflame, while on the soundtrack, Christine's lovers' promises intensify: "Let's go everywhere, even though we're scared—because this is life and it's really, really happening right now." Richard's hand becomes engulfed in flames; he stares at it in wonder before beating the flames out in the grass. The film then cuts to a medium shot of Christine holding her mic: "Now let's kiss to make it real, okay?" Next, in a close-up, Christine slowly kisses her left hand. Longing shapes her facial expression and, subsequently, disappointment. Performing a kiss that can never kiss back, her loneliness and desire for love register in her look and are reaffirmed by subsequent shots of her small bachelor apartment. The intercutting between Richard's wounded hand and Christine's tender and yearning one, along with the aural layering of the sounds of their embodied rituals, initiates the film's dyadic structure of wounding/healing: their wounded bodies are meant to come together for mutual healing.

Later that day, when Christine goes shoe-shopping and meets Richard for the first time, he notices her blistered ankles and tells her she "doesn't deserve that kind of pain." Instantly developing a crush on him, Christine

Richard's burning, wounded hand (*above*) intercut with Christine's kissed, healing hand (*below*), in *Me and You and Everyone We Know* (Miranda July, 2005).

aggressively pursues Richard throughout the rest of the film. She purchases a pair of shoes from him, and they later come to stand in for his body: she holds them and, during one lovely scene, uses the shoes to craft a short video expressive of her and Richard's close-but-so-far-away incipient relationship. Like his bandaged hand, however, Richard closes himself off to Christine. Once healed, the bandage comes off, and later, at the film's dénouement, their hands touch and, finally, their bodies embrace.

Other bodily vulnerabilities and negotiations transpire between the nine ensemble characters in *Me and You*. Richard's son Peter becomes the subject of a blow job experiment initiated by two curious teenage girls; Richard's coworker posts perverted signs on his window describing sexual acts to be performed between him and those same girls; Christine decorates her video-cassettes with pink dot stickers and touches them, as if to invest them with her own corporeality, before submitting them to the curator at the Contemporary Art Museum for potential exhibition. Nearly all of the characters in the film underscore and attempt to legitimate their desires, at different points, by speaking the phrase "I can feel it."

Perhaps the film's most memorable invocations of feeling and touch involve Robby, who is too young to be limited by the (often artificial) boundaries that separate disparate phenomena in the world, be it humans from other humans, humans from nature, or humans from inanimate objects. As one critic of the film eloquently describes it, "[Robby's] confusion over what he can control, over where he ends and the rest of the world begins, is the beating heart of this movie."[28] Polymorphously perverse, Robby imagines his body as being connected to everyone and everything. Online in digital space, where Robby and his brother "talk dirty" with an anonymous instant messenger, he describes a continuous "back and forth" exchange of "poop between butt-holes" as a gesture of warmth and care, and develops an ASCII drawing to visualize it:))<>((. Not knowing Robby's age, the turned-on anonymous IM'er, an adult, professional woman, meets him at a public park. The encounter between this boy and woman leads to one of the film's most tender gestures: a child reaching out and touching an adult's hair.[29] This same gesture appears during the crescendo of July's short video *Nest of Tens,* but takes place between a precocious adolescent girl and a flustered business-woman (played by July). The girl pulls a piece of lint from the woman's hair, blows it, and sets off a web of connections linking everyone who waits inside and outside of the airport. As the lint moves upward into the sky, a white line traces the lint's movements to visualize its subtle yet intimate connective power.

Like this white line in *Nest of Tens,* a visual manifestation of its characters' longing to be recognized and empathized with by others, the hand-touch sensibilities in July's films lay themselves bare and reach out to audiences, nudging them to access their own vulnerability and to recognize its (political) agency. As Butler tells us, "to ask for recognition, or to offer it, is precisely not to ask for recognition of what already is. It is to solicit a becoming, to instigate a transformation."[30] The dialogical encounter between July's films and audiences has the potential to incite political desires and actions: the desire to abandon and transform cultures of domination and violence; the ability to let down one's defenses, to be vulnerable, and to recognize one's connections to another (or the "Other"); and the knowledge that "I" am constituted by and tied to "you"—that "we're undone by each other . . . and if we're not, we're missing something."[31]

Hopeful Intentionalities

Situating July's multimedia-making in the reverberating history of U.S. feminist art and media, it becomes clear that her work, like that of the second-wave artists and media-makers she draws on, is one of hope and possibility. As feminist art historian Peggy Phelan proposes, "Successful feminist art beckons us towards possibilities in thought and in practice [that are] still to be created, still to be lived."[32] Phelan's words bring to mind a recurring image that appears in both *Nest of Tens* and *Me and You.* For me, this image is among the most compelling visual incarnations of contemporary feminist hope and possibility. Lying on a carpet, eyes looking up, a young girl gazes at the ceiling, and thus directly at the camera. Her intentionality, or bearing in the world, is radically open and curious. A tender, fully embodied subject, she is comported toward something hopeful and uncertain that exists from both within and outside of herself; she longs for something more, inventing the future through her imagination. Various critics of July's work have dismissed this image as "overly precious" or "quirky," but miss its poignancy. While this image itself may seem simple, its context should not be forgotten or overlooked. Produced during a moment in history when "security," "threat," and "defense" structured (as they continue to structure) U.S. politics and culture, the image of July's radically vulnerable, searching, and hopeful girl constitutes a true alternative to ideologies and systems of domination. She is both a challenge and a promise that none of us should ignore.

Notes

1. Jeanie Forte, "Women's Performance Art: Feminism and Postmodernism," in *Performing Feminisms,* ed. Sue-Ellen Case (Baltimore: Johns Hopkins University Press, 1990), 260.

2. Laura Cottingham, *Seeing through the Seventies: Essays on Feminism and Art* (Singapore: G+B Arts International, 2000), 126.

3. Mary Ann Doane, "Woman's Stake: Filming the Female Body," in *Feminist Film Theory,* ed. Constance Penley (New York: Routledge, 1988), 226.

4. See Schneemann's book *More than Meat Joy* (Kingston, NY: McPherson, 1979).

5. Judith Stein, "Collaboration," in *The Power of Feminist Art,* ed. Norma Broude and Mary D. Garrard (New York: Harry N. Abrams, 1996), 226.

6. Cottingham, *Seeing through the Seventies,* 164.

7. While some second-wave feminist art and filmmaking can indeed be described as "essentialist," upon closer inspection, much of women's art and film from the 1960s and 1970s seeks to fiercely question and unsettle stable conceptions and categories of identity. For example, in many of the films and performance pieces by Schneemann, Ono, Yayoi Kusama, Ana Mendieta, Eleanor Antin, Adrian Piper, Hannah Wilke, Yvonne Rainer, Joan Jonas, Jan Oxenberg, Barbara Hammer, Hermine Freed, Lynda Benglis, and others, a stable identity is asserted only to be unraveled and exposed as fluid and indeterminate. For further discussion, see Amelia Jones, *Body Art: Performing the Subject* (Minneapolis: University of Minnesota Press, 1998); and Helena Reckitt, ed., *Art and Feminism* (New York: Phaidon, 2001).

8. Matt Wolf, "New Queer Live Art," *LTTR: Practice More Failure* 3 (2004): 2.

9. Ibid.

10. In *Outlaw Culture: Resisting Representations* (London: Routledge, 1994), bell hooks uses the expression "commonality of feeling" when discussing coalitional politics.

11. Judith Butler, *Precarious Life: The Power of Mourning and Violence* (New York: Verso, 2004), xiii.

12. Alexandra Munroe, introduction to *Yes Yoko Ono,* ed. Alexandra Munroe (New York: Harry N. Abrams, 2000), 13.

13. Julia Bryan-Wilson, "Some Kind of Grace: An Interview with Miranda July," *Camera Obscura* 19, no. 1 (2004): 196, 188.

14. Ibid., 182.

15. Miranda July, Joanie 4 Jackie, http://joanie4jackie.com.

16. Ada Calhoun, "Do-It-Yourself Girl Revolution: Performance Artist Miranda July," *Austin Chronicle,* September 17, 1999, http://austinchronicle.com/gyrobase/Issue/story?oid=oid%3A73926.

17. July qtd. in ibid.

18. Laura Lark is a participant on Learning to Love You More, and she posted her life story for assignment #14.

19. Maurice Merleau-Ponty, *Phenomenology of Perception,* trans. Colin Smith (London: Routledge, 1962), 354.

20. hooks, *Outlaw Culture,* 217.

21. July's short experimental video *Nest of Tens* (1999) operates quite similarly to *Me and You* in that it features a racially diverse and multi-age ensemble cast. In a recent interview with Rachel Kushner, July described *Nest of Tens* as the "primordial version of *Me and You.*" Rachel Kushner, "Miranda July," *BOMB* 92 (Summer 2005), http://www.bombsite.com/issues/92/articles/2739.

22. Butler, *Precarious Life,* 20.

23. Ibid., 27.

24. Ibid., 30.

25. Ibid., 27.

26. Vivian Sobchack, *Carnal Thoughts: Embodiment and Moving Image Culture* (Berkeley: University of California Press, 2004), 71.

27. Laura U. Marks, *Touch: Sensuous Theory and Multisensory Media* (Minneapolis: University of Minnesota Press, 2002), xx.

28. Annie Wagner, "You and Everyone You Know," *The Stranger* 14, no. 42 (2005): 77.

29. For those of you reading this chapter who have not yet seen the film, I refrain from revealing the identity of this anonymous woman in order not to ruin the affective surprise of this lovely scene.

30. Butler, *Precarious Life,* 44.

31. Ibid., 23.

32. Peggy Phelan, "Survey," in *Art and Feminism,* ed. Reckitt, 20.

The Archivist Tango

Sally Potter Collects Herself

Sally Potter has been dancing the archivist tango as long as she has been making creative work. She first introduced her audience to the figure of the Archivist in "The Archivist Goes to Buenos Aires," a short story included in the screenplay accompanying her 1997 film *The Tango Lesson.* In that story, SP (an avatar of Sally Potter) is visited and advised by her friend the Archivist while she is struggling to make a film in Buenos Aires. The Archivist brings with him a number of boxes containing ideas, kisses, and tears that SP has sent him, a magical realist conceit for Potter's determination to situate the ephemeral, emotional, and embodied as signifiers of process that argue for the archive as unfixed and open-ended.

Defining the Archive

Found footage documentarist Joel Katz writes of his archival material:

Because the consequences of their difference are both economic and ideological, the terms "archive" and "archival" themselves merit some discussion. Archive is defined as "a place where public records, documents, etc., are kept" . . . all archives perform a selection process which is inherently ideological. . . . In vernacular usage, "archival" is used to describe certain attributes of age, status of preservation, and ascribed importance, and does not dovetail completely with its root word: not all which may be considered archival is to be found in a formal archive.[1]

Potter's films insistently address the gap between the official archive and the

34

vernacular archival in a way that operates as a corrective to performance theorist Diana Taylor's stern distinction between the archive, which she asserts is always invested with and in (maintaining) hegemonic power, and the repertoire, which is embodied, versatile, resistant, oral, displaced, contestatory, open-ended, and politicized.[2]

Taylor associates the "repertoire" with the (anti)traditions of feminist, queer, and postcolonial performance art that resist hegemonic spaces and forms; she includes film among such forms, identifying it as a "fixed" record whose technological aspect, early use in anthropology, and apparent "objectivity" align it with the archive as purveyor and recorder of dominant histories. Yet as Katz points out, "whether because of the instability of early nitrate stocks, the archivist's perception of popular culture as 'pedestrian,' or the deliberate exclusion of certain materials from historical canons, it is safe to say that millions of feet of filmed history have been lost or destroyed."[3] In identifying film's ambiguous archival status, Katz reads the archive through what it omits.

A 1974 program note for "Park Cafeteria," created by Potter's Limited Dance Company for a performance art festival at London's Serpentine Gallery, challenges the reader and potential viewer to rethink the institutional archive exactly in terms of its omissions. The show is described as a "series of arbitrary afternoons spent chewing possibilities, refreshments, and light snacks. . . . Into this two exiles return . . . searching out old faces, researching the tea archives, acknowledging the contradictions, lost for words. We spit it out: what next?"[4] This playfully unprogrammatic program note deftly outlines the place of the archive in Potter's work. The word "archive" echoes in the piece's title (P*ar*k C*af*eteria) as it will through her film career from 1979's *Thriller* onward, and it will stand for and announce similar thematic concerns: the archive as a resource for "chewing possibilities"; as a location of exile and return, of searching and researching, of sensory and bodily nourishment; and, most important, as a site from which to issue a challenge to the future.

Limited Dance Company mocks the idea of the archive by suggesting that one could "research . . . tea," but the idea of a "tea archive" evokes the potential of the archive for recording the embodied and the "arbitrary": what Ann Cvetkovich refers to as "an archive of feelings" and illustrates by way of a scene in Cheryl Dunye's film *The Watermelon Woman* (1997) in which Cheryl, the protagonist, visits the Women's Herstory Archives in New York seeking personal information about Fae Richards, an African American actress. Both the archive and the material found there are spoofs, but Cvetkovich reads the scene as exploring the importance for feminist historiography of the intimate, ephemeral archive.[5] In Potter's short story, the Archivist similarly tells SP that his "line of work and [the tango's] fancy footwork . . . are merely two faces of the same research . . . [into] the ephemeral."[6]

Rather than the privileging of the archival "final" form, the archive stands principally in Potter's work for the feminist cultural practice of incorporating the ephemera of process into the finished work. As well as continually and visibly employing both her own and others' archival material to build counterhistories, Potter also argues for a reclamation of the archive as an open-ended, continuously evolving resource, an imaginative model not only for feminist historiography but also for feminist generative artistic practice.

As in *The Watermelon Woman,* unpublished archival ephemera can provide an insight into Potter's process, and into the importance of archives in (re)constructing the recent and unrecorded history of feminist filmmaking. Each of Potter's feature films representationally see(k)s Taylor's ephemeral, embodied notion of repertoire in the archive, and thus redefines the idea of a "fixed" archive, or what I term the "hierarchive," in opposition to a fluid constellation of more ephemeral tropes of memory, history, and heritage that resonates with Katz's notion of the "vernacular archival." Potter's oeuvre speaks and braids vernacular film languages to create the potential for a feminist archivist tango that will "move like a dancer itself . . . lyrical and agile."[7]

Orlando (Tilda Swinton) contemplates the archive in *Orlando.* (Photo by Liam Longman, Adventure Pictures Ltd., 1992.)

Reviving the Archive

Uriel Orlow begins his essay in *Ghosting: The Role of the Archive within Contemporary Artists' Film and Video* with an epigraph from Pierre Nora, who coined the phrase *lieux de mémoire* (realms of memory) to rethink a postcolonial relationship between history and memory: "Modern memory is, above all, archival. It relies entirely on the materiality of the trace, the visibility of the image."[8] Orlow's essay, which considers the "film/video work as keeper of archival matter," highlights and inverts the concerns that I address here.[9] His concern with "the materiality of the trace" and film/video as its "keeper" confirms Taylor's alignment of moving image media with the hegemonic archive, set against the repertoire of performance. Orlow's conceptualization of archival-based cultural production thus holds out little potential for those whose material traces or visible images have been, as Katz writes, "lost or destroyed."

It is exactly at this point of exclusion that Potter begins her cinematic negotiations with the archive via *Thriller,* a short film that bridges the multiple artistic and activist modalities with which Potter was (and is) involved: dance-based performance art, vocal performance, and Expanded Cinema, as well as a commitment to socialist feminism. *Thriller* employs all of these modes to investigate the ways in which marginalized cultural texts enter and can transform the received archive through its reinvention of Mimi, the consumptive heroine of Puccini's opera *La Bohème.* The film consists of a few moving sequences and a series of black-and-white stills filmed with fades; some of these are Potter's photographs of her cast, including black French actress Colette Laffont as Mimi, while others derive from two archives. The first source is the (nationalist, hegemonic) Royal Opera House (ROH) archive, which provided stills from a production of *La Bohème* that are juxtaposed with Potter's very different restaging. Profoundly different images from the National Labour Archives show women working in garment sweatshops, marking the way in which the exploitation of such women is "archived" by Puccini's romanticized characterization of Mimi as a seamstress, and the ways in which that archiving not only is inadequate but obfuscates the material conditions of women workers. As Mimi says, "the truth of [her] death is written in their texts" by the thorough erasure of her historical existence *via* the construction of a cultural product that becomes her "final" form.

The truth of her death is that it is utter, whether in opera, ballet, or *Tel Quel*'s critical theory (from which Mimi quotes), and it is invisible. The film suggests an archive of feelings specifically in the realms of the invisible, with its borrowing of the menacing strings of Bernard Herrmann's theme from

Alfred Hitchcock's *Psycho* (1960). Juxtaposed with Puccini's score, the "thrilling" strings question the place of the popular and cinematic in the musical archive and underline the way in which both *Psycho* and *La Bohème* use musical thrills to score femicide. The musical score is both emotive and motive, a rare material "trace" of kinesis in a film largely composed of still photographs. Yet it works, like Mimi, to enliven or revive gestures and histories immobilized by Western culture's misogyny and elitism. The photographs of Potter's cast performing parodic ballet lifts are brought to life by the constant movement of the music and Laffont's voice-over. One gesture breaks the stillness: an arabesque performed by Rose English, which combines the lift of Musetta's "little foot" and Mimi's pose for the artists. Performing this arabesque on moving film in the same room as, and for, Laffont, English's reorientation of a gesture from the repertoire of classical ballet models the fleeting, embodied queer archive of affect Cvetkovich proposes.

The presence of dance, and of dancers such as Rose English, makes the film like an archival record of one of Potter's performances with Limited Dance Company, with photographs, score, and voice-over insisting on repertoire's place in the archive, through its incomplete but necessary record of liveness. The ROH's stills reinforce this connection of cinema and photography to live performance, negotiating an intersection or thirdspace between the ephemeral feminist repertoire of performance art, which is in danger of disappearing like Mimi, and the hegemonic and deathly archive of high culture, that—even so—contains material traces of the excluded and invisibilized, if you know (if you can learn from Mimi) how to see(k).

Repertoire as Archive

Like *Thriller,* Sally Potter's second film, *The Gold Diggers* (1984), is an investigation. Femicide has been replaced by the connection between the movements of global capital and women as trade goods. Dance performances by Jacky Lansley and Siobhan Davies, diegetic musical performances by a comedic orchestra and Colette Laffont, and marvellous pastiche of both Charlie Chaplin's *The Gold Rush* (1925) and D. W. Griffith's *Way Down East* (1920) combine to form a unique cinematic experience. It proved too unique for several male reviewers, who lambasted it. Thus, despite its rapturous reception at women's film festivals in Canada and Australia, as well as a season at the National Film Theatre in London, *The Gold Diggers* has roughly the same (un)archived status as Potter's performance work, as it was withdrawn from distribution, and exhibition prints are rarely made available.

Patricia Mellencamp cites it in *A Fine Romance* as a model for a feminist formal filmmaking revolution that never occurred, because of the film's eradication from what could be called the cinematic repertoire. Reviews, interviews, and striking images in the mainstream and alternative media, as well as festival programs and a few academic articles, form a partially legible Cubist collage of the film. Accounts by feminist film theorists and historians who engaged with the film during its festival circuit, including Mellencamp, Kaja Silverman, and B. Ruby Rich, offer passionate descriptions of the film—narrative, psychoanalytic, and anecdotal, respectively.[10] Rich cited *The Gold Diggers* as her "hidden gem" in an issue marking *Sight & Sound*'s seventy-fifth birthday.[11] Her selection points to the film's central position in a feminist film historiography, while simultaneously alluding to (and maintaining) its erasure from the cinematic archive, which is mobilized as repertoire via its circulation through cinematheques, repertory cinemas, academic institutions, television, and digital media.

The film's problematic relationship with the archive is visible in the way in which the cinematic archive framed the film's release. The National Film Theatre, the exhibition venue of the British Film Institute, which co-funded the film, asked Potter to program a season of films that influenced *The Gold Diggers*. These films ranged from the Chaplin and Griffith films cited earlier through musicals such as *Kuhle Wampe* (Slatan Dudow, 1932) and *Singin' in the Rain* (Stanley Donen and Gene Kelly, 1952) to the work (rarely exhibited in the UK) of North American feminist filmmakers Yvonne Rainer and Joyce Wieland.[12] It seems fitting that the film should have been broadcast in the context of such a wide-ranging archive, as the film itself draws on, and reconstitutes, the cinematic archive. The film excavates cinematic icons by both casting Julie Christie and having her perform made up with huge kohl rings around her eyes, parodying Lillian Gish, and it redefines genres as diverse as the backstage musical, the costume drama, and the buddy movie. Recirculating cinema's narrative and semiotic economy is instrumental in the film's larger investigation into the role of women in the circulation of global capital.

As in Bertolt Brecht's films and musicals, the political message of *The Gold Diggers* draws together economic, social, and cultural discourses, utilizing the form of the cabaret to introduce various opinions rather than to motivate a linear narrative. One particular skit specifically stages the (self-)importance of the institutional archive. Celeste (Laffont) and Ruby (Christie) are on interlinked quests. As their alchemical names indicate, this quest is both metaphysical and material, exploring the multiple significances of gold in Western culture.[13] Celeste, who rescues Ruby from an Austenesque ball in the film's opening sequence, does data entry for an international bank. She is curious about the routes and destinations of the money that "passes through [her] body" as digital figures. Celeste's curiosity and determination lead her to the Ministry for Information, a parodic bureaucratic enterprise headed by an expert who begins with intimidation, addressing Celeste from a behind a desk on a raised platform, and ends in hilarity, as his performed authority is shored up with model Greek columns, a miniature desk, and a model of a ship, which he sinks.

Alongside the model of the ship is another model, one of a finely attired woman in a gilded cage: the woman is (suggestively) the information he will not give Celeste. Yet this model is also a reference to the film's repertoire of images, as it will be seen later at full scale, with Ruby as the caged woman being carried to the (information) bank alongside bars of gold, while the bankers sing. The scale model trapped in the Kafkaesque Ministry is liberated into performance, yet the woman is still trapped. The ball has to be repeated in order for Celeste to ride in on a white charger and rescue Ruby, again. In this iteration, although the same waltz is playing, the men fall to the ground one by one, liberating their female partners to dance with one another. Taylor would argue that this is a moment in which performance art's repertoire, its capacity for difference and surprise, asserts itself. Yet the cinematic image, as in *Thriller,* draws on the cultural archive (eighteenth-century novels and their adaptations as well as classical musicals) to constitute its difference and, in doing so, redefines the way in which the viewer receives the films that informed and framed *The Gold Diggers* as it was received into the cinematic archive. Moving from feminist performance into the more resistant medium of cinema, Potter chiasmatically employs repertoire as memory and the archive as movement. This is the archivist tango getting into its stride.

Resisting the Archive

In her postscript to *The Tango Lesson* screenplay, "First Steps," Potter repeats the adage that "Ginger Rogers did everything Fred Astaire did, only backwards and wearing high heels."[14] This describes the director's role in the archivist tango, particularly when it comes to adaptation. Potter goes on to describe the "joy of being a follower" as "be[ing] completely in the present."[15] An Australian poster used the tagline "At last! At last! Free from the past!" to advertise Potter's adaptation of Virginia Woolf's novel *Orlando, A Biography.* As the tagline suggests, this is one of *Orlando*'s most striking qualities, ending as it does in "The Present," which is not Woolf's present of 1930s department stores and biplanes but a postmodern present (and even presentiment) of glass-and-steel architecture, heritage tourism, and video cameras.

Woolf's—and *Orlando's*—position as high cultural commodity was altered by a film that moved it from a recherché academic text identified with second-wave feminist archival work to the front lines of queer pop culture. Not only does the film share Tilda Swinton as a performer with Derek Jarman's *Edward II* (1991), a contemporaneous film that revived the populist and/because queer aspects of a canonical text about British national history, but it also shares *Edward's* strategy of including popular queer performers. Quentin Crisp as Elizabeth I and Jimmy Somerville as the Herald/the Angel reinsert *Orlando: A Biography* into a grassroots, populist queer entertainment culture that is as much Soho bar as Bloomsbury set.[16] This is the culture too ephemeral and contestatory to archive that Cvetkovich documents: a culture predicated on performance and masquerade, on culturally feminine and ephemeral acts associated with fashion and pop. Artificial Eye's tenth anniversary DVD re-presentation includes a second disc featuring three making-of documentaries.[17] One connects to the film's queer/pop culture status, charting the involvement of Somerville and his transformation into an angel for the film's closing sequence.

The other two connect back to Potter's own intimate archive, as they document her shooting in Russia and Uzbekistan, an act made possible through connections that Potter had established on her trip to the USSR in 1986 as part of a delegation of British filmmakers, including Jarman, organized by the British Film Institute. While there, Potter researched *I Am an Ox, I Am a Horse, I Am a Man, I Am a Woman* (1987–88), a documentary on images of women in Russian cinema, which involved extensive archival research as well as interviews with contemporary women filmmakers. *Orlando* shares with *I Am an Ox* its productive excavation of the past as context for a future-present, and its intimate encoding of Potter's imaginative investment of Russia signals the way in which *Orlando,* the most commercially successful of Potter's films, also archives gestural and thematic intertexts from her experimental work.

The DVD documentary about Uzbekistan shows the process that Potter went through in casting several local sets of twins as extras to underline the theme of doubling (the Khan of Khiva, played by Lothaire Bluteau, is a visual double for Charlotte Valandrey's Sasha). This is reminiscent of an early Potter short, titled *Play* (1970), which features three sets of twins playing in the street. The official paratexts that, by their existence and deluxe presentation, canonize the film also suggest more intimate and resistant pathways through Potter's archive. They do so first by connecting implicitly to her creative process and oeuvre and second by underlining the way Potter's early political affiliation to socialist feminism alters Woolf's *Orlando,* informing

Ghosting/doubling: Twins in *Play* (1970). (Photo by Sally Potter, Adventure Pictures Ltd., [1970] 2006.)

formal experimentation and Potter's relation to the economics both on set and within the diegesis.

In the novel, Orlando herself enters both the canon and the marketplace with a prize-winning poem that s/he had begun in Shakespeare's day. Potter's Orlando turns an untidy manuscript over to her present-day publisher. It is unclear whether the manuscript contains a poem (as in the novel), the novel *Orlando,* or indeed the screenplay for the film that we are watching, given that "The Present" is represented by Orlando's daughter's video camera. She lets go of her lifework, as she has let go of her property, whose retention is the quest and success of Woolf's Orlando, apparently for no financial remuneration or fame. Invested in the creative process rather than in the product, the film argues for a different kind of archive than the gilt-bound library (where we see Orlando reading poetry after his first melancholy sleep) transformed to hide-bound costume drama. The passage of Orlando's life from quoting Shakespeare amid the books to writing her own story is emphasized by the difference in framing: behind the modern Orlando is a plate glass window overlooking a train—symbol of modernity—traversing urban space. No longer perched precariously on the archivist's ladder, Orlando sits confidently facing the publisher, played by Heathcote Williams, who also played Nick Greene, the poet who ridiculed the earlier Orlando's sub-Shakespearean doggerel. Greene, a poet who sought Orlando's patronage in order to enter the library, is now its guardian and is shown opening its gates. This twist—a complicity sealed by Orlando's silent gaze to camera as the publisher/producer comments on how to deform the resistant, intimate, ephemeral archive of Orlando's extraordinary life to conform to Hollywood standards—connects the film to *The Tango Lesson,* in which the "life" of the protagonist SP becomes, despite Hollywood interference, the film that she is going to make/has actually made.

Desiring the Archive

Like *Orlando, The Tango Lesson* is made "backwards, in high heels," not in a tango with a canonical text, but with the film world that, having accepted *Orlando* into the canon, expected Potter to produce a certain kind and amount of cinematic work. Potter is also dancing this tango with herself, or with the version of herself who is pulling away from Hollywood pressures and turning to tango as a respite from the pressure of making work that conforms to mainstream modes of production. Potter, who plays a semi-autobiographical character called Sally, enters the dance of feminist autobiography, in which any reportage of the self is complicated by a theoretical insistence on the self as subjective, fragmented, deconstituted by the recording it attempts.

This is not the place to enter into discussion as to *how* biographical *The Tango Lesson* may or may not be, except to say that the film itself raises the question, Can the tango (or love or life) be archived? Feeling's absence from the archive is foregrounded through the film-within-a-film that Sally is writing and pitching to Hollywood producers. Called *Rage,* the film takes place in a campily stylized yet threatening version of the fashion world, its garish primary colors clashing with the rich black-and-white of *The Tango Lesson*'s framing narrative. *Rage* takes as its theme the fashion world's punishment and victimization of women. *The Tango Lesson* documents the process by which *Rage* is gradually abandoned as Sally's next project in favor of a film about tango and her dancing teacher and partner, Pablo Veron (playing [a version of] himself), so the stylized, Technicolor excerpts of *Rage* are from a film (and an anger) that, in the archival sense, does not and cannot exist. The excerpts have to be read as internal visions, Sally's fantasies, just as the frame narrative is both a documentary about its own coming into being and a feature film that recognizes its own process in the mirror.

Rage, which transformed over a decade into Potter's most recent film *Rage* (2009), has an archival trace that underlines the connection between feeling and process in Potter's feminist auto-archiving. *Rage* is also the title of the final, and most feminist, part of her four-part TV documentary miniseries on emotions. *Tears, Laughter, Fear, and Rage* (1986) featured a late interview with the director Michael Powell. In a development document for *The Tango Lesson,* Potter cites Powell and Emeric Pressburger's ballet film *The Red Shoes* (1948), which is excerpted in the "Tears" episode of the documentary series, as a key visual and tonal referent for her film. Describing *The Red Shoes* as "the story of an impossible conflict between love and art, at the heart of which lies the obsessive compulsion to dance, on and on," Potter simultaneously demonstrates *The Tango Lesson*'s archival ancestry as a film about obsessive dance and love and marks her film's difference, as the female protagonist, Sally, does not have to choose between love and dance, escaping the fairy tale narrative that imprisons Victoria in the earlier film. Claiming comparative status to one of the classic films about classical dance, Potter opens the hierarchive to her feminist, postmodern cinema. In doing so, she insists, following the Archivist, that dancing in the archive renders it a repertoire in which socially accepted "moves," such as women dancing backward to their death, can be altered by recognizing the place of the ephemeral, in the sense of both the fragmentary and the emotional.

This is the claim of the tango itself, existing as both (recorded yet ever-changing) music and (performed yet gesturally fixed) dance. Music records emotion but also solicits it: in the film's most magical scene, a tango playing on the radio of a cab in Buenos Aires, an instance of the archive of recorded and repeated culture, breaks the ice after an argument between Sally and Pablo following a stage performance. They spring from the cab and begin dancing in the rain. Tango is freed from the constraints of public performance and returned to its roots as an expression of feeling, as the music is both foregrounded as part of Argentinean popular culture (in its broadest sense) and set free from its meanings to form part of a fleeting moment, passing from the cab's radio to the film's nondiegetic soundtrack as if including the viewer in this private moment: making it archival.

Sounding the Archive

Music as an ephemeral, unarchivable, and emotive mediator of cultural and personal memory is a repeated theme in Potter's work, from early performance pieces such as *Aida* (1974) and *Who Is Sylvia?* (1974), which used well-known pieces from the classical repertoire to explore women's absence as creators through their presence as muses. In *The Tango Lesson,* Potter drew on the archive of a singular musical form to exploit its complex web of associations, both emotional and cultural. When Potter engages most explicitly with transnational history in World War II (melo)drama *The Man Who Cried* (2000), her access is through music. In the liner notes to the soundtrack, she describes her obsession with a cover version of "Gloomy Sunday" by a Roma musician. The song's history of translation and re-recording operates as a microcosm for the film's narrative, in which a Yiddish girl called Fegele

(Claudia Lander-Duke, then Christina Ricci) is transplanted to England and renamed Suzie, journeying via Paris cabarets and the Nazi invasion to the United States, where she finds her father, who recognizes her *as* Fegele when she sings to him in Yiddish.

Suzie does indeed sing "Gloomy Sunday" (in English) precisely in a moment of translation, on the boat from Paris to America. It is a moment whose pure musicality foregrounds and connects the multiple instances of musical cross-pollination that narrate the film. Over the precredits sequence, Suzie's father sings, "Je crois entendre encore" from Georges Bizet's *The Pearl Fishers,* in Yiddish, an aria that Suzie will later hear sung in its original French, provoking an emotional response comparable to Sally and Pablo's spontaneous dance in the rain. Suzie also possesses a signature song, "Dido's Lament" from Henry Purcell's opera *Dido and Aeneas.* She first sings it to her assembled English schoolmates, a performance that cuts, with a sound bridge, to an older Suzie completing the song for the doyenne of a Parisian dancing troupe, who hires her. Through another dancer, Lola (Cate Blanchett), Suzie meets Dante (John Turturro) and is hired for his opera company, where she meets Cesar (Johnny Depp), a Roma horse trainer. She sings her lament a third and final time alongside elderly musicians at the Roma encampment where Cesar lives. The musicians, played by the legendary Roma orkestar Taraf de Haïdouks, improvise vocally and finally turn to Suzie, who sings the lament in an unaccented classical style, until she comes to the most famous lines. As her voice descends between "Remember me" and "Forget," it breaks and catches, picking up the half-notes of the Roma singers and her own Yiddish musical heritage.

This pivot between remembrance and forgetting is exactly the film's territory, concerned as it is with the hidden and lost histories of the Jews and Roma who were murdered by the Nazis, and with the ways in which, through oral history and music, both the peoples and their cultures resisted the eradication by the Nazis. Unlike *Orlando* or *The Gold Diggers, The Man Who Cried* contains no visible archives, with the exception of a Parisian government office outside of which papers are being burned, only aural ones. Music, with spoken language as its corollary, is a talisman against amnesia: Suzie recalls her Jewish heritage when she hears Yiddish spoken by her landlady Mme Goldstein. Language encodes remembering when shared, suggesting that collective memory is the most powerful archive. When Suzie arrives in New York to search for her father, his name is not on the official records, but he is recalled by fellow immigrant workers in a garment factory.

Oral and aural histories become both refugee and refuge under the weight of the film's historical research and setting. The hierarchive is made as invisible as it made the people represented by the film's characters, while the high cultural archive of opera is revealed as repertoire: infinitely changing and changeable, even to the point that Suzie/Dido *survives* her prescribed fate as a woman (and a Jew) and leaves both her lover and the burning city/ boat to reconnect with the most intimate archive of her self: her childhood name, language, and her father, who first gave her music. Memory is a shared act, like the tango, like watching a film.

The Archivist as Alchemist

On the online message boards for *YES* (2004), "sally potter" answers a question about the influence of James Joyce on *YES,* in particular Molly Bloom's closing monologue from *Ulysses.* To do so, she enters her personal storehouse of memory, which includes a visit to a cinematic archive: "In moscow . . . on a private tour of the Eisenstein museum, (which was housed in an apartment as if Eisenstein had just stepped out for a moment), I came across his battered, well thumbed copy of Ulysses on one of the crowded bookshelves. this too was a moving experience."[18] Eisenstein's museum, his library, takes its place in a new kind of archive: the Internet. Potter's move to the digital foregrounds new developments to the idea of the archive, particularly regarding access. Unlike a film, or even a DVD collector's edition with additional material, the online archive is seemingly limitless. Added to the privately archived paratexts surrounding earlier films, there is now a public archive of reactions to *YES.* Unlike Taylor's "fixed" institution, it is open-ended, emotive, and dialogic, appropriately so for a film about a conversation between (and undoing of) binaries of East and West, male and female, Muslim and Christian.

YES itself is a double, having begun life as a five-minute segment for a portmanteau film called *Paris, je t'aime* (2006). Potter shot the segment in Paris but withdrew the finished short. The script for the short appears as an appendix to the *YES* screenplay, but it also appears as an echo within *YES,* as the dialogue for the short is an extended version of the "car park" scene at the heart of the film, a scene that is also the subject of a production documentary, "Finding Scene 54," on the DVD. This process of reworking is audible in *YES* through the repetition of lines between internal diegetic voice-over and diegetic dialogue. The ways in which we repeat ourselves, drawing on our intimate archives and the possibility of entering into one another's archives, are part of the film's thematics, even as the film is the least connected to the kind of archives that Potter's previous films have engaged with so explicitly and artfully.

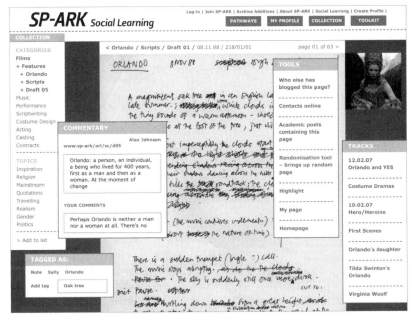

Potter archives herself on the SP-ARK website demo (Adventure Pictures Ltd., 2006).

Yet the digital technology that is both instrumental to the film's production and complicit in the oppressive global politics that the film speaks against makes *YES* the most intensely archived of Potter's films. What has been transformed in the process is not the archive on which it draws for its images or narrative (as with *Thriller* and *Orlando*), nor the archive whose absences it charts (as with *The Gold Diggers* and *The Man Who Cried*), but the archive of cinema itself. Potter proposes the filmmaker as a postmodern archivist, one who is, as she sings in *The Gold Diggers,* "searching for the secret of transformation," looking in the archive for that which will alter it.

When SP meets with the Archivist in Buenos Aires, he opens boxes of material (kisses, tears) that SP has sent him.[19] This material, "ephemeral" in both its fantastic form in the short story, and its visualized form in the film, is the basis of both film and archive. The archivist tango between the two states is "a moving experience," the archival material arranged for us in her films "as if [Potter] had just stepped out for a moment." In an expansion and continuation of her feminist working practices from the 1970s on, Potter demonstrates that she has stepped out of the picture to create a space in which the viewer, "chewing possibilities," can form her own intimate archive. She has also stepped out from *behind* the picture to share with us her creative process, asking an open-ended and inviting "What next?"

Notes

Thanks to Sally Potter and Adventure Pictures for access to private archival materials.

1. Joel Katz, "From Archive to Archiveology," *Cinematograph* 4 (1991): 96–97.

2. Diana Taylor, *The Archive and the Repertoire: Performing Cultural Memory in the Americas* (Durham, NC: Duke University Press, 2005).

3. Katz, "From Archive to Archiveology," 97.

4. Festival of Performance Art program (London: Serpentine Gallery, August 1974). Sally Potter, private collection.

5. Ann Cvetkovich, "In the Archive of Lesbian Feelings: Documentary and Popular Culture," *Camera Obscura* 49 7.1 (2002): 106–47. Reprinted in *The Archive of Feelings: Trauma, Sexuality, and Lesbian Public Culture* (Durham, NC: Duke University Press, 2003): 239–71.

6. Sally Potter, *The Tango Lesson* (London: Faber & Faber, 1997), 94.

7. Sally Potter, "The Tango Lesson: If Tango Is the Answer, What Is the Question?" (unpublished tactical document, 1995), 15. Sally Potter, private collection.

8. Qtd. in Uriel Orlow, "Latent Archive, Roving Lens," in *Ghosting: The Role of the Archive within Contemporary Artists' Film and Video,* ed. Jane Connarty and Josephine Lanyon (Bristol, UK: Picture This, 2006), 34.

9. Ibid., 35.

10. Patricia Mellencamp, *A Fine Romance: Five Ages of Film Feminism* (Philadelphia: Temple University Press, 1995), 159–69; Kaja Silverman, *The Acoustic Mirror: The Female Voice in Psychoanalysis and Cinema* (Bloomington: Indiana University Press, 1988), 178–86; B. Ruby Rich, *Chick Flicks: Theories and Memories of the Feminist Film Movement* (Durham, NC: Duke University Press, 1998), 326–36.

11. B. Ruby Rich, *"The Gold Diggers"* in "75 Hidden Gems," *Sight & Sound* 17, no. 8 (August 2007): 23.

12. National Film Theatre program, May 1984. Sally Potter, private collection.

13. The "celestial ruby" is the philosopher's stone, which held the property of transforming base metal into gold.

14. Potter, *Tango Lesson,* 84.

15. Ibid., 85.

16. Anne Ciecko, "Transgender, Transgenre, and the Transnational: Sally Potter's *Orlando,*" *Velvet Light Trap* 11 (1998): 19–34.

17. I refer here to the Region 2 DVD (Artificial Eye, 1997).

18. Post by sallypotter, *YES* talkboard, March 24, 2006, http://www.yesthe-movie.com/forum_thread.jsp?articleType=Content.TALK%20TO%20SALLY. Poetry&threadId=161.

19. Potter, *Tango Lesson,* 94.

Interactions

Toward a Feminist Coney Island of the Avant-Garde

Janie Geiser Recasts the Cinema of Attractions

You hear Janie Geiser's cinematic diorama installation before you see it. Drifting out of a darkened room are the suspenseful flourishes played on a piano when a damsel is in distress in a silent film, punctuated every so often by a thunderous clap. Produced by a motorized contraption that would be right at home on the grounds of a country fair—a large box hanging in mid-air whose side flaps are hoisted up by a rope on pulleys, then released with a violent *slam*—this is a sound that stops you dead in your tracks. It rings in your ears, runs down your spine, and makes you feel suddenly trapped. These sensations have a political dimension. Their hold on the body offers a lesson in history and invites a kinesthetic insight into the freedoms and limitations experienced by women in early American films.

"The Masculization of Girls"

It is precisely this tension between female liberation and restriction that is the subject of Geiser's *The Spider's Wheels,* created for the tenth anniversary exhibition of the City of Los Angeles Individual Artist Fellowship Program. When Geiser moved to LA in 1999 to become the director of the Cotsen Center for Puppetry and the Arts at CalArts, she was struck by the fact that Hollywood's first generation of female stars was quickly dying out. Intrigued by the glimpses into the once-adventurous lives of now unknown actresses from the 1910s and 1920s afforded by their obituaries, she began to investigate the careers of Pauline Curley, Laura La Plante, Ruth Clifford, Allene Ray, and their more famous counterparts, the "serial queens" Pearl White, Helen Holmes, and Ruth Roland. Several of these stars survived well into

51

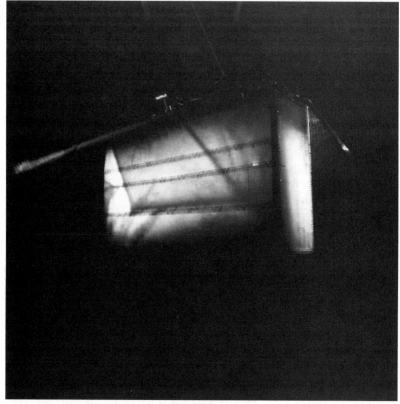

The Spider's Wheels, part 1, "Box opening" (Janie Geiser, 2006).

their nineties, while others, like White and Holmes, barely reached middle age; most saw their careers eclipsed by the coming of sound in 1927. During their heyday, however, one actually replaced another—Ray became the Pathé Company's leading lady when White retired in 1923—and all were in some sense doubles for one another. Athletic, strong, and self-reliant, these "New Women" frequently performed their own stunts, and were as accomplished in real life as the heroines whose exploits they enacted on screen. In their roles as spies, detectives, reporters, and telegraph operators, they flew in air balloons, raced cars at full throttle, leapt from speeding trains, and jumped off rooftops, sometimes engaging in fist fights or wielding pistols as they devised clever means of escape from dangerous situations. In their own lives, the women portraying these fearless heroines were equally untraditional: Roland, star of *The Girl Detective* (1913), was fond of fishing and handled firearms with ease; Kathlyn Williams, of *The Adventures of Kathlyn* (1913), loved baseball, fencing, and motoring; and White, who played the unflappable heiress Pauline Marvin in *The Perils of Pauline* (1914), famously proclaimed, "For recreation I love beefsteak and aviation," flaunted her dislike of domestic tasks, and openly supported new "companionate" relationships between men and women.[1]

As both Ben Singer and Shelley Stamp have pointed out, the press regarded Roland, White, and other New Women with a curious mixture of admiration and anxiety. While White wrote a series of articles under her byline recommending that young women interested in working in the film industry cultivate strength, courage, and physical fitness, fan magazines like *Motion Picture Classic* ran celebrity profiles at once praising White's unconventional acts of daring and emphasizing her "simplicity and womanly charm."[2] Assuring readers of the modern woman's customary femininity was obviously an issue, as a 1911 article titled "The Masculization of Girls" and another from 1919 asking "What Sort of Fellow Is Pearl White?" made clear.[3] Modern women were energetic, independent, and extraordinarily mobile: they liked to walk, row, ride, motor, jump, and run, but "not daintily with high heeled, silk-lined elegance."[4] Mentioning the softer side of serial queens in profiles showcasing their heroic feats helped assuage cultural anxieties about the possibility of declining femininity. In the serials themselves, such contradictory tensions were echoed in plotlines alternately empowering and imperiling their daring heroines. Their ambivalent condition—as characters and as New Women—became the basis of Geiser's installation.

Utilizing found imagery from serial films and 16mm black-and-white footage of a contemporary actress playing a silent film heroine, dispersed across three distinct object/projection areas, *The Spider's Wheels* focuses on the forgotten star of a fictitious serial about a female detective known as the Spider. Although her name conveys a potentially dangerous femininity, this mistress of disguise, Geiser writes, "alternately relishes her power and is frightened by it."[5] The central element in the installation is that compelling contraption, an opaque Plexiglas box with perforated metal flaps that also serves as a silver screen. Superimposed on both sides are luminous images of a determined Pearl White and her double Andrea LeBlanc crawling back and forth through a tunnel that gradually gives way to an apocryphal landscape. Meanwhile, the screen, as its sides lift, transforms temporarily into a house. When the roof descends with a violent slam, our heroine is stuck. In this situation, she appears hopelessly boxed in.

Elsewhere in the installation, she has other options. In one corner of the room, she reclines in her "web," a paper and wire mesh screen on which

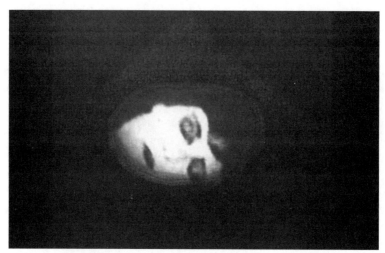

The Spider's Wheels, part 2, "Floating face" (Janie Geiser, 2006).

The Spider's Wheels, part 3, "Door with Peephole Projection" (Janie Geiser, 2006).

is projected an uncanny image of her head. In another miniature projection she is engaged in detection. Adjoining the house-screen is a closet-diorama that seems to belong on the set of a Technicolor version of *The Cabinet of Dr. Caligari* (Robert Wiene, 1919). Constructed in the foreshortened perspective favored by German Expressionist films, a deep blue corridor leads to a mysterious red door at the top of a small staircase. A latched peephole invites us to peer in on an inexplicable scene: a man's hands crush and conceal an unidentified document, before dropping an inkwell deliberately onto the floor, causing a spectral female figure abruptly to open a door. The wide-eyed Spider witnesses these events, and then, unexpectedly, looks directly at *us*—as though she is acknowledging our presence as viewers. Like her, we are left wondering how these incidents add up, and, more important, what they might mean.

"Anything but Pure"

The Spider's Wheels, a video installation exploring the representation of women in silent film whose spectacular form has all the appeal of a fairground attraction, is such a wild hybrid that fits simultaneously into so many histories, it is hard to know where to begin. On the one hand, its seamless fusion of film and video places the work squarely within the new genre of

The Spider's Wheels, part 3, "Spider on Woman's Face" (Janie Geiser, 2006).

cinematic moving image installation made possible by the widespread availability of the video projector in the 1990s. Video's pedigree may be "anything
but pure," as Doug Hall and Sally Jo Fifer noted at the outset of that decade,
but those who were drawn to it in the 1960s and 1970s were performance
and conceptual artists, electronic musicians, sculptors, and social activists
interested in community-based television or documentary rather than filmmakers.[6] Experimental film had its own history, and during this same period
the "heroic," visionary avant-garde that championed radical abstraction, rejected Hollywood narrative style, and was most associated with the work of
Stan Brakhage was at its peak. Crossover between the two media was rare.
More recently, however, as Chrissie Iles put it, "the languages of film and
video have become conflated into a single cinematic aesthetic."[7]

This conflation signals the third distinct phase in the history of moving image installation. Following the phenomenologically oriented works
of the 1960s and 1970s and the sculptural arrangements of the 1980s, the
wall-sized projections of the last two decades recall the large-scale, "expanded
cinema" events and slide installations of thirty-five years ago. Shot on 16mm
film or video and digitally projected, often on enormous, contiguous screens
that require frontal viewing rather than encouraging movement through
space, some of these new works utilize installation as a tool for interrogating
Hollywood cinema, and each engenders a unique form of affect. Douglas
Gordon's *24-Hour Psycho* (1993), for example, meticulously deconstructs
Alfred Hitchcock's famous thriller by slowing the film down to two frames
per second and stripping it of sound, thus exposing nuances of movement
imperceptible to the naked eye and making our experience of each gesture
more unsettling. Isaac Julien's *Baltimore* (2003) does something different.
Made in the wake of *Baaadasssss Cinema* (2002), his documentary about
the history of Blaxploitation films, this three-screen work intersperses dialogue from *The Mack* (1973) throughout 16mm color sequences featuring
the genre's founder Melvin Van Peebles on an urban journey that brings him
face to face with his own effigy at the Great Blacks in Wax Museum in Baltimore, Maryland. When his adventure ends with this shock of recognition,
visitors to the installation feel it too. *On Chapels, Caves, and Erotic Mystery,*
by Christian Tomaszewski (2007), returns to a more sculptural configuration
to evoke the mysterious world of David Lynch's *Blue Velvet* (1986), juxtaposing life-size and miniature recreations of key film locations with objects
drawn from the film's mise-en-scène, like the famous severed ear that sets the
narrative in motion. The installation's conceptual approach to the film's eerie
atmosphere inspires a critical attitude in visitors to the work.

The Spider's Wheels likewise utilizes a more three-dimensional assembly of elements to interrogate an earlier period in Hollywood's history, thus transforming a number of experimental film traditions while taking Janie Geiser's eclectic body of work in a whole new direction, one that makes her unique feminist aesthetic particularly forceful and explicit. If her first installation resembles a stage set, this is perhaps no surprise, as Geiser is a master of puppet theater, and what drew her to puppetry twenty-five years ago—its ability to invent, as she says, "an incredibly visual world apart, where image, object, movement, sound, and text are all equal players"—sounds remarkably like a definition of moving image installation.[8] Her comment also alludes to what she loves about experimental cinema, especially the genre of collage animation: its capacity for creating self-contained worlds.

Geiser has moved fluidly back and forth between experimental film and theater since 1990, when she made a short, black-and-white animated film titled *The Royal Terror Theatre* and a toy theater segment for *Half a World Away,* a diorama performance dramatizing British naval officer Robert Scott's fatal voyage to the South Pole in 1912, co-created with A. Leroy (aka Dick Connette). Since that time, she has made ten animated films that collage found imagery with found objects, and has often included films in her works for puppet theater, projecting them on characters and elements of mise-en-scène and sometimes borrowing footage from Hollywood films. *Ether Telegrams* (1999), for example, a "theatrical collage" inspired by the dramatic use of gesture in nineteenth-century spirit photographs and by the ghost stories of Edith Wharton, projects imagery from the dreamlike opening sequence of Alfred Hitchcock's *Rebecca* (1940) onto a masked performer flanked by a screen to construct the winding, moonlit terrain through which she walks to a haunted mansion.[9] More recently Geiser has integrated film and theater via *Automata,* a company co-founded with CalArts colleague Susan Simpson in 2004 to explore the common ancestry of puppetry, miniature theater, and experimental film in earlier kinds of popular entertainment like the cinema of attractions, nineteenth-century toy theater, magic lantern shows, and cabinets of curiosities.[10]

The Spider's Wheels offers a new twist on these intertwined histories, recasting the cinema of attractions for the twenty-first century by plumbing film's original penchant for spectacle, fusing it with found footage's skillful critique, and tapping into installation's kinesthetic aspect: its sensual effect on an ambulatory body, moving through the immediacy of a spatial here and now. Fuelling all of this is an investigation of gender as it was constructed by Hollywood cinema in the mid-1910s. As women continued to fight for suffrage, the film industry embarked on its first major campaign to solicit female patronage, through serials whose sensational action-adventure format showcased the heroic feats of the Progressive era's New Women, while relishing the spectacle of their distress.[11] Probing the films' political unconscious (bypassing scenes of lurid victimization and leaving diabolical villains behind), Geiser extracts a female archetype—an image of a woman engaged in struggle, crawling back and forth again and again—and by recontextualizing it in space, adding riveting sound, and providing a shocking but entertaining mode of presentation, creates a spectacular, feminist "Coney Island of the avant-garde."[12] Film historian Tom Gunning coined this phrase. Let me explain its pertinence here.

If experimental film has often functioned as a pedagogical intervention or mode of reception capable of interrogating the codes and conventions of Hollywood cinema as thoroughly as film theory or history, as Bart Testa suggests in *Back and Forth: Early Film and the Avant-Garde* (1994), then one of the most striking examples of this tendency is the recurring interest by members of the French, Russian, and American avant-gardes in cinema's facility at harnessing visibility or, as Fernand Léger put it in 1922, for "making images seen."[13] Films produced before 1906 exhibited this quality most intensely. Shocking, spectacular, and virtually without plot or characterization, these short erotic and trick films, often demonstrations of cinematic techniques or recreations of current events, were designed to incite viewers' visual curiosity and to provide pleasure through acts of display. Frequently displayed was the act of looking itself, as actors ruptured the film's illusion of continuity and stared out at spectators, acknowledging their presence. This nonnarrative, exhibitionistic cinema of attractions, as Gunning called it, directly addressed and engaged its spectator.

"Jolting Us into an Encounter"

"Attraction" is a fairground and circus term for a surprising or illogical novelty act, and Gunning borrowed it from Soviet filmmaker Sergei Eisenstein, who outlined his ideas in "Montage of Attractions" (1923). He called for a politically agitational form of theater that would replace the melodramatic illusionism of the bourgeois stage with a method that subjected audience members to sensual and psychological impact, rather than encouraging them to identify with characters. Along with acrobatic clowns, a short film, and a tightrope act that disrupted the proscenium and extended over the heads of spectators, Eisenstein envisioned a salvo exploding beneath their seats, catapulting them into revolutionary consciousness. The spectator was the theater's most important material, and attractions, he argued, worked by establishing interrelationships: with other attractions and with viewers whose intellectual process was a dialectical synthesis of the relationships between those attractions and their own perceptions. These ideas became the basis of his "dialectical approach to film form," which emphasized the collision of antithetical elements. As he wrote in his notes in the late 1920s for an unrealized film of Karl Marx's *Capital* (whose "formal side" was inspired by *Ulysses* [1922] and therefore dedicated to modernist James Joyce), Eisenstein's goal was instruction in Marx's method. He wanted to teach workers to "think dialectically" by drawing upon cinema's spectacular properties, and by creating novel attractions, like those found at the circus or fair.[14] If films could generate physical sensations with genuine political significance, then a truly critical cinema should seek to *astonish*.

No wonder Gunning turned to Eisenstein for terminology: the word "attraction" perfectly embodies both the confrontational spirit and pleasurable appeal of early-twentieth-century forms of popular entertainment, from circus to cinema, and highlights the direct mode of address they shared with Eisenstein's later avant-garde. Convinced of spectacle's radical potential for stimulating insight, and committed to the political efficacy of an aesthetics of shock, Eisenstein was "tapping into a source of energy" that had always been part of film history but that had been absorbed by narrative features since their rise to prominence in the mid-1910s.[15] A diverse group of filmmakers with different styles and agendas have joined Eisenstein in this discovery over the years: Buster Keaton, Salvador Dalí and Luis Buñuel, Jack Smith, and, most recently, Janie Geiser have each realized that the cinema of attractions is still an "unexhausted resource" capable of fuelling spectacular forms of critique.[16]

By embracing theatricality, harnessing visibility, and especially utilizing strategies of direct address (from the startling moment when the Spider breaks the frame and meets our gaze, to that dangling house-screen's unforgettable slam), *The Spider's Wheels* refashions the cinema of attractions into a three-dimensional installation that cultivates an attitude of critical distance by employing techniques that leave us in awe. But instead of catapulting us into revolutionary consciousness through a salvo that literally hurls us out of our seats, Geiser creates a form of kinesthetic consciousness-raising. She raises our consciousness as female spectators by reworking a number of strangely familiar images, and by subjecting us to a series of physical jolts that lead to surprising historical insights. And this, as various scholars have suggested, is the very stuff of *wonder*. "A historical phenomenon differently valenced and valued (and experienced) in different times and different places," writes Mary Baine Campbell; wonder nonetheless has a deep structure.[17] Unpredictable and jarring, if not overwhelming, wonder may be difficult to recognize or understand, although it has long been associated with specific bodily reactions. Philosophers and scientists from Descartes to Darwin have noted its capacity to immobilize the body temporarily (especially during an encounter with something completely new) and to engender a wide-eyed response manifested in physical gestures such as trembling, gasping, and shortness of breath.[18] At once personally illuminating and culturally significant, the experience of wonder, as Caroline Walker Bynum suggests, operates by "jolting us into an encounter with the past that is unexpected and strange."[19]

What better way to describe the effect of *The Spider's Wheels* could there possibly be than this, given the work's effect on the body and examination of film history? To answer this question one must first ask two more, both concerned with the issue of spectatorship. If, as Gunning points out, "every change in film history implies a change in its address to the spectator, and each period constructs its spectator in a new way," then how are we addressed and constructed as spectators, or more aptly, as visitors, in and through the genre of moving image installation, at the dawn of the twenty-first century?[20] And what is the nature of our experience as female visitors, as we move from station to station in a cinematic diorama installation that explores the representation of women in the American silent serials that once thrilled so many female fans?

"Space-in-Between"

In the early 1990s, just as video installation was becoming less sculpturally oriented and more inclined to utilize large-scale projections, Margaret Morse outlined a preliminary poetics of the medium, noting that only by experiencing installations when they are installed do we get a sense of their atmosphere: the elusive mood or feeling that cannot be captured in photographs and that is generated by and palpable within the charged "space-in-between" each work's unique sculptural or projected components.[21] And yet, like other experiential arts only temporarily anchored in the present, video installation is a remarkably fugitive medium, and therefore its potentialities have been "discovered at a very slow rate."[22] As a result, and even after what at the time of Morse's writing was a twenty-year history of widely varying works, we still lacked a critical vocabulary for "kinesthetic 'insights' at the level of the body ego and its orientation in space."[23] To flesh out the specificity of video installation, she concluded, "requires each experience and its interpretation."[24]

That is one of the goals of this essay: to provide for posterity that somewhat paradoxical thing, a textual analysis of a fleeting experience whose particular resonance, in Morse's phrase, "you had to be there" to perceive.[25]

Evocative description is enriched by context, however, and corporeal sensations offer lessons in history, while opening onto new forms of theory that finally begin to give us the vocabulary for the embodied experiences alluded to by Morse. Before elaborating upon these theories in detail, let me return for a moment to the place where I began, to the shocking slam that boxes in our heroine, and echoes throughout the space-in-between the sculptural components comprising *The Spider's Wheels*. Here, in Janie Geiser's deconstructed chamber of cinema, the mood is one of serious exhilaration, but the longer you linger the more an initial sensation of delight is punctuated by pangs of dread. Every time the roof goes up it is hard not to anticipate that crash back down or to sigh or to cringe and think "not again!" Other visitors to the installation seemed to feel the same: they gasped or winced or stopped in their tracks, reacting each time the Spider was trapped. And while such reactions are not gender-exclusive—I saw both men and women respond in similar ways—they may be especially gender-poignant. The image of a woman engaged in struggle is nothing less than archetypal, and seeing this struggle repeatedly thwarted may be painful, if not traumatic, for female visitors. It is something that has happened consistently throughout history (in the United States it took feminists seventy years of activism to achieve the right to vote), and it is a condition women know all too well in the world.

The Spider's Wheels, part 1, "Woman Crawling" (Janie Geiser, 2006).

That *The Spider's Wheels* allows us to experience this struggle "at the level of the body ego and its orientation in space" is significant. It suggests that the act of viewing may be perceived haptically, as Laura U. Marks puts it, as a form of sensuous contact with a moving image medium, rather than as a disembodied process of mastery through physical distance. In this phenomenological model the eyes function as organs of touch, roving across richly textured surfaces, and subjects are understood as material or embodied. They engage in a series of "intercorporeal relationships" with other material "bodies" like those of film and video, each of which is an ideal haptic medium: film, when it slows down or speeds up imagery, enlarges grain, or enhances deteriorating nitrate; video, because of its low contrast ratio, capacity for electronic and digital manipulation, and susceptibility to decay.[26]

Given the way it fuses film and video, *The Spider's Wheels* would seem to be an ideal haptic work of art. Add to this the increased graininess produced by large-scale projection, the additional image texture provided by Plexiglas and mesh screens, the three-dimensional phenomenon of installation, which requires bodily movement through physical space, and of course the slam that ricochets around the room and reverberates in your chest, and you have the potential for multiple sensory insights equipped with an instructive historical edge. By following Marks's eclectic gesture in *Touch,* which is less about "bringing objects in line with ready-made principles" than forming numerous points of contact with them through the creative fusion of critical methods, we can arrive at an understanding of the kinesthetic aspect of Geiser's installation through another eclectic critical synthesis.[27] The one I have been developing throughout this essay begins with Morse, is expanded by Marks, shares affinities with the cinema of attractions as informed by Eisenstein, and bears an interesting relationship to the responses of female fans who adored serial films in the 1910s.

As Stamp explains, serials were so popular in their heyday that one distributor called the craze "serialitis," thus likening it to an ailment.[28] If reactions to these tales of female independence laced with peril bordered on the obsessive, it is perhaps because their pleasures were unique. Consisting of installments ending at each plot line's most interesting moment, serial films deliberately deferred desire and suspended traditional narrative closure. Their popularity also hinged on their ability to generate specific kinds of affect. Repeatedly described in the press as "hair-raising," "heart-thumping," "nerve-gripping," and "awe-inspiring," serial films caused female spectators to sit on the edge of their seats, rise up out of their chairs, feel somewhat out of breath, and gasp in amazement: bodily reactions that register experiences of wonder and are driven by anxiety, excitement, and fear.[29]

The sudden stopping, gasping, smiling, flinching, and wincing register-ing the astonishment, anticipation, dread, frustration, and delight experi-enced by female visitors to *The Spider's Wheels* provides a historically distinct yet interesting echo of the physiological responses of early-twentieth-century female viewers to the serials themselves. Reacting with equal passion to the unresolved fragments of a plot involving scenarios of entrapment, struggle, detection, and relaxation, to the intriguing cinematic dioramas elliptically presenting these lines of development, and to the political insights into the status of women that the work engenders through such spectacular means, visitors to *The Spider's Wheels* were invited to use their imaginations to envi-sion their own crises, climaxes, denouements, and endings in the space-in-between the physical elements of the installation.

Wandering through Geiser's chamber for rumination, trying to fathom what will happen to the Spider, and wondering how much longer she will have to keep crawling, it seems suddenly striking that she also has *wheels*. Neither represented in the projections nor by the dioramas, but alluded to, nonetheless, in the title of the work, perhaps these wheels are her means of transportation, a way of getting around that we must imagine. After all, New Women were known for their mobility: they moved through the world with unprecedented freedom, relishing their ability to fly, drive, and cycle. Maybe they are the ghosts in the machine, as their energetic independence is so palpable in the room, even as that slam reminds us of their struggle. Here, then, is a final exhilarating image of the Spider, drawn from an imagined heroic scenario that further defers narrative closure: confident at the wheel, the wind in her hair, racing at breakneck speed through the streets of Los Angeles, in fearless pursuit of a dangerous criminal. Between the sculptural components of Janie Geiser's installation is an interval charged with per-petual desire.

Notes

An earlier version of this essay was published in *Afterimage* 34, no. 4 (2007): 21–27.

1. Ben Singer, *Melodrama and Modernity: Early Sensational Cinema and Its Con-texts* (New York: Columbia University Press, 2001), 221–62; and Shelley Stamp, *Movie-Struck Girls: Women and Motion Picture Culture after the Nickelodeon* (Prin-ceton: Princeton University Press, 2000), 102–53. References to the untraditional pastimes embraced and remarks made by Roland, Williams, and White may be found in Stamp, *Movie-Struck Girls,* 143, 144, and 147. Chapter 8 of Singer's book, "Power and Peril in the Serial-Queen Melodrama," was an important resource for Geiser in thinking through her ideas for *The Spider's Wheels,* especially regarding the

New Woman's cultural and physical mobility. Interview with the author, Los Angeles, May 2006. See Singer, *Melodrama and Modernity,* 235–43 for more information on the New Woman's mobility.

2. Stamp, *Movie-Struck Girls,* 145.

3. Singer, *Melodrama and Modernity,* 242; Stamp, *Movie-Struck Girls,* 146.

4. Singer, *Melodrama and Modernity,* 242.

5. Janie Geiser, unpublished "Residency Statement," Atlantic Center for the Arts, New Smyrna Beach, FL. Geiser developed *The Spider's Wheels* during her residency at the Atlantic Center for the Arts, October 10–30, 2005.

6. Doug Hall and Sally Jo Fifer, eds., *Illuminating Video: An Essential Guide to Video Art* (New York: Aperture, 1991), 14.

7. Chrisse Iles, "Video and Film Space," in *Space Site Intervention: Situating Installation Art,* ed. Erika Suderburg (Minneapolis: University of Minnesota Press, 2000), 257.

8. Geiser in Melinda Barlow, "Interview with Janie Geiser." *Animac* 3 (2004) (Spain): 3.

9. Geiser, unpublished program notes for *Ether Telegrams,* 1999.

10. For more on *Automata* and Geiser's role in the international revival of miniature theater, see Melinda Barlow, "Size Matters: In the Micro-Universe of Toy Theatre, Startling Shifts in Perspective Require Audiences to Look Closely." *American Theatre* 22 (February 2005): 60–64.

11. Stamp, *Movie-Struck Girls,* 102.

12. Tom Gunning, "The Cinema of Attractions: Early Film, Its Spectator, and the Avant-Garde," in *Early Cinema: Space Frame Narrative,* ed. Thomas Elsaesser (London: British Film Institute, 1990), 61.

13. Fernand Léger, "A Critical Essay on the Plastic Qualities of Abel Gance's Film *The Wheel,*" in *Functions of Painting,* ed. Edward Fry, trans. Alexandra Anderson (New York: Viking, 1973), 21, cited in ibid., 56.

14. See Sergei Eisenstein, Maciej Sliwowski, Jay Leyda, and Annette Michelson, "Notes for a Film of *Capital,*" *October* 2 (Summer 1976): 3–26.

15. Gunning, "Cinema of Attractions," 61.

16. Ibid.

17. Mary Baine Campbell, *Wonder and Science: Imagining Worlds in Early Modern Europe* (Ithaca, NY: Cornell University Press, 1999), 3.

18. See Stephen Greenblatt, *Marvelous Possessions: The Wonder of the New World* (Chicago: University of Chicago Press, 1991) for a thorough account of these various approaches to the aesthetics of wonder.

19. Caroline Walker Bynum, "Wonder." *American Historical Review* 102, no. 1 (February 1997): 1.

20. Gunning, "Cinema of Attractions," 61.

21. Margaret Morse, "Video Installation Art: The Image, the Body, and the Space-in-Between," in Hall and Fifer, *Illuminating Video,* 153–67. Since 1991, there have been other books and essays also exploring the phenomenology of installation—but not moving image installation—and these do not discuss what Morse isolated in her essay and what most concerns me here: that elusive thing called atmosphere.

Significant, however, for their examination of the "nomadic" aspect of installations are James Meyer's "The Functional Site; or, The Transformation of Site Specificity," and Miwon Kwon's "One Place after Another: Notes on Site Specificity," both in Suderburg, *Space Site Intervention*, 23–37 and 38–63, respectively. Another useful source on kinesthetic insights is Caroline A. Jones, ed., *Sensorium: Embodied Experience, Technology, and Contemporary Art* (Cambridge, MA: MIT Press, 2006).

22. Morse, "Video Installation Art," 167.

23. Ibid., 153.

24. Ibid., 166.

25. Ibid., 167.

26. Laura U. Marks, *Touch: Sensuous Theory and Multisensory Media* (Minneapolis: University of Minnesota Press, 2002), xx. Chapter 6, "Loving a Disappearing Image," 91–110, provides an especially rich account of the haptic qualities of decaying film and video imagery.

27. Ibid., xx.

28. Stamp, *Movie-Struck Girls,* 102.

29. Ibid., 114–15.

Michelle Citron   *Chapter 4*

Slipping the Borders/Shifting the Fragments
A Working Paper

Memory/history, fiction/documentary, fragments/narrative cohesiveness, bodies/ideas, visual pleasure/text, life/art, linear film/interactive digital: I start with paired ideas, seemingly opposite, sometimes contradictory. It's in the narrow current created by "/" that the truth breathes. It's at the border I learn. I hold these pairs, and explore the borders, with tightly structured works: controlling/unruly.

• • •

My artwork slips across the mediums of film, writing, performance, and new media with two consistent underlying ideas: the examination of borders and the tension between fragmentation and narrative coherence. Borders are where contradictions flourish. Fragments are the building blocks of all narrative. We assemble fragments into a whole to construct a memory, to recall a dream, to create a film, or to piece together a story of our life.

• • •

The tension between fragmentation and narrative unity has been central to my art since the beginning—even before the beginning if I include my doctoral work in cognitive psychology, where I investigated how the mind creates narrative coherence out of the mass of fragmented stimuli that constantly flood us.

An early film, *Integration* (1975), takes twenty-five still images of a solitary woman violinist and optically prints them to give unity, temporality, and movement to that which was fragmented, discontinuous, and still. In *Parthenogenesis* (1975) fragmentation is created through the interweaving of documentary and experimental images: a formal expression of the conflicted feelings the young musician/subject has toward her work. In *Daughter Rite* (1978) and *What You Take for Granted . . .* (1983) fragmentation is created whenever the documentary, fictional, and experimental threads interrupt one another. In this way, the stories of mothers and daughters, and of women working in traditionally male jobs, are constructed through shifting and contradictory points of view. The fragmentation creates unexpected juxtapositions, allowing for the expression of complexity and contradiction. Fragmentation and borders are intimately linked. This is a different kind of telling from the seemingly seamless unfolding of most narratives we experience in our media culture.

● ● ●

When I screen *Daughter Rite* I'm always surprised by how many in the audience read unity into a film that was narratively disjointed at every stage of its creation: writing, editing, and finished movie. But the audience strives for coherence. The home movies become those of the sisters, Stephanie and Maggie, and the voice-over is attributed to one of them, usually Stephanie. This is cognitive gymnastics. The story narrated in *Daughter Rite*'s voice-over is not the same as the one told in the faux cinéma vérité scenes, and the voice-over is clearly read by a different actor. But the longing for narrative coherence is strong. How much is this driven by cognitive processes or habits of narrative construction with dreams, with memory, with daily life? How much is this influenced by the conventions of mainstream media, with television being little more then illustrated radio and most mainstream films tightly structured by cause and effect action, three-act architecture, and tidy endings?

● ● ●

Though always central to my media work, these ideas of fragmentation and narrative wholeness were unformed, or at least undertheorized, until I wrote *Home Movies and Other Necessary Fictions.*[1] The process of writing brought to the foreground what had been largely unconscious. *Home Movies* is an experimental memoir, juxtaposing fiction with autobiography with home movie images with cultural critique. Different discourses weave through the book, sometimes on the same page, forcing readers to pick their own way through the story: one of the relationship between lived experience, trauma, art practice, home image–making, and identity construction. The fragmented form of the book was my way of expressing how fragmentation lies at the core of trauma, but also everyday lived experience. The book exploded

67

my ideas of narrative. Linear film no longer held my interest. I embraced the digital as a way to create stories that lie in fragments until constructed in the mind of the player/viewer/reader.

• • •

The digital work I've created over the last eight years juxtaposes text with image, and the personal with the cultural, in a fluid and dynamic way. I use the nonlinear and interactive qualities of digital technology to further explore questions about fragmentation and narrative. How can I maintain fragmentation and still provide narrative pleasure, which is perhaps derived from narrative coherence? What is narrative's power and seduction: cause and effect or instances of strong emotional and/or intellectual engagement? What is the relationship between the emotional and intellectual pleasures of narrative? How can different performance styles and genres enhance the emotional stakes of fragmented narratives? How can players/viewers be sensitized to narrative's constructed nature? How can narrative be structured to respect and foreground contradiction and paradox?

• • •

Formally, I use the nonlinearity inherent in digital media to examine the tension between fragmentation and narrative coherence, a question central to film art, where an illusion of wholeness is built from the edited bits and pieces of visual and sound material. In our digital age of TV channel surfing, interactive games, hypertext novels, and complex Internet websites that we must navigate, issues about narrative seem even more pressing. In this sense, the five interactive digital narratives that I've created represent an evolving experiment in narrativity.

• • •

These digital narratives, created at the intersection of film's materiality and digital media's fluidity, explore the contradictions of identity and the paradoxes of narrative itself. Since these artworks express lived experience in all its messiness, form melts into content.

• • •

The five digital narratives were never whole. I wrote each one as a series of scenes that never, in my mind at least, aligned into a linear story structure. I wrote each work as moments remembered or fragments imagined or dream bits recalled. The scenes are pieces of a character's real or imagined life, creating a puzzle that must be assembled. The narrative lies neither in the work itself nor in the mind of the player/viewer. Rather, these are narratives cre-

Woman wearing red sweater with her back to camera, *Cocktails and Appetizers* (interactive CD-ROM by Michelle Citron, 2001).

ated in the space between: author and audience, computer screen and user, artist and viewser.

• • •

"Jewish Looks" (2001) is a web-based "essay" on American Jews, photography, and identity, created for the online journal *The Scholar and the Feminist Online.*[2] It is an interactive meditation on identity, immigration, and the function of family photographs: a dynamic way of preserving and understanding family images, honoring the lives lived, the photographs seen, and the desires they represent.

"Jewish Looks" blends and contrasts the personal with the historical, the psychological with the political, and the image with the text. Using as its focus four photographs—of my paternal great-grandparents and two of their children—"Jewish Looks" is structured on five levels: the textual ("what you see"), the familial ("what I know"), the historical ("what was"), the mythical ("what we believed"), and the psychological ("what we desired"). A viewer can navigate vertically or laterally through the work, exploring an individual photograph in depth or a theme across images.

• • •

Queer Feast, a further exploration of the complexities of identity, is a series of intersecting, interactive digital narratives on CD-ROM. Each is a stand-alone work. Collectively they create a multi-course meal, a mosaic of lesbian life played out through its contradictions of class, desire, and the minutiae of daily life. The recipe is an algorithm, at once a sly reference to the inter-activity of these works and a procedure for making something—in this case narratives—from the ingredients of scenes. But I'm also a cook, and so food often fuels my imagination. Each of the four pieces that make up the *Queer Feast* uses a different recipe to explore questions of narrative.

As American as Apple Pie (1999)—of course I made dessert first—sits on the border between melodrama and sitcom and builds its story from fragments overheard. It is a tale of food, sex, family, and what happens after the first kiss is over. The story is told through twenty-two scenes, randomly accessed by the viewer, from which a narrative of the characters' family life can be constructed. Monica and Lucille make love, fight, work, raise their son, and, of course, commit adultery. *Apple Pie* is genuinely open-ended; a different story is constructed on each viewing. "Played" one time, Monica and Lucille might live happily ever after; another time, their relationship clearly will not survive; and in yet another "play," ambiguity prevails. The one constant: you learn how to make my grandmother's apple pie.

Cocktails and Appetizers (2001) builds on this work with a more complex structure. The viewer eavesdrops on a multitude of conversations during a cocktail party. From these snippets of both relevant and inconsequential overheard moments, the viewer constructs a story of the main characters, their ever-changing relationships, and their milieu. *Cocktails and Appetizers* explores the pleasures of voyeurism, the performance of gender, and falling in love.

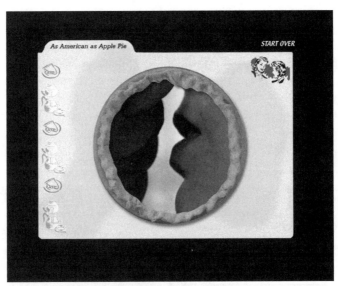

Photo of two women almost kissing, *As American as Apple Pie* (interactive CD-ROM by Michelle Citron, 1999).

Mixed Greens (2004) is a do-it-yourself movie about identity, belonging, and the things we desire. It is a tasty buffet of forty-eight scenes that presents two narratives: four generations of my Irish-Jewish heritage played against four decades of lesbian life in America. Using both documentary and fiction, scenes are mixed and matched by the viewer to interrogate identity versus assimilation, social versus personal history, and discrimination versus accommodation. *Mixed Greens* explores articulations of identity being simultaneously negated and constructed, across sexual and ethnic lines.

Mixed Greens can be navigated to compare and contrast different inflections on a similar issue, for example, the tension between assimilation and maintaining one's identity. My Uncle Oscar joined the IRA and fought alongside Catholics for Irish independence. Oscar, a secular Jew, guarded Michael Collins while writing his diary back-to-front like a Jewish prayer book. Lesbian commitment ceremonies, attendant gift registries, and same-sex partnership benefits all suggest mainstreaming, while the butch/femme scene at the baths, drag kings, "packing," and other Queer possibilities work toward acceptance of differences, or perhaps not giving a damn about acceptance at all.

Alternatively, a viewer can fully construct each of *Mixed Greens'* eight stories sequentially, to reveal deepening knowledge of a character, a culture, or a particular identity formation.

Leftovers (2008) contemplates the aging lesbian. At the center are Norma and Virginia, a real-life couple of forty-five years who died, one after the other, alone in their home, the vibrant dyke community of their youth long gone. Their story is shaped by the objects they left behind, stuffed in their Chicago bungalow: letters and poems, matchbook covers of bars where they danced, paint-by-number paintings left half-finished, clothing (Norma was a softball player in the women's professional softball league as well as a champion bowler; Virginia saved every one of Norma's uniforms packed carefully in tissue paper), trophies, and thousands of snapshots of lesbian life in Chicago from the 1930s through the 1970s. *Leftovers* explores how we use objects to construct our identity and what it means to grow old at the margins of society.

• • •

All five of these pieces are interactive; four are non-linear. Lev Manovich would name these works data-based narratives. He defines the database as a collection of unordered elements—objects, images, words, scenes—that a user can sort or move through in different ways. A website is the obvious example of such a database. In his model, an interactive narrative allows a user multiple paths through a database, usually a collection of scenes, in the process of creating a story.[3] This accurately describes the architecture of interactive narratives and the process of assembly by a viewser of my (and others') interactive stories.[4] It does not, however, adequately address the viewser's experience.

While Manovich acknowledges the more active role of a user in navigating a database narrative, his focus is on the database itself and its cultural meaning. I am more interested in the cognitive experience of the viewer, and understanding why such a database might be compelling. These are the questions that my interactive narratives explore. To that end, I use the term "viewser" for the database negotiator, implying a debt to both the digital world and cinema. Viewsers actively construct database narratives: physically by clicking a mouse and cognitively by watching, and making sense of, their constructions.

• • •

Manovich sees the database as the appropriate cultural form and metaphor for our historical moment. For him, the computer age, which signals the end of master narratives, requires a new way to "structure the experience of ourselves and our world."[5] I think that the process of structuring elements into narratives is a very old process for human beings; it's only the metaphor that's new. Whether constructing narratives is hardwired into our brains or, as Jerome Bruner argues, the main cultural process by which we "organize our experience and our memory of human happenings," narrative is fundamental to our experience as human beings.[6]

• • •

Interactive narratives are challenging to make. They require coherent characters created without the safety net of narrative cause-and-effect determined by the author; narrative forward motion is created only in the mind of the viewser. Interactive narratives demand holding the ambiguity of story puzzle pieces that don't seamlessly fit together—for me as author, and for the viewser. This is not an unfamiliar process. You do it every time you meet someone new: you observe her interaction with a friend, perhaps you then hear a snippet of gossip about her, later you meet and she reveals an intimate moment in her life, and out of these fragments you try to piece together her story, though the pieces rarely create a coherent whole. And yet there are instances of happenstance, what I think of as juxtaposition perfection, when pieces collide and the story momentarily coheres, allowing insight and depth before it inevitably breaks apart. There is liveliness, disorder, and mystery to

Polaroid in interface, *Mixed Greens* (interactive CD-ROM by Michelle Citron, 2004).

these narratives, much like life itself. I find comfort in their unpredictability and ambiguity.

• • •

Truth be told, I was also bored with conventional storytelling. Cause and effect became reductive. Or maybe I just couldn't hack it. I realized that I was unable to write endings. Or at least I couldn't imagine ones that weren't sentimental or cynical or clichéd.

• • •

After *Apple Pie* I no longer desired to make an "indie" feature film. No more writing scripts that would be optioned, yet never produced. No more meetings with development people who, flummoxed by my stories, would start our meeting with questions such as "What kind of car does your protagonist drive? Don't you know that's an important symbol of character? And where are your three acts?" I was tired of the pitch, which I was never good at anyway, tired of trying to find obscene amounts of money, tired of being rejected by Sundance. The interactive narratives showed me a way out. They're small, contained.

• • •

For each course of *Queer Feast* I pressed CD-ROMs and sent them off to festivals, sold them to universities, handed them out to friends. They've won prizes in online digital festivals, been exhibited in kiosk installations in museums, and even been projected. I've shown *Mixed Greens* in a large film theater, where I "performed" the work with the help of the audience who waved large flash cards emblazoned with vegetable icons to indicate their scene selections, creating an experience of communal interactivity. And all of *Queer Feast* is destined for the web at http://www.queerfeast.com.

• • •

I love the camaraderie of a film shoot, the feeling that comes from collective work well done, the intense friendships that often develop. I hate waking up at 5:30 a.m. to get to the set, the sixteen-hour days, day after day after day. The interactive narratives are created on a human scale—five days of shooting, not thirty. Or maybe ten days of shooting over a year's time; what's conceptualized in fragments can be shot in fragments. After shooting I spend at least a year editing the scenes, designing the interface, and creating elements: Photoshopping the interface icons for *Apple Pie;* scanning backgrounds for the composited movies in *Mixed Greens,* or photographing vegetables for its interface; animating the Flash movies for *Leftovers.* Yet the CD-ROMs are collaborative too: I work with programmers who create the interactivity and stitch the pieces together, graphic designers who realize my interface, illustrators, sound designers, composers, digital compositors, and all-around digital helpers, like the ones I'm indebted to for scanning over seventeen hundred photographs for *Leftovers.* Many of these people, artists in their own right, have worked with me on multiple courses; they have become friends. This slower, more intimate process of CD-ROM creation allows me time to think, breathe.

• • •

Is this maturity? Wisdom? Or just aging? Thank god, I don't look my age. All my women friends in the business lie about how old they are, shaving five to ten years off, depending on what they can get away with. It's survival. They're competing for jobs with young men in their twenties.

• • •

Making movies is not easy. Making them with no money is truly difficult. And it only gets harder the older you get. A feature film shot on a shoe-string budget seems a young person's art. It's not that I can't do it. *Mixed Greens* has eight stories, seven separate shoots over an eighteen-month period, thirty-two actors, and a crew of thirty-five. But mostly my interactive narratives are small works: two actors in one, six actors in another; two days shooting documentary or live action, or five days shooting mise-en-scène that will play under a voice-over. I like the intimacy of these smaller works. The latest course, *Leftovers,* has no actors at all: one voice-over that I read, and more than two years of sitting in front of my computer writing, manipulating images, thinking, discovering. It's as if over time my work has stripped down to the essentials of character, events, and feeling.

● ● ●

For the moment, I am content.

Notes

1. Michelle Citron, *Home Movies and Other Necessary Fictions* (Minneapolis: University of Minnesota Press, 1998).

2. http://www.barnard.edu/sfonline/cf/citron.htm.

3. Lev Manovich, *The Language of New Media* (Cambridge, MA: MIT Press, 2001), 218–44.

4. There are many database narratives: e.g., Adriene Jenik, *Mauve Desert* (Los Angeles: Shifting Horizon Productions, 1997); Carroll Parrott Blue, Kristy H. A. Kang, and the Labyrinth Project, *The Dawn at My Back: Memoir of a Black Texas Upbringing* (Los Angeles: USC Annenberg Center, 2003); Pat O'Neill, Rosemary Comella, Kristy H. A. Kang, and the Labyrinth Project, *Tracing the Decay of Fiction: Encounters with a Film by Pat O'Neill* (Los Angeles: USC Annenberg Center, 2002); and Marsha Kinder and Kristy H. A. Kang with John Rechy and James Tobias, *Mysteries and Desire: Searching the Worlds of John Rechy* (Los Angeles: USC Annenberg Center, 2000).

5. Manovich, *Language of New Media,* 219.

6. Jerome Bruner, "The Narrative Construction of Reality." *Critical Inquiry* 18, no. 1 (1991): 4.

Networks

"Each Film Was Built as a Chamber and Became a Corridor"

Maya Deren's Film Aesthetics as Feminist Praxis

With the issuance of her experimental films on DVD, the publication of Bill Nichols's anthology *Maya Deren and the American Avant-Garde,* and the release of Martina Kudláček's documentary *In the Mirror of Maya Deren* (2002), Maya Deren has reemerged as a key auteur of the twentieth century. Deren's innovations in the name of film art stand as an historical counterpoint to the Hollywood product but also pose an implicit critique of contemporary American independent cinema. With decreasing difference between the two, Deren's idea of making a film "for what Hollywood spends on lipstick," as she once famously phrased it, or using her New York apartment for exhibition purposes seems nearly unthinkable.[1] It is this very exceptionality that makes Deren and the various activities she undertook in the name of independent and experimental cinema all the more significant today. Much of the historical work on Maya Deren, feminist and otherwise, has been "inquiries into the individual subject and her textual products," but, as Lauren Rabinovitz goes on to suggest, "the direction of radical political analysis must reach beyond" this limited scope if it is to articulate effectively the ever-expanding influence of Deren on filmmaking today.[2] Yet, even a feminist film historian like Rabinovitz, who presents a thorough discussion of Deren's work beyond her film texts, equivocates as to Deren's authorial agency. Claiming her to be "unconscious" of the ideologies against which she worked, Rabinovitz postulates that Deren "remained prisoner of an ideology that even constructed [her] position of resistance within traditional roles."[3] Rabinovitz suggests, accordingly, that in mapping the "discursive struggles" that shaped Deren's praxis, film historiography is better served by reassessing "the politics of power relations" than the examination of "intentions as politics."[4]

In vitiating Deren's agency, Rabinovitz repeats the gesture made by Laura Mulvey years earlier in her history of feminism and the avant-garde. Mulvey argues that "there is a difference between an interest in women's traditions—the individual or group achievements which women have to their credit, despite a hostile environment—and a belief in a feminine sensibility, tied to the domestic and then freed only into a similar orientation in art."[5] For Mulvey, Deren falls into the latter category, reduced to a parenthetical aside in her history of women's cinema.[6] Consequently Deren herself is frequently delinked from the discursive resistances apparent in her films.

Yet a feminine sensibility—originating in the domestic and redirected to the art world—found expression not only in her films but also in her activism, particularly her establishment of the Creative Film Foundation (CFF), a fact that renders disavowals of Deren's agency moot. Thus my goal here is to radicalize the analysis of Deren's function as film auteur by rethinking her various roles in the history of independent cinema in terms set out by feminist film theory. Deren's historical significance is much more complex than simply a name attached to a body of texts. In her film theories, her promotion of film art, her lobbying for alternative modes of distribution and exhibition, and the themes of her experimental films, Deren contested the extant film system and patriarchal society as a whole. By theorizing these interventions as a concatenated practice, I propose a feminist epistemological inquiry into the discourses that shape current understandings of the history of independent film and Deren's place in it.

Cutting across Deren's innovations as a filmmaker and activist, I contend, is a coherent "chamber" aesthetic formed as a critical response to the sexual division of public and private space that shaped her existence, both as a woman and an artist. Deren's biographers have noted, "architectural imagery serves throughout Deren's early films as a dominant visual metaphor."[7] However, I aver that the physical geographies represented in her films are in fact metonymic of Deren's broader spatial aesthetics, an aesthetics aimed at remapping social geographies circumscribing women's psychic, artistic, and physical mobility. In this way, what manifests in her films as a visual metaphor is actually a synecdoche for a broader conceptual metaphor informing Deren's various activities throughout her career as a filmmaker.

Ideological Premises and Social Geographies

Although much attention has been given to Deren's life, especially in the expansive biographical project *The Legend of Maya Deren,* and a great deal of critical work has been written on her films, the aesthetic relationship between the two remains largely unaddressed. That is, critics tend to approach Deren studies with an implicit split between "life" and "art," which produces *either* biographical discussions *or* formalist critiques.

Over twenty years ago, Teresa de Lauretis urged feminist film critics to reconsider their object of study toward a redefinition of aesthetics that, among other things, foregrounds the production of gender difference: "The emphasis must be shifted away from the artist behind the camera, the gaze, or the text as origin and determination of meaning, toward the wider public sphere of cinema as a social technology."[8] This shift in emphasis has yet to take place fully in Deren historiography. When attention is directed away from Deren's film texts and toward her activities in transforming film culture, they appear as self-evident and transparent, stated as simple historical fact: "Since the war there had been several attempts to organize the independent film community in New York, most of them fueled by the energy and initiative of Maya Deren. In response to her vision of an extensive artists' support system, the Film Artists Society was founded in 1953 . . . while her Creative Film Foundation attempted to secure grants for independent filmmakers from 1955 to 1961."[9] Clearly, such practices speak directly to Deren's influential role in the wider sphere of cinema as a social technology. Nonetheless, Deren's activism and her productions as a filmmaker have yet to be theorized as a unified body of work. Regina Cornwell, for example, points out that Deren "is acclaimed as important; yet, seldom is the real significance of her role as an activist in the avant-garde explained."[10]

In the brief discussion of Deren that follows, Cornwell posits that "if Deren was influential through her filmmaking it was only so because she began the process of establishing, almost single-handedly, a milieu for the avant-garde film in this country—ways and means by which her works could be seen, ways and means taken up in turn by other artists."[11] Cornwell's thesis proposes a cause-and-effect scenario linking Deren's influence as a filmmaker and her (supplementary) role as a film activist. However, while she did take steps to create alternative forms of exhibition and distribution early in her career, much of Deren's efforts to invent these "ways and means" actually took place several years *after* her films had been widely screened. To this extent, reconsideration of the relationship of Deren's filmmaking to her activism requires a more nuanced historical analysis that resists certain teleological assumptions that imply Deren was inconsistent in her praxis. Deren's committed activities in the 1950s in terms of exhibition, distribution, and organization are rarely seen as a continuation of the immense productivity that marked her filmmaking in the 1940s. On the contrary, the waning of film production after *Meditation on Violence* (1948) is frequently perceived as a cessation in Deren's creative process.

Deren's strides to create a public forum for film art need to be placed in sociohistorical context. If her film activism figured centrally in the period 1955 to 1961, it did so in relation to the apex of patriarchal ideology, which, as feminist historians have persuasively argued, attempted "to redefine women's roles in accordance with the new industrial order," effecting "the consolidation of the suburban nuclear family and the separation of the predominantly female sphere of consumption from the predominantly male sphere of production in the period after World War II."[12] This social context endows Deren's praxis with specific (counter-)cultural meaning. After World War II, institutional machineries were set in motion to shepherd women into emergent roles as suburban housewives whose redomestication was imperative to the shifting socioeconomic situation in the United States. Deren's interventions in terms of artistic practice and aesthetic commitment are redirected by this profound ideological shift. Yet discussions of Deren's historical significance rarely reflect the effects the war's changing circumstances had on her textual production and activist work, much less the social technologies bridging these concomitant discursive activities. What is needed to redress this oversight is an analytical framework that resists seeing life, history, and art as separate categories.

A feminist epistemology of aesthetics provides such a framework insofar as it links together pro-filmic tropes, gendered subjectivity, and the sociohistorical discourses from which they emanate. By informing film analysis with the larger questions of sexual difference, feminist reconfigurations of aesthetics pointedly depart from strictly formalist definitions. As Mary Ann Doane has summarized, "there is at least one basic question that subtends the entire project of feminist film criticism . . . the question of the relations between aesthetics and politics."[13] Initially confronted with this question in the 1980s, Doane, along with other scholars who were actively involved in establishing said project, formulated a response that pointed beyond purely textual concerns by conceiving of feminist aesthetics as a social practice and thereby broadening its scope "to the axis of vision itself—to the modes of organizing vision and hearing which result in the production of that 'image.'"[14] In other words, the significant intervention of feminist film theory was to redefine aesthetics in such a way that it took account of the larger fields of artistic and political practice that together constituted women's cinema. Doing so led de Lauretis to characterize women's cinema "as a form of political critique or critical politics . . . that women have developed to analyze the subject's relation to socio-historical reality," and to identify its central project as constructing "other objects and subjects of vision, and [formulating] the conditions of representability of another social subject."[15] It is this definition of feminist aesthetics that I want to return to and renew in the analysis of Deren that follows, for it invites feminist film historians to rethink Deren's various discursive activities as part of a constellated interventionist project, one that bespeaks a unified aesthetic in response to the historical discourses central to the production of sexual difference.

The Effective Creation of an Idea

Deren's fluidity between artistic undertakings, political praxis, and community organizing fundamentally reconceptualizes the very notion of aesthetics in that these activities emanate less from "an aesthetic centered on the text and its effects" than from "an aesthetic of reception, where the spectator is the film's primary concern."[16] This concern with reception is overtly stated in Deren's concept of the "chamber film" as articulated in her "Statement of Principles": "Just as one is prepared to listen, in chamber music, for different values than one expects of symphonic orchestrations, so the use of the program title CHAMBER FILMS is intended to alert the eye of the audience towards the perceptions of values quite different from those of feature films."[17] What makes up these "different values" goes beyond the obvious formal challenges to the Hollywood system. The "chamber" in music indicates either a small, intimate performance space or music to be performed in the private sphere. The evocation of the chamber in Deren's own definition of her work raises the question of the ways in which her art transgresses the demarcated spaces of private and public. In this way, the concept of the chamber takes on a wider signification as a structuring principle in Deren's praxis, a principle directly concerned with the production and reception of "different values" made possible by the reconfiguration of subjectivity and space.

Deren's chamber aesthetic is most explicit in her early films wherein the male protagonist is "the mover of narrative while the female's association with space or matter deprives her of subjectivity."[18] As a site of domesticity, the chamber carries with it the cultural meaning that inscribes gender in its "proper" place. Manifest in Deren's cultural practices is the inseparability of spatiality and sexuality, which historically cohere in the figure of the domesticated woman. Deren's thematic engagement with femininity and domesticity appears early on in her poetry and experimental portraiture but clearly culminates in her film work, most famously in *Meshes of the Afternoon* (1943), as I have discussed in detail elsewhere.[19] Beginning with *Meshes,* her early "narrative" films reflect on how "the apparent mobility of the man is produced by the confinement of the woman, who is at once necessary to the maintenance of the house and the greatest threat to it."[20] During what her biographers call her "chambers years" (1942–47), her best-known films often juxtaposed images of interiors with nature, constructing these spaces as oppositional.[21] In *Meshes* and *At Land* (1944), Deren herself is predominantly filmed either by the sea or enclosed in the home, with distinct meanings accruing to these contrasted spaces. Domestic space in both films is infused with danger for the female protagonist, but while *Meshes* conveys this threat through editing to make objects appear ominous, *At Land* embodies the threat in the male characters that populate interior spaces. Maria Pramaggiore interprets Deren's pro-filmic "concern with bodies and movement" as a deconstructive response to heteronormativity, but I would suggest that the "hostile and threatening" men in these films—particularly in their "attempt[s] to limit her mobility"—also stand as an immediate creative response to the historical situation of women in the United States at the time.[22]

If, as Patricia Erens asserts, aesthetics "deals with the relationship between art and life and becomes the perspective from which an artist creates," then the guiding aesthetic principle that emerges from Deren's films and that continued in her film activism is the interrogation of, and resistance to, the gender arrangements that shaped her life as a woman and an artist.[23] Emphasizing ideological import, Deren argued that her "concern with space and time is not purely technical" but rather articulates "the curious dislocation of the individual in a suddenly and actually relativistic world, and her inability to cope with its fluidity or to achieve a stable, adjusted relationship to its elements."[24] Deren articulates only too clearly the (political) meanings that subtend her aesthetic devices, such as slow motion and staccato editing, that ground her "new film realities" in the actualities of the world.

This disequilibrium is descriptive not only of *At Land* but also of the social situation of women during the war years more broadly. Deren's most productive deconstructions of the narratives of gendered domesticity flourished during the years when women were encouraged, in the guise of patriotism, to enter public life to benefit the war economy. The necessities of the war produced the dislocation of women by reversing the specific ideology of feminine domestication, bringing out into the open the actually relativistic spatial distribution of power along gendered lines. In fact, the U.S. government used the medium of film to disseminate these inversions of gender expectations: *Rosie the Riveter* (1944) is the most famous example. If Deren's pro-filmic women were made to negotiate a "stereotypically feminine space," "in the sexualized, emotionalized, personalized, privatized, erratic sphere of the home and bedchamber rather than in the structured, impersonal public realm," Deren herself, at least during the war years, was not.[25] In 1946, Deren rented out the Provincetown Playhouse to show her 16mm films—something never attempted before—and was immensely successful with the event. Deren, who had often challenged social codes publicly, legitimated herself as an artist by bringing her work boldly into the field of public art. She screened her films at universities and theaters, wrote for magazines and journals, and won a Guggenheim grant and honors at Cannes, breaking new ground in both institutions as a woman and an independent filmmaker.

While the 1940s afforded a window of opportunity for women to seize the mechanisms of cultural representation, the 1950s announced the closing of this window, with the intensification of the discourses of domesticity and the family. "In the postwar period," simultaneous to Deren's establishing a presence in the public realm, "an intense ideological campaign was waged . . . calling for women to abandon the workplace and return to 'traditional' family values."[26] Deren's public life and art were greatly altered by the reclamation of public space by men returning from the war, as her biographers explain: "Deren may have made a breakthrough, in 1946, in legitimizing cinema as an art form, but her triumph was short-lived. In this year she received more support from the public and from private foundations than any other time of her life. She never received another grant. . . . Her subsequent screenings at the Provincetown were never as successful. The last seven years of her life were largely devoted to running the Creative Film Foundation," a foundation, significantly, run from her home.[27] The conflation of "home" with acceptable forms of femininity policed women's access to public space, which only a few short years previously women had been chastised as unpatriotic for *not* entering. For Deren, the spatial limitations imposed on women meant the public delegitimization of her work and position as an artist.[28] Deren was displaced from the public realm and found herself "projecting [the film] for people here at home almost every night."[29] This shift back into the home, however, provided the grounds for Deren's resistance to such a dislocation.

An Act of Inestimable Public Importance

Although Deren was prolific in making "chamber" films during and right after the war years, the discursive contingencies following the war channeled her energies into creating a "chamber" form of collectivity and distribution. It was during the 1950s, at the height of the newly restructured cult of domesticity, that Deren founded the CFF, "a non-profit foundation that awarded filmmaking grants to independent filmmakers. Naming herself the executive secretary, Deren ran a one-woman operation, seeking funds to underwrite the grants, organizing film screenings and symposia, and publicizing film as a creative art form . . . she ran the entire organization out of the Greenwich Village apartment."[30] Deren may have run her organization from home, but in so doing she negotiated the hegemonic concepts that defined this space for women. In line with the themes and imagery of her early films, Deren used the CFF to transform the very space constitutive of the "feminine," the private "chamber" of the home, into a viable site of contestation. One particular instance of how Deren accrued funds for the CFF exemplifies the ways in which her praxis resignified the domestic, private roles ascribed to women: "Deren convinced Shirley Clarke that if Clarke's wealthy father contributed $1,000 he was going to give to Clarke anyway, Deren would see that Clarke got a fellowship for $800. Deren netted a $200 cash contribution and the publicity attached to a substantial anonymous donation, while Clarke benefited from the attendant publicity as well as the status of receiving an artistic honor."[31] Shirley Clarke, one of the only other female filmmakers in the Greenwich Village art world, would go on to make two significant independent films, *The Cool World* (1964) and *Portrait of Jason* (1967). Deren's shifting of funds appears innocuous but in fact effects a significant reworking of the flow of cultural capital upon which gendered power relations rely, a reworking that Clarke herself continued as the co-founder of the Film-Makers' Distribution Center.

Key to men's regaining the public realm was the desire for sole control of economic resources that require the dependency of women upon men. This patriarchal control makes women turn to private forms of economic support, provided to them in familial roles such as wives and daughters. Deren rechanneled the flow of capital from the confines and secrecy of the home through a public foundation, which appears to esteem the work of women like Clarke and Deren, thereby challenging the very enclosures of the family and its economic substructure that keeps women tied to the domestic situation. In one gesture, Deren enacts a complex transvaluation of the economies of the domestic sphere, transforming Clarke's reception of her father's money from private, paternalistic "gift" to a respectable, public "honor" for artistic practice. This intervention on the part of the CFF exemplifies what was demanded of Deren as a woman working in the 1950s, not only to establish alternative routes for funding independent cinema, but also to make a place for women outside of the normative patriarchal familial structures. Deren's resistance enabled her to link together the kind of behind the scenes organizational work commonly done by women in the home with the social order and, in this way, allowed such unofficial practices to accrue cultural capital and public validation. The CFF's cultural legitimacy nevertheless needed to be officially sanctioned by male authority; the names of public figures (almost all male) on its board of directors were used as metaphorical chaperones to grant the foundation tacit legitimacy. Deren turned to the established names in the arts, such as Jean Cocteau, Martha Graham, Joseph Campbell, and Clement Greenberg, whose "personal endorsements of the CFF authorized independent cinema's rightful place among the postwar vanguard arts."[32] These public figures, whose relationship to the foundation was often just a name on a letterhead, lent credence to Deren's work as an authoritative public arts discourse despite the fact that it was generated in the private sphere.

In a rare critical analysis of Deren's activism in the history of independent film, Rabinovitz posits that "the CFF may have been in practice a nominal apparatus of the independent cinema but its discursive value obscured its limited economic function."[33] This discursive value does indeed transcend the history of independent cinema. Deren's interventions signify a transgression of the implicit gender boundaries between the public and the private. Using Clarke's father's money or turning to the men of the public art world, Deren appropriated the authoritative privilege granted to men by a phallocratic political economy to make space for women artists like Clarke and herself in the public imagination. The role of artist not only granted women like Deren a certain (limited) access to public discourse but also provided versions of community in opposition to the patriarchal family structure. Deren's "role in the apparatus extended beyond that of the producer" in that her artistic and activist practices attempted to redefine both private and public space for women, standing as a viable and necessary response to the patriarchal discourses of her own time.[34]

The discourses enforcing sexual asymmetry in the 1950s and 1960s effectively silenced Deren as an artist and activist. Deren built her career and public fame on "ideas of the filmmaker's mutual support, exhibition, and distribution"; yet these ideas quickly fell out of favor.[35] The spatial ideologies of the 1950s and 1960s depended on the consolidation of discourses that yoked femininity to sexual reproduction within the confines of the patriarchal, suburban family home. The rigid sexual stratification reconfigured the art world as a male-only territory, foreclosing the cultural position of authorial subject to women. Significantly, it was feminist filmmakers of the

1970s and 1980s who strategically co-opted Deren's "chamber" aesthetics as a critical gesture to open a space for women in the avant-garde film establishment. As film historian Michael O'Pray notes, "It was in the late 1970s that women film-makers broke away from the London Film Makers Co-op and set up their own organization Circles in East London. . . . Interestingly the dissenting women cited Maya Deren, Germaine Dulac, and Alice Guy, who represent by and large a poetic narrative cinema and not a formal one. Thus the political split was also an artistic one."[36] This discursive reclamation goes beyond acknowledgment of the content of Deren's films. Circles, along with the many other organizations that arose in the name of "women's cinema," were indebted to Deren for inventing new forms of cultural communities and social subjects as well as producing tools, from cinematic narratives to theoretical models and economic structures, for ideological refashioning.

Deren's film activism, especially through the CFF, emerged from the knowledge that artistic "experiments . . . are next to impossible for individuals unconnected with a sympathetic institution."[37] Her praxis countered this by attempting to establish the ways and means of distribution that would enable her and others to continue making films. Most likely, it was the example of this praxis—more than Deren's "poetic narrative cinema"—that helped the Circles filmmaking co-op to go on making films. Deren made a space for herself as a woman and for the women filmmakers who followed by forging a critical social vision of the spatial discourses constitutive of the gendered subject and pursuing this vision in all areas of filmmaking, from production to distribution and exhibition. Contemporary lesbian-feminist filmmaker Barbara Hammer attests to Deren's continuing influence when she asserts that the exhibition and distribution practices Deren created, along with her critical writings and formal film aesthetics, have benefited her career immeasurably.[38] Whereas Deren's protagonists appear to be trapped in, or perpetually escaping from, the domestic sphere that defines the limits of their world, her activism in the name of independent film unfettered women artists from the domestic by staking a claim to the public discourse of the art world.

Deren quite consciously dedicated herself to the transformation of the social technology of the cinema by establishing a chamber aesthetic that shaped her filmmaking and organizing activities. Indeed, her social vision for independent cinema was clear. In July 1960, a year before she died, Deren wrote, "The artist, beginning in reality—in that which already exists—starts moving toward a vision, an idea, and with the cumulative momentum of that dedicated concentration, crosses the threshold . . . propelled by the dynamic of the idea, the limitations which he does not recognize do not exist, and so he transcends them and creates new worlds."[39] The idea, or "complex cluster" of ideas, that propelled Deren was a set of "ideological premises" in direct opposition to "to the corrupt artistic standards of . . . the Hollywood industry," premises gathered together and codified in "the concept of the *Chamber film.*"[40] The chamber stands as a critical concept for redefining (feminist) aesthetics to rethink the divide between formalism and activism that has structured the figuration of Deren in the history of American independent cinema. Focusing on the discourses that engendered her as an historical subject provides a means of connecting these apparently disparate activities. In her effective creation of a chamber aesthetic, Deren transcended the historical limitations designed to immobilize women and, in doing so, performed "an act of inestimable public importance" in the histories of women's cinema and independent cinema alike.[41]

Notes

1. Maya Deren, qtd. in *Esquire,* December 1946; reprinted in Catrina Neiman, VèVè A. Clark, and Millicent Hodson, eds., *The Legend of Maya Deren: A Documentary Biography and Collected Works,* vol. I, part 2 (New York: Anthology Film Archives/Film Culture, 1988), 331 and 418.

2. Lauren Rabinowitz, "Wearing the Critic's Hat: History, Critical Discourses, and the American Avant-Garde Cinema," in *To Free the Cinema: Jonas Mekas and the New York Underground,* ed. David E. James (Princeton, NJ: Princeton University Press, 1992), 270.

3. Lauren Rabinovitz, *Points of Resistance: Women, Power, and Politics in the New York Avant-Garde Cinema, 1943–71* (Urbana: University of Illinois Press, 1991), 5.

4. Rabinovitz, "Wearing the Critic's Hat," 277.

5. Laura Mulvey, "Film, Feminism, and the Avant-Garde," in *The British Avant-Garde Film, 1926–1995: An Anthology of Writings,* ed. Michael O'Pray (Bedfordshire, UK: University of Luton Press, 1996), 201.

6. Ibid., 214. For further discussion of Deren's place in Mulvey's article, see Theresa L. Geller, "The Personal Cinema of Maya Deren: *Meshes of the Afternoon* and Its Critical Reception in the History of the Avant-Garde," *Biography* 29, no. 1 (2006): 153–56.

7. Neiman, Clark, and Hodson, introduction to "Chambers" in *Legend of Maya Deren,* 2.

8. Teresa de Lauretis, *Technologies of Gender: Essays on Theory, Film, and Fiction* (Bloomington: University of Indiana Press, 1987), 134.

9. David E. James, introduction to James, *To Free the Cinema,* 9.

10. Regina Cornwell, "Maya Deren and Germaine Dulac: Activists of the Avant-Garde," in *Sexual Stratagems: The World of Women in Film,* ed. Patricia Erens (New York: Horizon, 1979), 185.

11. Ibid., 186.

12. D. A. Leslie, "Femininity, Post-Fordism, and the 'New Traditionalism,'" in *Space, Gender, Knowledge: Feminist Readings,* ed. Linda McDowell and Joanne P. Sharp (London: Arnold, 1997), 301.

13. Mary Ann Doane, "Aesthetics and Politics," *Signs: Journal of Women in Culture and Society* 30, no. 1 (2004): 1231.

14. Mary Ann Doane, Patricia Mellencamp, and Linda Williams, eds., *Re-Vision: Essays in Feminist Film Criticism* (Frederick, MD: University Publications of America and the American Film Institute, 1984), 6.

15. De Lauretis, *Technologies of Gender,* 134–35.

16. Ibid., 141.

17. Maya Deren, "Statement of Principles," *Film Culture* 22–23 (1961): 161–63.

18. Mary Ann Doane, *The Desire to Desire: The Woman's Film of the 1940s* (Bloomington: Indiana University Press, 1987), 6.

19. See Geller, "Personal Cinema," 140–58.

20. Mark Wigley, "Untitled: The Housing of Gender," in *Sexuality and Space,* ed. Beatriz Colomina (New York: Princeton Architectural Press, 1992), 337.

21. See Neiman, Clark, and Hodson, introduction to "Chambers," in *Legend of Maya Deren,* 1–2.

22. Maria Pramaggiore, "Seeing Double(s): Reading Deren Bisexually," in *Maya Deren and the American Avant-Garde,* ed. Bill Nichols (Berkeley: University of California Press, 2001), 249.

23. Patricia Erens, "Towards a Feminist Aesthetic: Reflection-Revolution-Ritual," in Erens, *Sexual Stratagems,* 157.

24. Maya Deren, "Program Notes," *Film Culture* 39 (Winter 1961): 2.

25. Richard Feldstein and Judith Roof, eds., *Feminism and Psychoanalysis* (Ithaca, NY: Cornell University Press, 1989), 2.

26. Leslie, "Femininity, Post-Fordism," 301.

27. Neiman, Clark, and Hodson, "Thresholds," in *Legend of Maya Deren,* 236.

28. For further discussion see Geller, "Personal Cinema."

29. Deren, "Letter to Sawyer Falk" in Neiman, Clark, and Hodson, *Legend of Maya Deren,* 250.

30. Rabinovitz, *Points of Resistance,* 82.

31. Rabinovitz citing Shirley Clarke, ibid., 82.

32. Ibid., 83.

33. Ibid.

34. Rabinovitz, "Wearing the Critic's Hat," 277.

35. Sheldon Renan, *An Introduction to the American Underground Film* (New York: E. P. Dutton, 1967), 214.

36. Michael O'Pray, introduction to O'Pray, *British Avant-Garde Film,* 16.

37. Deren, "Letter to Sawyer Falk," 251.

38. Barbara Hammer, "Maya Deren and Me," in Nichols, *Maya Deren,* 264.

39. Deren, "Movie Journal," July 21, 1960; reprinted in *Film Culture* 39 (Winter 1965): 53.

40. Ibid., 53–54.

41. Maya Deren, "The Hero's Life," in "Stairways (1942–3)," in Neiman, Clark, and Hodson, *Legend of Maya Deren,* 67. In Deren's poem, "He performs an act of inestimable public importance" while she returns to "the too familiar street of houses leading home."

Kay Armatage   *Chapter 6*

Material Effects

Fashions in Feminist Programming

This essay addresses the exigencies of feminist work on the inside of the film festival industry. It maps my own genealogy as a spectator, organizer of women's film festivals, and programmer of women's films and offers institutional analysis of festival structures and tactics in the international field. The strategic decisions, negotiations, and successes I recount here outline the work of a feminist programmer in a large international festival, the Toronto International Film Festival (TIFF), the largest in North America and currently considered one of the three most important festivals in the world.

Genealogy

As a graduate student I went regularly to England for summers to write my doctoral dissertation on Gertrude Stein, although I was already drifting rapidly to film studies. One August, I attended the Women's Film Week, the focus of the 1972 Edinburgh International Film Festival. This was the first event to highlight films by women directors (noted for the rediscovery of Dorothy Arzner and the first publication on a woman director), followed by a smallish—considering the location—New York Women's Film Festival (1972).[1]

As soon as I got back to Toronto that fall, my friend Phyllis Platt and I co-edited "Women's Cinema," a special issue of the Canadian film journal *Take One*.[2] At the time, the only published work in the field was a vastly incomplete filmography of 150 women filmmakers from the entire history of cinema.[3] We tracked down as many of them as we could, to survey their ideas about women in the industry and the new movement in feminism. We found many who, surprisingly, were willing to answer our jejune question-naire, including Anita Loos, Joyce Wieland, Shirley Clarke, Betty Box, and Stephanie Rothman. In the wake of that special journal issue and my knowledge of the Edinburgh Women's Film Event, I joined the group of women that was organizing the Toronto Women and Film International Festival (1973).

In retrospect, it is clear that, as with other "alternative" festivals founded in the 1970s, as Ragan Rhyne points out, "cultural production and the circulation of images are central to the legal and institutional practices of governance and liberation."[4] Feminism was then in its reminence as a governmentally sanctioned movement. The Canadian federal government had launched a Royal Commission on the Status of Women (1970), and, spurred by its recommendations, the National Film Board's Studio D—the women's studio—was launched in 1974 on a directive of films "by, for, and about women," hinging on the mode of realist documentation of women's struggles for liberation. The Toronto Women and Film International Festival was also financed through federal, provincial, and municipal grants dedicated to job creation for baby boomers and the instauration of cultural industries in Canada. Blithely and unwittingly celebrating governmentality, we had a great time.

Our stellar researcher found hundreds of unknown women filmmakers and tracked down prints of films long considered lost.[5] As B. Ruby Rich writes, "Back then, organizing a women's film festival was first and foremost a research project. . . . [C]abals of programmers were . . . literally rescuing films from a life on the shelf: they were dusting off the cans to show women's work for the first time in months, years, decades, *ever*."[6] We never found Dorothy Arzner's *Working Girls* (1930), but I still have Arzner's letters regretting that she could not attend. Even more important, many of the films found through those excavations were subsequently made available for study.[7]

We then made our programming selections in collective meetings, while haggling out the issue of positive women's content. This was the early 1970s, when the North American theoretical apparatus pivoted on the white liberal feminist agenda: positive role models, consciousness-raising, sexism, and gender inequities. I was a fan of Stephanie Rothman's *Student Nurses* (1970) and *The Velvet Vampire* (1971) but had to argue long and hard to program Rothman's newest, *Terminal Island* (1973), an early foray into masculinity set in a men's prison, among the uplifting feminist and avant-garde films. After much debate, we made the decision to concentrate on production by women directors, despite presence or absence of "women's content," with

Shirley Clarke's oeuvre and Rothman's latest as cases in point. We sought out women's filmic production on many subjects and in diverse cinematic modes.

The 1973 Toronto Women and Film International Festival was the largest women's film festival thus far (ten days, morning to midnight).[8] It was a fabulous hippie event, redolent with the 1970s zeitgeist: collective administration by avant-garde artists and grant-savvy girls, free admission, free full-time onsite daycare run by men, organic food concessions (sprouts!), and parties every night. Freude Bartlett, Joyce Chopra, Shirley Clarke, Martha Coolidge, Stephanie Rothman, Amalie Rothschild, Viva Superstar, and many others were guests. The festival was held in the St. Lawrence Centre, the newest and largest cultural edifice in Toronto, usually home to the ballet and the opera. As we were all proud of our newly liberated legs and armpits, we felt that we were taking Toronto mainstream culture by the short hairs.

In a workshop on directing, Stephanie Rothman (pastel sweater set and pearls) and Shirley Clarke (black skinny pants and turtleneck) traded tips. Clarke emphasized the importance of good solid shoes, and Rothman demonstrated a yoga posture to take the strain off the back over long hours of standing. In the workshop, they got along well, but later Clarke, who had never heard of Rothman, was horrified to discover the kinds of films Rothman directed: American International flicks. After Clarke saw *Terminal Island* on the first weekend of the festival, she didn't speak to Rothman again. This was, in spades, the standoff of avant-garde versus B-movie, New York versus LA, groovy versus square, and it was inflected by issues of class privilege, which were the opposite of what their chosen vestimentary codes might suggest: Rothman's was a masquerade.

Yet there was no discussion of "feminist content," which Rothman's early films would have won hands down. The abortion scene in *Student Nurses,* in which the inadvertently pregnant character hallucinates the evacuation of various domestic consumer goods, such as boxes of laundry detergent and fridges, is a case in point. While her films conformed to the Roger Corman model of sex or violence every seven minutes, they presented commanding women characters and dealt wittily with "women's issues."

The Edinburgh Style

I went back to the Edinburgh Film Festival every year from 1973 to 1979. Under the command of Festival Director Lynda Myles, in the heady years of the Anglo-French film theory revolution, Edinburgh became the epicenter of the intellectual film world.[9] Myles, coauthor of *The Movie Brats: How the*

Film Generation Took Over Hollywood (1979), was then not only the sole woman directing an international film festival but also an astute critic connected to the British Film Institute. The Edinburgh Psychoanalytic Event (1976) was the only festival sidebar I know to send out an advance reading list. This conference, in which Laura Mulvey, Claire Johnston, Stephen Heath, and others led discussion groups, had seismic repercussions in the world of feminism, film studies, and filmmaking. Mulvey's famous essay (1975) had introduced Lacanian psychoanalysis as a useful theoretical instrument for feminism, but for North Americans at the time, this was a startling development, one that produced both converts and critics.

One of the strongest negative voices was *Jump-Cut* co-editor Julia Lesage, who denounced Lacanian psychoanalysis as "an essentially patriarchal framework . . . used to drive women out of the film industry and keep them out."[10] B. Ruby Rich, who was aligned with the *Jump-Cut* group that boycotted the Milwaukee conference organized by Stephen Heath and Teresa de Lauretis (1978), asked, "How does one formulate an understanding of a structure that insists on our absence even in the face of our presence?"[11]

There was at least one Canadian casualty in the aftermath of the psychoanalytic revolution and Mulvey's call for new forms of feminist filmmaking. In 1976, there was an avant-garde program in parallel to the psychoanalytic event. Among the films programmed was Joyce Wieland's bold incursion into dramatic feature filmmaking, *The Far Shore* (1976). Wieland had stepped out of the small-scale artisanal production mode that was indispensable to the avant-garde to direct a period feature in 35mm with sumptuous settings and costumes, vintage automobiles, recognized Canadian actors, multiple locations, and a melodramatic narrative.[12] *The Far Shore* aimed for Claire Johnston's dictum of feminist entertainment rather than Mulvey's "thrill of negativity," which—ironically for Wieland, as a former structuralist filmmaker—advocated antinarrative, antirealist formalism as the appropriate cinematic mode for feminist expression. Wieland's former supporters in the avant-garde turned their backs on the film on account of its "mainstream" ambitions. Wieland later recalled her horrible time at Edinburgh that year, where her former supporters couldn't look her in the eye.

By the Edinburgh Feminism and Film Event in 1979, these tensions had come to a head. In her autobiography, *Feelings Are Facts* (2006), Yvonne Rainer sums up the "feminist theory wars" that took place that year: "The battles raged over issues of positive versus negative imaging of women, avant-garde versus Hollywood, distanciation versus identification, elitism versus populism, documentary versus fiction, transparency versus ambiguity, accessibility versus difficulty, and so on."[13] B. Ruby Rich's recollection of the conference in *Chick Flicks* is a treat. Although the general substance of the issues is well known, Rich's notes include details that, to my knowledge, have not been published elsewhere. Her chapter title "The Fury That Was Edinburgh" sets the tone for a recounting of debates that were mostly contentious and divisive and sometimes downright vicious.[14] Rich romps through the personalities, discussions, hierarchies, sexual divisions, and theoretical splits and in passing takes on her old adversaries from *Camera Obscura;* in the last pages of the book, she writes, "Old enmities die hard, perhaps; I've never published anything in *Camera Obscura* to this day."[15] In addition to great gossip (always a festival resource), Rich's article indicates the significance of Edinburgh in the period that ushered in the film studies revolution and psychoanalytic feminist film theory.

The chronicle ends with the party that Rich and her American flatmates threw, to which all the women at the conference were invited. "Is it surprising that a convincing chart of 'theoretical' differences could be drawn by tallying those who did or didn't attend?" she asks.[16] Her anecdote illustrates one of the important functions of festival social events: the formation of professional liaisons and canonicity. People often chat about movies at parties, but when the guests are scholars, critics, and festival programmers, who may write an article, produce a consumer review, or program a film in another festival, the stakes are quite high. Rich concludes, "It was a landmark event that ultimately was about process rather than product. No consensus was ever reached. *Daughter Rite* [Michelle Citron, 1979] and *Thriller* [Sally Potter, 1979] entered a new canon as feminist films that could both inspire emotion and support theory making. Numerous other films were forgotten. The conference ended and we scattered around the world again, friendships and relationships and antagonisms set in motion for the decade to come."[17]

Imagined Communities

I started working as a programmer with TIFF (then called Toronto Festival of Festivals) in 1982. Initially conscripted as part of the Canadian programming team and put in charge of American independents and documentaries, I moved to international programming in 1989, after curating a retrospective of Canadian women's cinema the year before. Unlike festivals such as Cannes that exhibited films offered by their national governments for many years or like New York, which determined their films by committee, the films at Toronto were chosen by individual programmers, each of whom had their own specialties. Although there might be pressure brought to bear on individual films, our personal critical choices were (almost) sacrosanct. I was therefore free to select work that not only demonstrated artistic innovation and achievement but also "hailed" a committed audience rather than catering to expectations of mainstream popularity.

In fact, as programmers, part of our mandate was to cultivate specific audiences, to let certain "imagined communities" know that we were looking out for them. The festival was promoting not just cinephilia but also, following Jürgen Habermas, countervisions of a good social life. Our programming cultivated, as Julian Stringer writes, "a sense of identity for minority communities, and . . . how that sense of identity is negotiated through specific festival activities."[18] Writing original program notes (rather than excerpting directors' statements, press releases, or other festivals' catalogs) was essential to this process. For many films, and certainly for North American premieres, these notes might be the first publications on the work, and often set the tone for critical reception. As Stringer observes, film festivals have "a particular kind of external agency that creates meaning around film texts."[19] The program notes served a three-fold function between audience and writer: understanding and definition, entertainment and display, and the creation and sharing of community.[20] Writing the notes was not easy: three hundred words were not many to give a sense of the narrative or subject matter as well as to position the film aesthetically, theoretically, and politically. The programmers signed the notes and were encouraged to develop a personal voice. We also introduced the films and filmmakers at screenings and moderated the postscreening Q&A sessions.

Despite our efforts, however, there were occasions when films defied audience expectations, especially once TIFF began building on its reputation as a hit-maker by propping even avant-garde films on sensational press releases. *The Man Who Envied Women* (Yvonne Rainer, 1985) got a fair bit of advance notice, resulting in a largely mainstream audience that was unprepared for Rainer's theoretical minimalism. As the film proceeded, I stood with Rainer at the back of the cinema watching the audience file out. "Let's go for a drink," I said. She replied, "It's OK. I'm used to it." As Rainer recounts of another screening, even feminists didn't get it:

Following a screening of *The Man Who Envied Women,* a well-known feminist who subscribed to Lacanian psychoanalytic theory asked me why I hadn't made a film about women. I was flabbergasted, having been under the impression that I had done just that. But she, taken in by the title and the prevailing physical presence of the male character, had discounted the pursuing, nagging, questioning female voice on the soundtrack. She didn't understand that I had taken Laura Mulvey's critique of Hollywood films . . . literally, and that by staying out of sight—beyond the reach of "the male gaze"—my heroine could maintain her dignity and avoid being caught with her pants down.[21]

Fashioning a Feminist Film Community

Although my beat also developed as low-budget independent, New York "underground," formalist documentaries, avant-garde, "new narrative," new Black British, and queer cinema, I was primarily known internationally on the festival circuit and to the Toronto audience as a dedicated programmer of women directors in many cinematic modes. In Toronto, you could count on seeing the most recent Potters, Akermans, Ottingers, and Rainers as they appeared, along with new voices such as Monika Treut, Julie Dash, Tracey Moffatt, Moufida Tlatli, Rose Troche, Samira Makhmalbaf, and Nicole Holofcener. In my festival selections, I averaged at least 50 percent women directors through the mid-1990s (I always counted), at which point the number of women's films on offer unfortunately dwindled. Nonetheless, my last year at TIFF, 2004, proved exceptional in this regard: many of the most well-established women directors as well as a handful of newcomers were there with their new films.

In the early years I relied on the German women directors from the 1970s since there were so many of them, rivaled only by the number of women directors at the National Film Board of Canada: *Marianne and Julianne* (Margarethe Von Trotta, 1981) was one of my first selections. Aside from the Germans—not only Von Trotta, but also Jutta Bruckner, Ulrike Ottinger, Helma Sanders-Brahms, and others—there were few other active women feature directors. Among that small pool was, of course, Sally Potter, whose work I knew from Edinburgh. Her second film, *The Gold Diggers* (1983) came in my third year with TIFF. Chantal Akerman was another exception to the worldwide paucity of women directors, and her work was a passionate commitment for me. I had seen *Hotel Monterey* (1972), *Je, tu, il, elle* (1974), and *Jeanne Dielman* (1975) in Edinburgh, as well as *News from Home* (1976), which had been a featured discussion in the Edinburgh Psychoanalytic Event.[22] I programmed all of Akerman's films as they came out, at least one of them unseen. For *Toute une Nuit* (1982) I wrote an enthusiastic catalog note that was chided in the press because I admitted I had yet to see the film: all I knew was that it was Akerman's latest work.

Programming Akerman films in the 1980s was somewhat difficult, as they were rarely promoted to North American or mainstream festivals. I routinely began the year's programming search with phone calls to producer

Marilyn Watelet in Brussels and Akerman in Paris. Eventually I had myriad phone numbers that could access Akerman. One year I left many messages on Akerman's home answering machine, none of them returned. In frustration, I set my alarm for two a.m. (eight o'clock in Paris) and phoned her neighbor with the intention of asking him to leave a note on her door. Akerman happened to be having coffee with him, and he put her on. I forget which film I got that year, but I got it. Later it was easier; Akerman seemed to know what a Toronto screening could mean for her films. TIFF had become not only a friendly environment for women directors but an important North American outlet as well.

Network Nodes

Over the years I necessarily cultivated strong working relationships with other critics and programmers as well as directors. I often depended on my colleagues for tips. In the 1980s Rich had become the film officer for the New York State Council on the Arts (NYSCA) and was one of my most valued sources in the field of independent American production. I consulted with her every summer about interesting films that were coming down the pike. In her position at NYSCA, as a writer for the *Village Voice,* and as a respected film curator of many years, Rich saw everything and knew everybody. We sometimes disagreed about the films, but her generosity in sharing her knowledge and opinions was one of my continuing resources as a festival programmer. Other major sources were Debbie Zimmerman (Women Make Movies), Sande Zeig (New York Gay and Lesbian International Festival), Lynda Hansen (New York Foundation for the Arts) and, for a time, Berenice Reynaud (*Cahiers du Cinéma*).

The festival industry depends on this sort of networking, as well as high secrecy in cases such as Telluride; a festival programmer's currency is information exchange, as Thomas Elsaesser indicates in his designation of film festivals as "network nodes" in the transnational circulation of cinema.[23] In this vein, one of my strategies at TIFF was to organize receptions for the women directors, festival professionals, and press attending the festival. Through these events, women directors were introduced to programmers and key women press, and I developed a friendly cadre of knowledgeable contacts.

The reception for Potter's *Orlando* (1992) was a huge women's event. There were about forty of us at dinner preceding the *Orlando* premiere, including Potter and Tilda Swinton, who was wearing her pink embroidered

Orlando shoes. I handed out tickets to the screening as we left the restaurant. It had been hard to get so many tickets, as word of the Venice success was out among the festival cognoscenti, long after TIFF scheduling had taken place. Potter's films had been a more specialized taste to that point, so *Orlando* was scheduled only in a four-hundred-seat theater, which was mobbed with the brightest and the best. The film was adored: huge standing ovation. After *The Gold Diggers* (1983) and *The London Story* (short, 1986) had received nondescript responses, I was thrilled that the glamour end of the industry had finally recognized Potter and Swinton as the extraordinary artists that they are. Mainstream attention to a film by a woman director changed the tenor of these women-only receptions at TIFF: suddenly they were effective in feminist power-brokerage rather than minoritarian social gatherings. For a time at least, powerful women were in the ascendancy.

Tapes of women's films addressed to me began to flood in, and I was invited to every private screening of a woman's film; the Australian Film Commission held them frequently in Cannes, showcasing films that were not in the official selection, such as *Bingo, Brides, and Braces* (Gillian Armstrong, 1988). A momentous invitation was *Antonia's Line* (Marleen Gorris, 1995). Gorris's films *A Question of Silence* (1982) and *Broken Mirrors* (1984) were feminist landmarks, but the mainstream press had castigated them as man-hating diatribes. World sales agent Carole Myers understood that Gorris's work needed special treatment, so she concocted a strategic promotional scandal at Cannes with a private screening and grand luncheon for about fifty women from the international film world; no men were invited, an unheard-of event at Cannes. Even the progressive male press howled at their exclusion, although they might well have ignored the film at a regular venue. Immediately after the screening, I invited *Antonia's Line* to Toronto for its official world premiere.

Gorris came to Toronto, but she was extremely nervous about potential negative reaction. I had to work for a couple of hours to get her to agree to say a few words before the screening, promising her that she would not have to take questions later. No need to worry: the audience response was ecstatic. *Antonia's Line* won the Toronto audience award, a North American distribution contract was signed during the festival, and Gorris's filmmaking career, which had appeared to be moribund, was revived.[24] After its launch in Toronto, the film went on to win the Academy Award for Best Foreign Language Film: the only film by a woman director to win a major Academy Award.

Material Effects

As exemplified by the case of *Antonia's Line,* I found that working as a feminist programmer could have material effects for women working in the film industry. Over the course of my work with TIFF, the most far-reaching interventions I made on a regular basis were in the debates around representations of female sexuality and censorship law. My start at TIFF coincided with the beginning of the sex wars. The United States–based Women against Pornography movement had been imported to Canada by the cultural feminists of NFB Studio D, and debates about censorship were raging in Canada as well in the many conferences and publications that ushered in the MacKinnon-Dworkin era.[25]

In the sex wars, *Variety* (Bette Gordon, 1983) was the first to tackle porn and women's sexual fantasies. A few years later, *Seduction: The Cruel Woman* (*Verführung: Die grausame Frau,* Elfi Mikesch and Monika Treut, 1985) featured a beautiful dominatrix catering to a wide range of fetishistic desires. Based on Sacher-Masoch's 1870 novel *Venus in Furs,* the subject of Treut's doctoral dissertation, the film's SM role-playing broke new ground in terms of sexual expression. The luminous stars were Sheila McLaughlin, New York underground player and director (*Committed,* 1984; *She Must Be Seeing Things,* 1987); Udo Kier (long loved from creepy roles in Fassbinder films); and incandescent-white-skinned and black-haired Mechtild Grossmann (Pina Bausch dancer/diva) playing the dominatrix. I had seen the film in the Forum at Berlin. A day later, I saw Treut and Mikesch sitting in the festival café and rushed up to invite the film to Toronto.

Mikesch and Treut arrived at the festival on opening weekend clad from head to toe in black leather; I greeted them in a white linen pantsuit. Under Treut's influence, I soon changed my sartorial system, to the point that I was lampooned in a Toronto weekly for my fishnet stockings, black vinyl bustier, and spiky hair. Many years later, Treut told me that I had also influenced her (although in her career, rather than in what she wore). I was shepherding her around the gigantic opening night party, introducing her to people I thought would be important to her. She was snarling at everyone, telling them what shit their films were, and generally playing the hostile butch. At some point, she told me recently, I said that it was important to festivals not only that her film was liked but that she should be liked as well. Treut made a subsequent change in her modus operandi and became one of the best-loved guests at every festival thereafter, resulting in constant travel, co-productions, and lucrative gigs all over the world (including visiting filmmaker at Vassar and Cornell). Treut's films were all invited to TIFF as they came out, in turn greeted ecstatically by the audiences that were the new face of feminism in the 1990s.

In 1985, the year of the North American premiere of *Seduction: The Cruel Woman,* Ontario was still in the grip of state film censorship, to which Lizzie Borden capitulated by cutting *Working Girls* (1986).[26] In the early years, all films had to be screened beforehand in order to be "passed" for festival exhibition, but lately the festival director had negotiated a "voluntary compliance" mechanism through which we were obliged to alert the censor board to problematic films. I had to "justify" *Seduction: The Cruel Woman.* My defense argued that the film was an important intervention in a significant feminist debate about sexuality and representation. The Censor Board allowed it, but those same arguments have been necessary again and again, as women filmmakers have faced up to assumptions about feminine sexual desire, middle-class morality, and the boundaries of representation.

The skirmishes with the Ontario Censor Board continued. In 2000, I invited *Baise-moi* (Virginie Despentes and Coralie Trinh Thi), commercially exploited under the title "Fuck Me." The film had opened in Paris in June that year but had been withdrawn three days later from commercial screens and slapped with an X rating (porno), confining it to exhibition in sex shops. A faithful adaptation of Despentes's 1995 novel, *Baise-moi* produces a compound female subject by bringing two women with disparate histories together by chance. They embark on a road trip, fucking and killing as they go. Although the novel was a best seller in France, the film version blasted open once again the old debates about pornography, violence, female sexuality, and the division between what was acceptable in the novel's written words and in cinematic images. It was allowed to be shown at TIFF, which by this time was in possession of a blanket exemption with no more "voluntary compliance" forms necessary. It was banned outright, however, for commercial distribution by the Ontario Censor Board.

Fat Girl (*À ma soeur,* Catherine Breillat, 2001) was the final challenge. After the festival screening, it was banned in Ontario for theatrical distribution, but a crusading lawyer mounted a constitutional challenge that enlisted me in an affidavit.[27] I argued that the seduction scene

interrogates the question of "ownership" of the girl's virginal body, which she desperately seeks to claim for herself in the midst of the demands of the young man who seeks to possess it as a badge of his own patriarchal rights over women's bodies in general. . . . In terms of women's social and legal equality, our sense of identity and independent authenticity, our right to dominion over our own bodies, this film makes an important philosophical and political statement. That both girls are adolescents determined to challenge the injustice of women's social inequality pushes the political import of the film into a terrain that has remained unexplored for too long.[28]

In my defense of the film, I returned to the concerns that have structured my viewing and programming practices since that first Edinburgh festival in 1972: feminist issues, cine-cultural context, and the political horizons of representation. While the Ontario Film Review Board had been challenged previously, it was finally brought down on the *Fat Girl* case, and today operates merely as a rating system. Although my letter was only one of many documents presented in the legal brief, I like to think that my dual credentials as a university professor and international programmer in a major festival helped to produce significant social effects.

Notes

1. Claire Johnston, ed., *The Work of Dorothy Arzner: Towards a Feminist Cinema* (London: BFI, 1975).

2. Platt, formerly the editor of *Take One Magazine* and later the vice-president of CBC, is now an independent television producer.

3. Richard Henshaw, "Women Directors: 150 Filmographies," *Film Comment* 8, no. 4 (1972): 33–45.

4. Ragan Rhyne, "Pink Dollars: Gay and Lesbian Film Festivals and the Economy of Visibility" (PhD diss., New York University, 2007), 7.

5. Anne Mackenzie, later second in command at TIFF and then creative director at Telefilm Canada.

6. B. Ruby Rich, *Chick Flicks* (Durham, NC: Duke University Press, 1998), 29.

7. E.g., *The Blue Light* (*Das Blaue Licht,* Leni Riefenstahl, 1932), *Peasant Women of Ryazan* (*Baby ryazanskie,* Olga Preobrazhenskaya, 1927).

8. Although Créteil's Festival International de Films des Femmes is now the longest continuing festival of women's cinema, it was not established until 1978.

9. Under the direction of Lizzie Francke (1997–2001), Edinburgh was revivified briefly. It is now a local event, not a player on the world film festival stage.

10. Rich, *Chick Flicks,* 59.

11. Ibid., 60. See also B. Ruby Rich, Chuck Kleinhans, and Julia LeSage, "Report on a Conference Not Attended: The Scalpel beneath the Suture," *Jump Cut* 17 (April 1978): 37–38.

12. Budget of nearly half a million dollars, perhaps equivalent to five million dollars now.

13. Yvonne Rainer, *Feelings Are Facts: A Life* (Cambridge, MA: MIT Press, 2006), 447.

14. Rich, *Chick Flicks,* 156–68.

15. Ibid., 381.

16. Ibid., 165.

17. Ibid., 166.

18. Julian Stringer, "Regarding Film Festivals" (PhD diss., University of Indiana, 2003), 241.

19. Ibid., viii.

20. Ibid., 244.

21. Rainer, *Feelings Are Facts,* 456.

22. See "On Suture," in Stephen Heath, *Questions of Cinema* (Bloomington: University of Indiana Press, 1981), 98–101.

23. Thomas Elsaesser, *European Cinema: Face to Face with Hollywood* (Amsterdam: Amsterdam University Press, 2005).

24. Gorris's subsequent film *Mrs. Dalloway* (1997) had its world premiere as a TIFF Gala, as did her *The Luzhin Defence* (2000).

25. See B. Ruby Rich, "Anti-Porn: Soft Issue, Hard World," in *Gendering the Nation: Canadian Women's Cinema,* ed. Kay Armatage, Kass Banning, Brenda Longfellow, and Janine Marchessault (Toronto: University of Toronto Press, 1999), 62–75.

26. Borden cut the second-long shot of an erect penis being fitted with a condom. The shot was in a montage sequence depicting women's work.

27. The Ontario Film Review Board gave the following reasons: (1) minute 18: Young girl's (fifteen years old) breasts are exposed while young man fondles them; (2) minute 22: Young woman's lower genital area is exposed while young man continues to fondle; (3) minute 23–28: Female frontal nudity and implied anal sex; (4) minute 38: Young girl simulating fellatio; young man refers to "getting caught for being in a sexual manner with someone so young"; (5) minute 50: Caressing of young girl's exposed breasts; (6) minute 59–61: Full female frontal nudity of fifteen-year-old girl; young man's erect penis (putting on condom); simulated sexual activity with a fifteen-year-old girl; (7) minute 80–82: Sexual assault of thirteen-year-old girl (violent); partial female frontal nudity (breasts).

28. Author's letter to Robert Warren, Ontario Film Review Board, November 16, 2001.

Dialogues

Sophie Mayer

Chapter 7

Shooting for Change

An Interview with Kim Longinotto

Kim Longinotto's documentary *Sisters in Law* (2005) won the Prix Arts et Essais at the Cannes Film Festival in 2005, bringing the director to international attention. Like all of her previous documentaries, *Sisters in Law*, shot in and around a legal practice staffed by women in Cameroon, was created through Longinotto's artisanal practice of working as cinematographer, with a crew consisting only of a locally informed co-director and her sound recordist, Mary Milton. Longinotto has directed several films in this way, which creates access without intrusion through local knowledge, including two films in Iran—*Divorce Iranian Style* (1998), set in a divorce court in Tehran, and *Runaways* (2001)—with anthropologist Ziba Mir-Hosseini and *The Day I Will Never Forget* (2002), about women working to abolish female genital mutilation (FGM) in Kenya, with Fardhosa, a Kenyan health worker.

Longinotto has been making films since completing her training at the UK's National Film and Television School in 1976, where she was part of a globally oriented generation of British documentary makers whose best-known representative is Nick Broomfield. Longinotto has negotiated the changing waters of documentary over the last thirty years, raising money independently, screening her documentaries in factual programming strands on the BBC, and working toward cinematic exhibition through the burgeoning documentary festival circuit. Her film *Hold Me Tight, Let Me Go* (2007), made for a BBC documentary strand, screened at the London International Film Festival and opened the BritDoc festival in Oxford.

Politically aware and engaged, Longinotto has traveled around the world to document women's lives, beginning with a series of films about women emerging from patriarchal structures in Japan (*Eat the Kimono* [1989], *Dream Girls* [1994], *Shinjuku Boys* [1995], and *Gaea Girls* [2000]). These films and others played in her first ever retrospective, accompanying the launch of *Sisters in Law* at the Institute of Contemporary Arts (ICA) in London in 2006. I interviewed her during this season, shortly before she left for Pakistan to begin work on her next documentary.

> **SOPHIE MAYER:** I'm really enjoying this season of your documentary films at the ICA. Do you have a feeling that there's a thread running through all the stories that you tell?

> **KIM LONGINOTTO:** What I'm looking for is change. If I'm going abroad, I've only got a certain amount of time, six or eight weeks, and I've got to bring a story, so the most obvious way to do that is to film something where there is a very dramatic change taking place, like going through wrestling school—the character's going to make it or she's not.

> **SM:** Are there films where you have changed your mind, or had your mind changed, while you were making it?

> **KL:** With *Dream Girls,* which I made in a theater in Japan, when we went, I'd seen pictures in a magazine, and I'd heard about Takarazuka, and I'd seen these amazing women playing men. They looked so incredible and confident and brash, I thought they would be like that in the rest of their lives, very in control. It was a shock of going there and realizing that the whole setup of Takarazuka was like a model of Japanese society where the men were in charge, where they whittle away at your self-esteem and try and break you in order to create a star that they can then manipulate.

> **SM:** So that changed the story of the film . . .

> **KL:** It was all a real shock, and I remember when we first saw it, Jano [Williams, Kim's co-director on her Japanese films] and I were really disappointed because we wanted the film to be a celebration of Japanese women becoming more powerful. But then we thought we have to go along with it. I think the film's more interesting because it's not a celebration of anything; it's an exploration, and it's full of contradiction.

SM: There's a wrestling school in *Gaea Girls,* the theater school Takara-zuka in *Dream Girls,* Simalo's boarding school in *The Day I Will Never Forget,* and they're all very strict. Does that reflect your experience of school?

KL: I went to a boarding school that had all these stupid rules. They talked about the working classes and how we were better than them, and yet treated us with such contempt, and tried to break us.

SM: Given that you had an upbringing with a certain amount of privilege, what was it that made you aware of how power works, and compelled you to give voice to people who don't have a voice?

KL: I think it was the experience of being a child, which I hated, and living at home with a father who hated anyone who was even slightly different, and a mother who was an incredible snob. I really identified with people that were somehow outside things, but didn't meet them until after I'd run away from home. I think people change you.

SM: Is that true of the people in your films too?

KL: Vera [Negassa] and Beatrice [Ntuba] [a lawyer and a judge in Cameroon, the main characters in *Sisters in Law*] had a great influence on me. Fardhosa, the district nurse, in *The Day I Will Never Forget* . . . I really swore after I got to know her, that I would be gentler about my convictions, that I'd try and be more like her, more open-minded and softer and gentler. So I think people impress you, and you see things about them.

SM: Fardhosa is gentle, but she also has very clear politics. Are your films an expression of your politics, or do you suppress your position in order to hear other people's?

KL: It depends. *The Day* was the closest to wanting to make a campaigning film. I'd had friends who'd had FGM, and told me how it had ruined their lives and made them then not trust their parents. It seemed to be a crystallization of this idea of tradition: that you're meant to accept things just because they're old and part of your culture. I wanted to show the falseness of that. I knew that I didn't want to have victims, that I wanted there to be young girls and women fighting, not just people just talking about them.

SM: Your films put women at their centers, and it seems to me like they have a feminist background or leanings. Were there any works or texts that were particularly influential?

KL: One of things that really influenced me was a book by Nawal al-Sadaawi, *The Hidden Face of Eve,* and I thought that was an amazing book, which is why I went to make a film about her. My friend Safra and I went to make a film about Nawal, except that she'd become a big celebrity and had become drunk on her own power. It was very disturbing, and she behaved very badly to the people on whose side she was meant to be.

SM: Do you think that happens to anyone who gets power?

KL: Vera and Beatrice have become more and more powerful and successful, but they've never become compromised or affected by self-importance. They never think of themselves as better than anybody, and they're continually working for what they call the underdogs. They're special, those two.

SM: Vera and Beatrice have an unusually high degree of cooperation for a prosecution lawyer and a judge. Were you drawn to them partially because of your own collaborative model of filmmaking? Do you work as closely with your co-directors as Vera and Beatrice work with each other?

KL: I think it would be hard for me to work with another filmmaker because the way I work is so particular. You can see from the films that they're all made in the same way. So a lot of the other people I've worked with haven't had any film training at all, or haven't got any expectations of how you make a film. Ziba [Mir Hosseini, who co-directed *Divorce Iranian Style* and *Runaway*] is a writer, an academic, and Jano [Williams], who I made the Japanese films with, is working as a landscape gardener now. Claire Hunt, who I worked with on quite a few films, is a sound recordist. Somebody like Ziba and somebody like Jano, who really do have a big input into the film, I feel that it's fair to put them as having made the film with you. It just seems that often people aren't recognized for what they do.

SM: Can you give me an example of how the collaboration works. How does an academic who has never worked on a film before adapt to a very different world?

KL: Ziba would say, "Let's go and hang out with Mariam, [one of the plaintiffs seeking divorce in Tehran]." She was completely comfortable with that. That's what she likes doing. She's an anthropologist; she's written books, and she loves observing things and hanging out with people and seeing what happens next. She's very laidback and very easy-going with people, and isn't always thinking of how can we drive this forward so we've got something to film.

SM: Vera and Beatrice have been touring to festivals like Cannes with you and your co-director, Florence Ayisi. It seems like an unusually collaborative practice with documentary subjects, and also points to the increasing attention paid to documentaries at the big film festivals. Do you think this will influence other documentary makers?

KL: Yes, it's a wonderful shift; I absolutely adore it. I love seeing documentaries on the screen. I think it's also changed the way people are filming documentaries because they're thinking we've got to grip people, and we've really got to hold them. It's got to be more like a film, not a documentary. Even the word *documentary* sounds dry to me, whereas if it's a film and you're going through an emotional experience, it's a whole different way of making the film.

SM: It seems to me that Vera and Beatrice are really pivotal to that emotional experience in *Sisters in Law*. Even though, in a sense, it's the other characters, like Amina and Manka whose cases you document, who have the more dramatic narratives. Why do you think that Vera and Beatrice are so compelling?

KL: What I'm hoping is that when people watch the films, they get a sense that they're getting as close to those people as I have. That's why I filmed Vera when she was with her little son, because I wanted to show the soft side of her. It's choosing the moments to reveal the things you've grown to like about them and that have impressed you about them. What I want people to feel is a leap of recognition that these could be people that they know. To get that closeness through watching them is like what happens in fiction as well.

SM: Your films have really gripping narratives, they're very involving, because the characters are so clearly drawn. That's not always the case in documentaries, especially those that have as broad a canvas as yours. How do you maintain the films' structural integrity and the audience's focus?

KL: You get little twists, like with Lum Rose [a character in *Sisters in Law,* whom Beatrice sentences to jail for beating her niece almost to death]; you're very distant from her, and you can see that there's something very false about her. Then in that moment in the prison [when she begs Vera for medicine], you suddenly feel this jolt, you think, she really is devastated, she's been through something I can't even imagine. In *Gaea Girls,* we thought Nagayo [the wrestling teacher] was fabulous, we adored her, then we got scared of her, then we felt sorry for her. And hopefully that's what people feel as they go through the film, that people change.

SM: That happens to other characters in your films, like Simalo [a girl who has run away from her family after they circumcised her against her consent] in *The Day.* She seems to know what she wants so clearly; then at the end she wants to go back to her family.

KL: She's amazing; she's a real pioneer, somebody who's really trying to change her life, and really brave enough to go for change. But she's on her own, whereas the sixteen girls who join together [leaving their village to take refuge in a school], they're changing their village from the inside, so they're changing things in a bigger way, and they're going to be OK. But Simalo is always going to be an outsider, and she's going to feel a great loss at the center of her life—her family, her friends, her village, everything—her whole identity, she has to give it up, go and learn different languages and be completely on her own. At one point she says to her social worker that at least they respected her at home.

SM: I found N'Daisi, Simalo's social worker, really compelling, like the characters from *Sisters in Law.* They're a group of African professional women who you rarely see when Africa is presented in the media. You highlight them to the extent that they are not just subjects but collaborators in the films.

KL: Vera and Beatrice are so impressive, and so dedicated. For example, when we went to the prison for Lum Rose, it would have been impossible for us to have got permission to film there, and Vera just swept us in with her. It was very much her making things happen and us filming it. That's very close to what it was like with Fardhosa in Kenya; she was going around talking to women, trying to make change, and we were following in her wake and filming it. She was the one that was doing things, and we were just really privileged to be allowed to be with her.

SM: Your films show women with unexpected lives, not just performers in a wealthy nation, like the wrestlers and actors in Japan who are placing themselves in the public eye, but Muslim women fighting domestic violence in Iran and Cameroon. How did these women deal with being the subjects of a film at such a tough point in their lives?

KL: When Amina [a Hausa woman who successfully prosecutes her husband, and one of the main subjects of *Sisters in Law*] was going through her divorce, she would always say to Mary [Milton, Longinotto's sound recordist] and I, "Are you going to be there?" That makes sense, because there hadn't been any convictions before. Amina knew that Mary and I were there as witnesses, and also we were there supporting and encouraging her and that we were going to be there each step of the way.

SM: One of the things that really fascinated me about *Sisters in Law* and *The Day* is how many lessons there are to learn from grassroots women's movements and activism happening in Africa, rather than importing Western notions of feminism.

KL: I think of Fazia [who had been subject to FGM, documented in *The Day*] who is eight years old, asking her mother to help her sister [be exempt from FGM]. She'd read the Koran and had her whole argument mapped out, and she used me to make that happen. She insisted on speaking in English so that we were real witnesses to what was happening. She set the whole scene up. When I arrived, she told me where to stand, and just told her poem ["The Day I Will Never Forget," about her experience of FGM] into the camera. I felt like she was about sixty and I was about ten, a complete role reversal.

SM: It seems like those are the moments that define what documentary can do, not just cinematically, but politically, that documentary opens up a conversation that can't take place anywhere else because of the way in which a subject addresses the camera. And your camera is so patient, yet so engaged. Do those moments feel electrifying at the time, or is it only when you're editing or watching the film that you think, "Yes, this is what documentary is for"?

KL: It's like when we filmed the girls [who had run away together] taking their parents to court in *The Day*. There was a local Kenyan TV crew there, two guys with a little camera, and they started interviewing the girls. We spoke to those guys when we knew the court case was going to be delayed for two weeks and asked whether they were going to come back for the verdict, and they said, "It's not a big enough story." Yet in terms of that community, you could hardly get a bigger story! So I felt this great relief that we were there filming it, and other girls might get to hear about it that way.

SM: Is telling women's stories a conscious decision on your part to redress the balance of male-focused stories, which presume that masculinity is somehow a neutral or representative state, or are you particularly drawn to women's stories?

KL: Being a woman, I'm very drawn to filming women. It's just what I'm interested in, and I often find that in situations where women don't have the power, they are much more articulate and emotional because that's all they've got.

SM: Do you feel that your films could change that, even as they demonstrate it?

KL: It is a documenting. It is those people who are making change. Mary and I are just there filming it, which is much easier than to go home after you've taken your father to court and he's furious with you and you have to live in his house. Films hopefully can be a little part of change, showing what other brave people are doing. Lots of people have met Vera and Beatrice from *Sisters in Law* because of the film, but they are the ones who are doing everything.

SM: Your films are made on such an intimate scale, often shooting in close confines or at speed. How have the massive changes in equipment wrought by digital technology—whether with cellphones, cameras, or sound recording—changed your practice?

KL: Not at all, I haven't worked with those yet, because what I'm trying to do is make my films as close to fiction in the way they look as possible. My own films, they're always on film. But for my new film, I'm doing it on digi-Beta, because the production company doesn't want to pay for film. But I want my films to look like film.

SM: Does digital hold out any potential for broadening access to filmmaking?

KL: In that respect, I think it's brilliant. A friend of mine recently went off and shot something to show the broadcasters to get money. I think it's loosened everything up, and given a lot more possibility of making films to people who don't have a lot of money, whereas what I've had to do is raise money. I've always had to have the whole budget in place before going, which has meant it's taken me longer.

SM: You've funded most of your films outside of traditional structures; only *The Day I Will Never Forget* was made with a production company. It seems like they circulate through alternate structures too. In the U.S., for example, you're listed with Women Make Movies, a feminist distribution network. Can you tell me a bit about your relationship with them?

KL: Oh, they've been fantastic. They've been distributing my films for ages now, since I started. What I love about them is that they're really committed to films. Obviously, they want to make money, but that's not their main thing. So for example, when 9/11 happened, they immediately said [to their customers, who are largely academic institutions and political groups], "All our films about Muslim women, you can hire them for nothing." They wrote to the filmmakers and asked our permission. That was their response to it, which I thought was fantastic. I trust them completely.

SM: It's a very different model to traditional distributors. Was that a one-off for WMM?

KL: No. For example, If people don't have much money, they let them hire films cheaply, and they make sure that the films get into colleges and schools as well as the more glamorous things [like festivals], so I feel very comfortable having them as distributors.

SM: And do you think that their model is sustainable? I really hope that they'll be around!

KL: Well, they seem to have lasted ages. I think they started in the seventies. So it does seem sustainable. They send me a list every six months of where the films have been, with pages of screenings all over America, so they've obviously got a very good network.

SM: Good to hear. They increasingly seem like an anachronism, one of the few survivors of that wave of feminist small businesses from the seventies.

KL: There is still a place for specifically women's films, but I think it's getting less and less.

SM: What about the film industry itself: is there still a political point to creating all-women production teams like yours, or is it becoming a moot point?

KL: It's just finding the right people, whether male or female. But it happens because the stories I'm doing are women's stories, it makes more sense for me to work with a woman. I've found Mary and I work so well together, it's nice to stick to someone you know.

SM: Who's producing your upcoming film [set in a school in Pakistan]?

116

KL: A company called Films of Record. The producer, Roger Graef, brought me the story, and I just trust that he's going to be OK and it's going to work. It's only the second time I've worked for a film production company, and the first time was such a disaster that I swore I'd never do it again.

SM: Why?

KL: That was with *The Day I Will Never Forget,* and I had such a terrible time with the production company. I always thought that producers, in my foolishness, were meant to somehow work with you as a team, and you work together to make a film. But what would happen was, we'd be out filming something [in Kenya], and the producer, Paul Hayman, would phone me up on the mobile and say, "You've got to do an interview in a car," and I'd say, "None of them have got cars, Paul," and he'd say, "No, I want interviews in a car." He had very set ideas of how he wanted the film to be.

SM: In the end, there aren't any interviews in cars in *The Day.* Do you feel it became the film that you wanted? And how did you win out?

KL: I'd somehow fob him off, and hope that when he phoned next, no one would answer the mobile. When we were editing, Paul would come in and want lots and lots of commentary, but the commissioning editor was great. So I let the two of them argue it out. That was kind of weird, because I thought the producer was meant to be the buffer against the commissioning editor. But we had a nice commissioning editor, and a very old-fashioned producer.

SM: It sounds like you fight hard to make the film you want. Have audience reactions borne you out? Have people told you that your films have changed things for them?

KL: Mary and I went to Cape Town with *Sisters in Law,* and I'll never forget that screening. It was amazing; lots of girls came up after and said, "We've been raped and we're really proud that the little girl's standing up in the film and confronting her rapist. We've never told anyone we've been raped, and we're going to go home and tell."

Really amazing things. That was very moving and exciting. It was really exciting to know that women in Africa liked it.

Note

A version of this interview originally appeared in *Scumgrrls* 10 (Autumn 2006): 30–33.

Chapter 8

The Gleaners and "Us"

The Radical Modesty of Agnès Varda's *Les Glaneurs et la glaneuse*

In both its formal and thematic choices, *Les Glaneurs et la glaneuse* (*The Gleaners and I,* 2000) is one of Agnès Varda's most experimental films to date. The documentary's delicate themes of poverty, aging, filmmaking, and art warrant this shift toward a more unconventional style. *Gleaners* explores the agricultural tradition of gleaning, the legalized practice of culling leftover food from fields after the harvest. Varda journeys from France's rural fields to its urban markets to meet and, with her handheld DV camera, to chronicle the lives of gleaners of all sorts. Through her direct address to the camera, her voice-over commentary, and her associative editing choices, she reveals that some glean out of necessity while others glean as a lifestyle choice or in rebellion against commercialism and consumer waste. These diverse people, their life conditions, and their reasons for gleaning seem unrelated at first, but over the course of the film, Varda draws remarkable social connections among them. Such unusual connections question and upend conventions concerning subjects worthy of documentation, since Varda chooses to include not traditional documentary fare but quite the opposite: moments of banality, images of aging and decay, and interviews with social outcasts. *Gleaners* encourages viewers to connect the motives one might expect for gleaning, such as poverty and adversity, to more unexpected ones, such as resourcefulness, tradition, art, and activism.

Varda recognizes that her task as documentary filmmaker parallels that of other gleaners, though her voice-over says that instead of grains or fruit she gleans "acts, gestures, and information" with her camera. Moments selected from her travels and her many hours of footage self-reflexively acknowledge her own role as, in her words, a "gleaner of images": *la glaneuse*. By extension, Varda's methodology in *Gleaners* underscores that documentary filmmaking itself is always a form of gleaning, conditioned by what a filmmaker finds valuable while shooting on location, which footage the filmmaker selects for inclusion in a film, and how the filmmaker chooses to arrange those selections for an audience. Varda describes this approach to filmmaking as educational: "Every time you make a film, you learn something. You approach other people, other people's work, some landscape you never noticed before. It's like giving sudden life to what you see and capturing the beauty in it."[1]

What makes *Gleaners* unique is Varda's profound manipulation of address in the process of achieving these effects. By modifying the modes of address, identification, and narration particular to the documentary genre, Varda hails both her viewers and the people she films—including herself—as active participants in *Gleaners*. This narrational style, which I call "filming in the second person," creatively locates Varda within her arguments while maintaining a firm commitment to the people she talks to, gleaners and viewers alike. As a result Varda's film conveys as much about herself and her spectators as her many acquaintances who glean. She draws poignant connections among these seemingly disparate groups, and the resulting eighty-two-minute film engenders a complex but direct circle of communication among filmmaker, filmed subjects, and viewing audience. In this essay I examine how Varda's filming in the second person contemplates the social politics of gleaning while simultaneously using her innovative filmic "you" to scrutinize the structures of documentary representation itself.

Indeed, the film is full of not only people revealing themselves but people revealing themselves *to each other*. With her onscreen presence, Varda connects with the gleaners she meets, and her physical proximity to them serves as a reminder that she shares in the conditions of their lives. Varda explains, "I asked people to reveal themselves, to give a lot of themselves; so I thought that the film should also reveal a little about the filmmakers, that I should just use a little bit of myself in it."[2] Underscoring this association is one of the film's most self-reflexive moments, one wherein Varda playfully adopts the pose of Jules Breton's *La Glaneuse* for the camera, balancing a bundle of wheat proudly on her shoulder before dropping it in favor of her DV camera. Though seemingly whimsical, it is significant that she adopts the pose of the *subject* of the painting here: the gleaner herself, not the artist himself. In doing so, she creates an explicit connection with her interview subjects, breaking down the barriers between filmed subjects and filmmaker.

Meeting la Glaneuse and les Glaneurs

Furthering the investigative style she has practiced throughout her career—especially in *Sans toit ni loi* (*Vagabond,* 1985)—Varda is always present in *Gleaners,* whether she physically appears onscreen, asks questions offscreen, comments in voice-over, or frames the image as her point of view. Her insistence on placing herself within the film reminds us that Varda's gleaning and assembly of these images necessarily shapes the documentary story. Her connection to gleaning is further advanced by an onscreen interrogation of her own aging process. With clever wit and a good dose of humor, she often compares the rot of vegetables in fields or detritus in the streets with her own aging body, particularly her hands. These scenes are marked by an affable, bittersweet directness and by an extraordinary sense of visual and textural composition. Twice in the film, for example, the crisp, digital images slowly track over her wrinkled hands in close-up—first compared with the rotting, veined flesh of a potato and later with Rembrandt's mottled, aged flesh in a self-portrait. Varda's commentary makes the connections explicit: "That is to say, this is my project: to film with one hand my other hand. To enter into the horror [of it as it ages, decays], I find it extraordinary. . . . And here's

"This is my project: to film one hand with my other hand" (Agnès Varda, *Les glaneurs et la glaneuse,* Ciné-Tamaris, 2000).

Rembrandt's self-portrait, but it's the same thing in fact, it's always a self-portrait."

Similar moments feature highly abstracted close-ups of the roots of her graying hair, cabbages after the harvest, mangled cars after they have been crushed, a lucite clock missing its hands. The film's voice-over and cutting always relate these moments back to Varda's self-portrait of her own aging process, as she dryly comments that "my hair and my hands tell me the end is near" or "a clock without hands, that suits me. You don't see time passing." Again, although somewhat whimsical, the ensuing pauses in her commentary and elevated minor-key music render each of these confessions disquieting; yet these explorations of her own aging approach a more fascinated than fearful tone. Her close framings in loving detail almost fetishize these harbingers of death and, in an adept feminist move, revalue the physical signs of age that society chooses to malign.

This exploration of aging parallels that of gleaning in powerful ways. Considered together, both themes mark an interrogation and revaluation of what society deems worthy of regard and respect. They embody a kind of eco-feminist subversion of aesthetics, of what Western society considers beautiful and therefore valuable. For in our capitalist patriarchy, one learns to prize the new, the young, the beautiful, the marketable; Varda instead revalues the used, the aged, even the unsightly. She rebelliously asserts that she likes to film "rot, waste, debris." She finds the "horror" of her aging hands "extraordinary," comparing it not to concepts of shame or uselessness but to priceless artworks. She prefers the nonsaleable, misshapen heart-shaped potatoes to the perfectly rounded ones. She praises the Musée en Herbe's program *Poubelle ma belle* ("my beautiful garbage can/trash"), which teaches children to recycle and to appreciate that which is not brand new. The most sustained way in which she embraces this fundamental concept of "my beautiful trash," however, is by gathering the stories of those ignored by society, oppressed by corporations and governments. In short, she strives to increase social awareness of "waste and trash" but also to push that more important and compassionate question in gleaning embodied by "who finds a use for it?"[3]

Filming in the Second Person: From "I" to "You" to "We"

In hailing her audience as participants in an ongoing conversation about society's attitudes toward poverty, waste, and class, Varda is engaged in breaking the boundary between those onscreen and their viewers, and she does so by filming in the second person. Grammatical person, according to the

Oxford English Dictionary, indicates a participant's role as either the speaker (I/we in first person), the addressee (you in second person), or someone or something spoken of (he/she/it/they in third person). Second-person address, rarely used in traditional literature, is most commonly found in travel guides, letters, lyrics, and games. Like literature, cinema traditionally prefers first- or third-person narration, and *Gleaners* employs these strategies as well. Varda occasionally narrates in third person ("they get all their food from trashcans"), though her first-person narration comprises most of the film's spoken commentary ("I wanted to talk to him," "I like filming rot, waste, debris") and nearly all of the film's interviews offer first-person accounts of gleaning.

The most distinctive mode of address in *Gleaners,* however, is the second person. Obvious cinematic uses of the second person include direct address through an eyeline match with the camera and voice-over commentary or dialogue that speaks to "you," the viewer. Varda sometimes narrates in second person ("you don't see time passing"), and she looks at the camera often, but most effective are the gleaners who look and speak directly to the camera/viewer, such as François in his rubber boots and Etienne-Jules Marey's grandson at his vineyard.[4] As the spectator becomes more involved in the stories of these gleaners, the lines between "you" and "them" begin to soften, and Varda thereby encourages her audience to participate in the film's conversations and to care about the people speaking.

Yet *Gleaners* is engaged in an even more radical project than speaking directly to individual spectators about social issues. Arguably, the film's most important project is to interpellate you, the viewer, as an active participant and subject. This, however, is not Louis Althusser's repressive, dominant ideology hailing you.[5] Nor is it classical Hollywood's "textual hailing," as Kaja Silverman describes the "You are now in Bedford Falls" establishing shot of *It's a Wonderful Life.*[6] That is, this is not an address that encourages you to adopt the false subjectivity of another—especially that of a fictional Hollywood character—or to be Althusser's "subjected being . . . freely accepting of his [*sic*] subjugation" or even to acquiesce to the subjugation of others.[7]

Instead, *Gleaners* strives to raise your social consciousness in the Gramscian "spirit of scission [a redemptive break from social class, capitalism, or other forms of division] that must aim to spread itself from the protagonist class to the classes that are its potential allies."[8] Of course, many leftist propaganda films seek class reeducation and solidarity, but *Gleaners* differs in that it promotes a pensive, questioning spectator and a grassroots approach to social change that is *situated,* per Donna Haraway, and thus generative of "an epistemology and politics of engaged, accountable positioning."[9] By multiplying and revaluing the meanings of "gleaning," this documentary teaches us to recognize and reconsider our societal role in class, gender, and age practices, as well as in environmental, cultural, and filmmaking practices. Befitting Varda's lifelong commitment to countercultural activism, her film offers us an alternative, revolutionary model: *Gleaners* openly defies bourgeois ideologies by challenging class oppression, environmental destruction, ageism, and rampant consumerism. The film's sociocultural critique teaches us to reject our prescribed role under consumer capitalism. It is a counterhegemonic second-person address that might more aptly translate: "Hey, you, gleaning comrade! Value your fellow humans and the environment!"

Toward this end, *Gleaners* strives not simply to target the second-person "you" but to inspire our embrace of a stronger, communal sense of the first-person plural, "we." The film's novelty and efficacy lie in its subtle interweaving of these modes of address, all designed to hail you in the second person, and through this hailing to lead you to a humanist awareness of the first-person plural. That is, Varda wants "you" to join "us," a community of gleaners, humanitarians, fellow humans, in order to shift from separatist ideologies of "I," "you," and "them" to the more inclusive "we."

One of Varda's most overt expressions of this humanitarian goal appears not in *Gleaners* itself but in the DVD's follow-up documentary *Deux ans après* (*Two Years Later*, 2002), in which she revisits many of the original interviewees and other gleaners too. Moving beyond a simple then-and-now update, Varda reverently tells us that it was the astounding number of letters, stories, and gleaned gifts sent to her after the release of *Gleaners* that prompted her to continue the film's project two years after its completion. All of these letters share with the filmmaker how inspiring and life-changing her film is for their authors, and how it creates a new awareness and a sense of community among gleaners of all sorts. One viewer of *Gleaners* interviewed in *Two Years Later* clearly summarizes the success of the film's humanitarian project: "It makes you want to be a better person, to pay more attention to other people." Confirming this response, Alain, the market gleaner and English-as-a-second-language teacher first interviewed in *Gleaners,* reports that now more people stop to talk to him, praise his volunteer work, and buy his leaflets. Another interviewee who first appeared in *Gleaners,* the famous philosopher and psychoanalyst Jean Laplanche, compares gleaning to a radical practice of psychoanalysis; like gleaners, who must be open to possibilities, the doctor "must give up what he knows so he can be receptive to something that is completely new." Yet another viewer describes her experience of *Gleaners* and the inspirational impact of Varda's role in it like this:

Delphine: Seeing this film was like a rebirth . . . this film just completely put us back in touch with ourselves, with life.
Varda: But it talks about leftovers, things that are abandoned.
Delphine: Yes, but it's made by someone who is very much alive.

The original *Gleaners* develops this inviting, communal tone in multiple ways. In the remainder of this essay, I will analyze how three of these methods raise awareness of social class: Varda's use of second- and first-person address, her unobtrusive DV camera coupled with her onscreen role, and her persuasively engaging sense of humor.

Raising Class Consciousness: "Us" and "Them"

Clearly, Varda's project seeks to humanize groups of people who are routinely ignored by more privileged members of society. She asserts in one promotional interview that gleaning "is a subject matter that is vaguely gray. When you see these people in the street, you don't look at them. My idea was not only to find them but to let them speak. To show that they have thoughts and feelings and intelligence—a luminescence."[10] Initially, Varda's statement seems to take for granted a problematic position of dominance when she, as a middle-class film director, claims the authority to "let them speak."

By invoking the second person, however, she redirects that authority and addresses the very people who habitually ignore scavengers and gleaners. When she says, "you don't look at them" scavenging in the streets, she puts into question the identity of the "you." Most obviously, "you" refers to those people who do not need to scavenge for food, who can afford to ignore gleaners in the streets and so choose to. Varda's statement implies that she herself was one of these people when she began her documentary project, since she needed "to find them" before she could "let them speak." Yet her strategic use of the second person groups her largely middle-class viewing audience in this category with her. She thereby implicitly slips into the deliberately absented first-person plural by hailing us as complicit, which perhaps initially incites a slight defensiveness about our privileged class position. Simultaneously, though, this subtle first-person-plural address encourages all viewers to open our eyes and minds, to acknowledge and accept a class of people whom society trains us to ignore.

In fact, Varda complicates such issues of class consciousness throughout *Gleaners*. As one of her key political strategies, she strives to dismantle the lines that separate poor gleaners from higher-classed or recreational gleaners. As a shared practice, gleaning produces Antonio Gramsci's realignment of

"potential class allies." The film's disjunctive editing facilitates this break-
down of class boundaries through its surprising and often humorous juxtapositions. For example, Varda's interview with Claude, the poor and dispir-
ited yet persevering traveler who gleans from potato fields and trash cans,
immediately cuts to the gourmet kitchen of four-star executive chef Edouard
Loubet, who, the film soon reveals, also gleans. This shift from poverty-
stricken traveler to gleaning gourmet chef broadens and revalues definitions
of gleaning even as it offers a more comfortable point of identification for
bourgeois audiences.

Since the film's release in 2000, I have viewed *Gleaners* with public audiences and with my undergraduate film students more than twenty times in
Paris, New York, and Atlanta, and the response is unfailing: predominantly
middle-class audiences always laugh at this comparison of a poor traveler
and a gourmet chef. Considering the film's overt class analyses, I find this
moment of laughter highly significant: why do audiences feel compelled to
laugh at this comparison? It is true that Varda's abrupt juxtaposition here
creates a moment of visual shock as she cuts from Claude's dingy, cramped
trailer to Edouard's bright, spacious, stainless-steel kitchen. The polar class
associations of these locations alone locate a humorous irony in the moment.
At a deeper level, however, the laughter may also originate in Varda's direct
class comparison, one that necessarily calls attention to the viewer's own class
position.

Varda's carefully edited juxtaposition of these two differently classed
gleaners initially might seem designed to condemn middle-class viewers, as
the comparison easily could have set up a biting criticism of the chef's—and
the audience's—bourgeois privilege. More productively, however, this moment of awkwardness functions not as a slap at bourgeois audiences but as
a gesture of inclusivity in the first-person plural: we must situate ourselves
on a continuum of privilege ranging from the pristine, stainless-steel afflu-
ence of the chef as he prepares fetishized, expensive foods to the shabby,
trailer-bound poverty of the traveler who must scrabble for leftover fish from
garbage cans. Further, the surprisingly sensitive nature of Varda's interview
with Chef Edouard quickly reveals that he gleans out of economic frugality
as well, albeit under less dire circumstances. "Nothing should be wasted,"
he tells us. "We don't throw anything away [in my kitchen]. You have to be
economical." This bourgeois chef gleans for his herbs and fruits because he
refuses to pay for overpriced foods of lesser quality at the store. Moreover,
through gleaning he can ensure the freshness of his ingredients and honor his
grandparents, who taught him the tradition of gleaning when he was a boy.
Through the sincerity and sensitivity of Varda's interviews with both of these

gleaners, the film allays any class defensiveness or judgment on the viewers' part and once again invites us to align ourselves with all gleaners.

Varda's equal treatment of impoverished and bourgeois gleaners alike creates a connection among diverse people because they value frugality and resourcefulness. She accentuates this connection by cutting from the potato gleaner to the chef by way of a clever graphic match: the two scenes end and begin, respectively, with similar shots of Claude and Edouard holding food. Such visual rhymes typify the film's overall editing pattern, subtly but effectively likening the motives for gleaning among poverty-stricken travelers and gourmet chefs, as well as other gleaners. Through such parallel edits, *Gleaners* sutures us into identifying with all of the gleaners interviewed: the film's kaleidescopic montage asks us to redefine gleaning by drawing connections among its seemingly disparate motives of necessity, tradition, kindness, activism, artistry, and resourcefulness, regardless of class distinctions that would separate us from them.

In her interviews with gleaners Varda shows compassion and appreciation, inspiring a sympathetic response from viewers in turn. She poses open-ended and concerned questions to the gleaners—"What happened to you [to necessitate gleaning for all of your food]?" or "Did you know that once they're through picking potatoes, you're allowed to take leftovers?"—and devotes extensive screen time to their responses. In Beauce, for example, she meets Claude's group of travelers, who must glean their staple diet from leftover heaps of potatoes, several tons deemed unfit for sale by corporate growers and so dumped in fields, left to rot. She conducts several lengthy interviews with these travelers. Close framings and longer takes in this scene, particularly the tighter shots inside Claude's small trailer, reveal his dignity and resourcefulness. For almost six minutes of screen time, Claude discusses the hardships of his living conditions, the wastefulness of markets and corporate growers, and the difficulties of gleaning out of necessity. Since Varda is posing her questions about gleaning to audiences as well as to the gleaners, her second-person address of "you" during these interviews invites a productive shift to first-person plural, carefully building a measure of intimacy among filmed subject, onscreen filmmaker, and viewing audience.

Documentary Modesty and Digital Video

Throughout *Gleaners,* Varda interrogates gleaning with a sense of wonder, humility, and, as she puts it, "modesty": "The people I have filmed tell us a great deal about our society and ourselves. I myself learned a great deal while I was shooting this film. It confirmed for me that the documentary film is a discipline that teaches modesty."[11] She asserts that modesty, which she strives to inculcate in the audience, was one of her primary motivations for using a DV camera. Eyeline matches and slightly oblique camera angles stitch us into her conversations with her interviewees, but it is the small size and flip-out monitor of her handycam that allows us to get physically closer to people during interviews without intimidating them: "to look them in the eye," she says, without having "to hide behind the camera."[12] Nothing inherent in digital cameras leads inevitably to changed relations between filmmaker and subject, but the DV camera's unobtrusive size and secondary viewscreen offer possibilities for such a difference, and Varda's film embraces these possibilities.[13]

The sense of connection enabled by Varda's technical choices extends to the viewer as well, creating the film's remarkable first-person-plural feel. In effect, the camera is "us," the viewing audience seated at the table or walking through the field with Varda and her interviewees. When the gleaners talk with Varda, they address the camera's presence and hence our presence too. These choices turn the typical informant interview—a ubiquitous trope in documentaries—into something quite new. Varda's small DV camera, her casual on-location settings, and her onscreen presence trade not on the authority invested in the interviewer and the distanced objectivity of the staged third-person interview but on the situated communality and spontaneity among all conversing, including the overtly addressed viewer. *Gleaners* thereby fosters a more "modest" role both for the documentary *glaneuse* and the viewer, swaying our sensitivity subjectively toward the interviewees.

While *Gleaners* differs markedly from mainstream styles, so too does its mode of address differ from the subjective styles of other contemporary documentarians. As with these better-known filmmakers, Varda's own acknowledged presence as documentary director, aging persona, and gleaner of images helps to flesh out her film's meanings, but she prefers to emphasize the politics of poverty for the gleaners as the film's dominant theme.[14] She is careful to avoid the pitfall of over-emphasis on herself, a significant difference from other documentaries that prominently include their directors onscreen.

Ross McElwee's *Sherman's March* (1985), for example, humorously highlights its own derailment from its original topic (a historical documentary about Sherman's March) and its devolution into the director's "shameless alibi to pick up women," but it veers further into a masochistic, "hysterical" documentary, as Lucy Fischer terms it.[15] McElwee hides behind his camera for most of his film, often looking voyeuristically at women and then mocking himself for doing so. Varda, in contrast, conducts highly engaged onscreen interviews in *Gleaners* and engages far more explicitly with her film's political and social ramifications. In many ways her work is more akin to Michael Moore's documentaries. Like Moore, Varda wears her left-wing agenda on her sleeve and does not conceal her political biases during her interviews and voice-overs. Yet Moore often employs a rather egoistic and confrontational demeanor with his interviewees, one marked by "personal audacity," "self-righteousness," and a "principle of brash provocation," as Matthew Bernstein writes of *Roger and Me* (1989).[16] Moore's sense of humor often builds from the fallout from these confrontations, largely drawing on criticism and satire. Varda's sense of humor, on the other hand, stems mainly from her discoveries of odd, unexpected connections, found objects, and delightful absurdities.

Hailing Us with Humor

Varda's use of humor in *Gleaners* is one of her crucial rhetorical tools when invoking her second-person address, and it strongly engenders the film's shift to the first-person plural. Through humor, the film engages us in a modest yet compelling way. Varda's witty asides and amusing anecdotes enable her to approach us more directly than a traditional documentary might, much in the way that the flip-out monitor of her small camera allows her to speak more intimately with the people she meets. Further, the candor of their stories is disarmingly funny and thus puts the viewer at ease with the different people interviewed.

Toward this end, *Gleaners* often inserts small gifts for our amusement: a dog inexplicably sporting an enormous red boxing glove strapped under its chin, a lawyer dressed in full judicial regalia standing in the middle of a cabbage patch, a "dancing" lens cap. The last is perhaps the best example of the film's strategic humor, since Varda uses it as gentle mockery of the presumed infallibility of the documentary genre and its director. Having forgotten to turn her camera off after an interview, she films "the dance of the lens cap." The camera swings at her side as she accidentally films the lens cap dangling above the ground. Rather than disregard or delete this extraneous footage, however, Varda embraces it. As the cap dances wildly for nearly fifty seconds, the director humanizes herself by admitting a moment of forgetfulness. She pushes the scene further, however, by scoring the shot with jazz music and transforming a delightful found object that she too has gleaned into a prized moment of beauty for us to share. In these gleaned moments of humor, the film winks at us and engages us on its own offbeat terms.

The dance of the lens cap (Agnès Varda, *Les glaneurs et la glaneuse,* Ciné-Tamaris, 2000).

These funny asides and anecdotes strategically usher us into sympathy with the film's larger political issues, especially that we are all, in some sense, gleaners and therefore should not discriminate against those who glean out of poverty. Rather than lecturing, the film introduces us more fully to the gleaners Varda has met through its warm, humorous tone. Sometimes that humor simply entertains us while courting our political assent, as when Varda defiantly eats a stingy grower's figs; sometimes it relieves tension when comparing different living conditions, as with the potato gleaner and the chef. Most often, the film's humor serves as a common thread that unites the quirky *glaneuse* herself, the myriad interview subjects, and the film's diverse viewers—now reeducated as "modest" class allies—directly hailing us all as gleaners.

Notes

Sections of this essay were published in another form in "Beautiful Trash: Agnès Varda's *Les glaneurs et la glaneuse,*" *Senses of Cinema* 45 (2007), http://www.sensesofcinema.com/contents/07/45/glaneurs-et-glaneuse.html. Reworked and reprinted with thanks to the editors of that publication.

1. Agnès Varda, "The Modest Gesture of the Filmmaker," interview by Melissa Anderson, *Cinéaste* 26, no. 4 (2001): 27.

2. Richard James Havis, "Varda Gleans DV Style," *2-pop: The Digital Film-maker's Resource Site Online,* May 30, 2001, http://www.2-pop.com/library/articles/2001_05_30.html.

3. Agnès Varda, promotional materials for *Les Glaneurs et la glaneuse* (Paris: Ciné-Tamaris and the Groupment National des Cinémas de Recherche, 2000), 1.

4. The *Gleaners* shooting script (courtesy of Varda and Ciné-Tamaris) reads: "on ne voit pas le temps qui passe." My translation here to the second-person "you" follows the standard translation of the third-person French, "on" (one). The French "on" is commonly understood to address the reader in the second person, which the film's subtitles reflect as well.

5. Louis Althusser, "Ideology and Ideological State Apparatuses," in *Lenin and Philosophy and Other Essays* (London: New Left Books, 1971), 174.

6. Kaja Silverman, *The Subject of Semiotics* (Oxford: Oxford University Press, 1983), 49–50.

7. Althusser, "Ideology," 182.

8. Antonio Gramsci, "Cultural Themes: Ideological Material," in *Antonio Gramsci: Selections from Cultural Writings,* ed. David Forgacs and Geoffrey Nowell-Smith (London: Lawrence and Wishart, 1985), 390.

9. Donna Haraway, "Situated Knowledges: The Science Question in Feminism and the Privilege of Partial Perspective," in *Simians, Cyborgs, and Women: The Rein-vention of Nature* (New York: Routledge, 1991), 196.

10. Havis, "Varda Gleans DV Style."

11. Varda, promotional materials for *Glaneurs,* 2.

12. Havis, "Varda Gleans DV Style."

13. For further reading on Varda's use of the digital camera in *Glaneurs,* see Homay King, "Matter, Time, and the Digital: Varda's *The Gleaners and I,*" *Quarterly Review of Film and Video* 24 (2007): 421–29.

14. Agnès Varda, personal appearance, Paris, July 23, 2000.

15. Lucy Fischer, "Documentary Film and the Discourse of Hysterical/Historical Narrative: Ross McElwee's *Sherman's March,*" in *Documenting the Documentary: Close Readings of Documentary Film and Video,* ed. Barry Keith Grant and Jeannette Sloniowski (Detroit: Wayne State University Press, 1998), 333–34.

16. Matthew Bernstein, "Documentaphobia and Mixed Modes: Michael Moore's *Roger & Me,*" in ibid., 408–9.

Tableaux

Final Girls

Appropriation, Identification, and Fluidity
in Cindy Sherman's *Office Killer*

In 1995, Christine Vachon, the producer of noted independent films such as *Far from Heaven* (Todd Haynes, 2002), *Boys Don't Cry* (Kimberly Peirce, 1999), and *I Shot Andy Warhol* (Mary Harron, 1992), asked American art photographer Cindy Sherman to participate in the making of a horror film. Although Sherman was hesitant, accustomed to working alone in her studio taking pictures of herself, she recognized in Vachon an ideal collaborator and agreed to take on the role of director for the campy slasher that would eventually be titled *Office Killer*. She later commented, "I feel I've always been more interested in movies, in some way, than in art . . . but maybe that's true for most people."[1]

Sherman offered the film's general storyline, which was then written up by a team of writers that included Elise MacAdam, Tom Kalin, and Todd Haynes. The result of this collaboration was an independent, low-budget horror flick about Dorine Douglas (Carol Kane), a skilled but antisocial copy editor who becomes a murderer by chance rather than design. Due to a middle manager's embezzlements, Dorine and her coworkers are faced with corporate downsizing at the magazine *Constant Consumer*. Working late one night shortly before the office is to close its doors, Dorine causes the accidental electrocution of her employer, Gary (David Thornton). Apparently too nervous, or perhaps too inept, to call the authorities, Dorine takes charge of Gary's body and sets him up in the basement of the home she shares with her controlling yet ailing mother; there his corpse is eventually joined by others to form blackly comic tableaux.

Film, Still?

Despite clear thematic and formal connections between *Office Killer* and Sherman's oeuvre, the film has been largely excluded from critical considerations of Sherman's career. It was not included, for example, in the Serpentine Gallery's 2003 retrospective exhibition and accompanying catalog, titled *Cindy Sherman*.[2] It is only briefly mentioned, as "a box office flop," in Catherine Morris's *The Essential Cindy Sherman*.[3] Furthermore, even though a handful of screenings were offered as part of a 2006 retrospective in Paris's Jeu du Paume Gallery, the film was not mentioned by any of the authors of the exhibition's catalog.[4] That Sherman's foray into film has not been recognized as a work of art as such and thus has been symbolically excised from her corpus is ironic since the success of her art photography has much to do with an insistence upon a formal instability between various forms of visual cultural production, including film, art photography, advertising, pornography, portraiture, and fine art. To wit, Sherman's most celebrated series, *Untitled Film Stills,* upsets the distinction between popular and precious visual culture by taking up the industrial practice of the commercial film still. Produced between 1977 and 1980, this collection of sixty-nine black-and-white photographs appropriates many of the formal conventions of classical Hollywood cinema in ways that highlight the semiotic processes necessary for such conventions to make narrative and aesthetic sense and the apparent ease with which women—including Sherman herself—embody the feminine stereotypes they produce.[5]

Nonetheless, there clearly persists on the part of critics a desire to maintain a particular theoretical vision of Sherman's practices by patrolling the boundary between "high" and "low" cultural production. Further evidence of such normative distinctions lie in the commercial work Sherman has done with fashion designers Dianne Benson, Dorothee Bis, Rei Kawakubo, and, most recently, Marc Jacobs. Although the advertisements she and photographer Juergen Teller produced for Jacobs were eventually published in book form, they have been largely removed from critical examinations of her artistic oeuvre as well.[6]

For Sherman, however, boundary crossing is fundamental. Her refusal to contain her visual practices within the boundaries of a single medium produces a disorderliness that challenges lingering fantasies of the Romantic artist. As artist, model, performer, filmmaker, and photographer, she occupies multiple identities available within the field of cultural production. Additionally, she works comfortably in commercial venues, in independent cultural production, and in fine art, maintaining a willingness and indeed a desire to explore multiple fields and, moreover, to treat the borders between fields as fluid. As a result, Sherman's work makes most sense when viewed not through the theoretical paradigm of "art" but as visual culture. Encompassing a broader collection of visual practices, visual culture, as scholar Lisa Bloom points out, "by its very nature dispenses with hierarchical cultural distinctions such as high versus low, elite versus mass, modern versus folk."[7]

Approaching *Office Killer* from the perspective of visual culture studies provides a means of embracing and accounting for the ways it intersects with Sherman's other work, for the means by which it too reframes a familiar, commercial form so as to draw attention to feminine representational codes. Organized around a female killer and her relationship with mostly female victims, *Office Killer* explores interactions among women or, rather, among different feminine stereotypes. Thus it emerges as a text deeply concerned with questions of femininity, which is open to feminist readings due to its thematic and formal similarities to other visual practices in Sherman's oeuvre.

Tableaux Morts

The most compelling, and simultaneously repelling, scenes in the film reveal the gruesome, *Untitled Film Stills*–like tableaux of carefully arranged corpses that Dorine has constructed in her basement recreation room. Populated with colleagues, the basement becomes not only a place of recreation but also a surrogate for the office that served as a site of respite from Dorine's tortuous home life. Her need to maintain the fantasy is made clear when she brings her coworker Norah (Jeanne Tripplehorn), whose embezzlements are the likely cause of the office's downsizing, alive to the basement. Dorine instructs her, "We're working at home now, and it's all because of you. . . . I want you to explain to everyone." The basement operates as what feminist film scholar Carol Clover calls the "terrible place," which is simultaneously terrible and comforting, horrific and heartening.[8] It is here that Dorine, like Sherman in her studio, creates a place in which she can perform being herself, where she is in control, visited by "friends," and where she belongs.

The first time this macabre mise-en-scène is revealed, Dorine sits between her victims on the couch, munching popcorn. In subsequent scenes, the now-deceased workers are arranged in couches and chairs. Some are placed before a flickering television; her coworker Virginia (Barbara Sukowa) is set to work in front of a typewriter; and the two unfortunate young girls who had attempted to sell Dorine Girl Scout cookies are nestled together in a large comfortable chair. Oblivious to the deteriorating state of these oozing

137

Office Killer (Cindy Sherman, 1997). (Courtesy of Killer Films and Strand Releasing.)

bodies, Dorine giggles like a schoolgirl at dead Gary's imaginary flirtations ("Mr. Michaels, you shouldn't say such things to a girl!") and engages in macabre girl talk with a rotting Virginia ("You'd look much prettier if you put your hair off your face").

In constructing and performing in these scenes, Dorine echoes Sherman's role as photographer/model and director through her use of the representational strategies explored by the artist in other contexts. In the same way that Sherman pieces together scenes in her photographs, Dorine pieces together, and inserts herself into, a scene in her basement. In reference to her controversial *Sex Pictures,* Sherman explained in an interview with Graham Fuller that she "identified with [Dorine] setting up the bodies in the basement, because it's how I see myself playing in my studio with mannequins."[9] The mid-1990s *Sex Pictures* featured the body parts of medical mannequins arranged in grotesque and often sexually suggestive poses. Using mannequins rather than her own body, which had been featured in all her work up until this point, gave Sherman the opportunity to explore nudity, sexuality, and explicit content without having to expose herself or a model graphically to the camera. Dorine's careful arrangement of corpses is a moment of self-reflexivity on the part of a director who recognized the macabre and horrific nature of work that was, like *Office Killer,* largely treated with suspicion by critics, many of whom were awaiting a return to her "usual style" of (self-)representation.

Dorine's tableaux also draw on themes that emerge in Sherman's other work, specifically her exploration of identity and the nature of feminine subjectivity through strategies of disguise and playacting. Like Sherman's studio, in which she tries on new identities and plays with feminine stereotypes, Dorine's basement provides her the opportunity to playact, to try on different feminine personas. At the beginning of the film Dorine is, as her coworker Kim (Molly Ringwald) puts it, a "freaky little mouse," who is awkward, nervous, and almost incapable of speaking a sentence. She wears large-framed glasses and frumpy sweaters several sizes too large, and she pulls her hair back severely into two buns. Dorine's transformation into an independent "office lady" can be traced through her changed appearance, particularly in terms of dress. The film's emphasis on clothing and, in particular, on dressing up reflects the director's preoccupations with fashion. Sherman has made a career out of playing with clothing within both her fine and commercial art practices, as she explores the ways in which clothing is tightly linked to identity, particularly for women.

The issue of Dorine's clothing and her lack of contemporary fashion sense is raised within the film by Dorine's coworkers Kim and Norah, both attractive, well-dressed women who fit comfortably into the office culture of *Constant Consumer*. While Kim is quick to ostracize Dorine and to make fun of her appearance, Norah steps in to help. In the film's first scene, Norah comes upon a frazzled Dorine just as she has spilled copier toner all over her clothes and offers the use of an extra jacket. As the film progresses, Norah's attempts to extend kindness to Dorine include bringing her a bag of professional but out-of-date clothes. Surprised by Norah's attention, Dorine graciously accepts the patronizing gift, using it to initiate a process of self-improvement that culminates in self-transformation.

By the time the office computer manager, Daniel (Michael Imperioli), comes to the house to express concern for a missing Norah, Dorine's hair is tumbling past her shoulders, she wears Virginia's earrings and Norah's pearls and fashionable suit, and she is capable of mustering up the courage to ask Daniel to join her for dinner. Buoyed by new, narcissistic, gruesome relationships constructed and nurtured in her basement, Dorine's dress-up play allows her to identify with a persona that is constructed from qualities found in the women of *Constant Consumer*. This "freaky little mouse," while certainly still odd, has transformed into a self-assured and independent woman.

Her transformation takes a dramatic turn in the final scene of the film. Dorine's home, with all its gory contents, goes up in flames as she drives calmly along a highway. No longer mousy and unfashionable, she is a new, cleansed Dorine, nourished by her basement friendships. This Dorine wears a stylish suit, dark glasses, heavy eye make-up, brash lipstick, and a blond wig. On the passenger seat of her car rests a classified advertisement for an office manager. She is ready to start a new life for herself in a different city. If the basement tableaux are suggestive of the medical mannequins phase in Sherman's work, the final escape scene is suggestive of the use of costumes in *Untitled Film Stills* to engage in an exploration of self-representation and self-transformation.

Regularly celebrated for offering visual confirmation of a model of subjectivity as fluid, Sherman's work is typically perceived as a corollary to postmodern and poststructuralist assertions that dislodge surface from depth and call into question the fixity or authenticity of the self; in it subject positions are posed as relative, shifting, and almost endlessly negotiable. As curator Rochelle Steiner puts it, her work seems to confirm our capacity to "adopt any role we want" and to "change it on a daily basis."[10] In light of such critical assessments, Dorine's apparently easy appropriation of the qualities of her female coworkers seems to suggest a model of subjectivity in which unrestrained subjects are capable of virtually unlimited transformation. Yet I want to query that reading of Dorine—and Sherman's work more broadly—by arguing that Dorine's development be understood not as an absorption of her identity into that of another, a transformation in which she becomes a new person, but rather as a shift in identification that enables her to experience *herself* in new ways. She tries on Norah's clothes and tests out Virginia's earrings; she imagines herself not to be them but to be *like* them.

Sherman bears a similar sort of relationship to the personae she explores in her self-representational visual practices. A critical emphasis on playful and exploratory identification works against the conventional analysis of Sherman's oeuvre in which she is said to represent and signify the end of the stable subject. Sherman's representation of identification as multiple and fluid does not, I argue, correspond to what many critics have applauded as a postmodern theory of subjectivity as fluid, flexible, and mutable, however central these qualities may be to Sherman's work. Rather than argue that subjectivity is fluid, I suggest that it is identification that is fluid. In terms of *Office Killer,* this means not that Dorine transforms herself into a new kind of woman but that she explores, through (often gruesome) identificatory practices, what it might feel like to be another kind of woman. Dorine wonders what she would be like as a stylish office lady. Likewise, Cindy wonders what she would be like as a femme fatale or an aging starlet.

Integrating *Office Killer* into Sherman's oeuvre opens up the space for an analysis in which Sherman's visual practices are understood not as a visual representations of the infinite malleability of subjectivity but rather as work that considers the potential to explore the borders of self through identificatory encounters with others: with other women, with other fantasies, and with other caricatures or personae. Reading Sherman's oeuvre with an eye for fluid identification—rather than postmodern models of a "perpetually mobile subject"—avoids the simplistic celebration of the work as a model for the largely fantastic capacity of postmodern subjects to transform effortlessly.[11]

Sherman, Women, and Chainsaws

In the same way that Sherman appropriates film stills for *Untitled Film Stills,* *Office Killer* proceeds from an appropriation of the most maligned form of horror film, the slasher. According to Carol Clover, this form of popular film is a genre that rests "down in the cinematic underbrush," nestled between horror and pornography, drawing inspiration from both.[12] In the typical slasher, audiences are offered a story of "a psycho killer who slashes to death a string of mostly female victims, one by one, until he is himself subdued or killed, usually by the one girl who has survived."[13] Against conventional assumptions that the slasher is an expression of misogynistic social forces and thus is necessarily antifeminist, Clover argues that the kind of serious critical consideration that has bypassed this genre reveals a more complicated economy of gender identification and gendered roles. An initial pass through the genre uncovers male aggressors whose violence is a thinly disguised substitute for sexual encounters and female victims offered as signs for and sites of a deep vulnerability.

With the recurring figure of the girl who fights back against her attacker, and often outsmarts him, audiences are offered a contrasting vision of feminine strength. Clover names this figure the "final girl" and argues that she is a particularly provocative figure vis-à-vis representations of gender within the genre. The final girl is more than a positive feminine role model or a figurative male. She is a figure upon whom both masculine and feminine qualities are collapsed in a form of gender play and subversion. Clover suggests, in psychoanalytic terms, that the slasher turns on fluid identificatory viewing positions: "Our primary and acknowledged identification may be with the victim, the adumbration of our infantile fears and desires, our memory sense of ourselves as tiny and vulnerable in the face of the enormous Other; but the Other is also finally another part of ourselves, the projection of our repressed infantile rage and desire . . . that we have had in the name of civilization to repudiate."[14]

In the slasher film, identification is multiple; attacker and victim are "expressions of the same viewer."[15] The slasher thus invites a "fluidity of engaged perspective" that crosses and potentially subverts the boundaries of gender.[16] The mostly male audience members of conventional slasher films are at first encouraged to identify with the aggressions of the killer but by the end of the film find themselves not only cheering for the figure of the final girl but also identifying with her. Her presence, though not a sign that the slasher is a feminist mode of cinema, constitutes, as Clover states, "a visible adjustment in the terms of gender representation."[17]

Sherman's appropriation of the slasher genre highlights its potential as a field of feminist cultural production. *Office Killer* is a "Shermanesque" slasher, a postmodern feminist approach to the genre that capitalizes on the fact that the very operations at the heart of Sherman's larger body of work—play, masquerade, and dissimulation—accord with the slasher genre's "fluidity of engaged perspective." In an interview with Graham Fuller, Sherman explained that she was eager to transform the predictable narrative structure of the slasher, which so frequently pits male villains against female victims, into terms that would resonate with women viewers.[18] Sherman explains:

I came across a book called *Men, Women, and Chainsaws,* by Carol Clover. She talks about the "final girl" theory, which applied to many horror films in the '70s where the audience was primarily young males, the killer was male, and the hero a goody-goody girl who doesn't have sex, kills the killer, and survives. I decided to make the killer a middle-aged woman because it was something I could identify with and because there aren't many films in any genre about women my age.

Sherman's key innovation is that in her slasher, the murderer is a woman and her victims are not nubile young women but adult office workers, both male and female. Moreover, in Sherman's hands the figure and function of the final girl persists but is dramatically transformed. The central tasks of the final girl are to stand as a sign for fear and vulnerability and, through a confrontation with the killer, to stand simultaneously as a sign of strength in the face of terror. Dorine is not subdued by the final girl but rather uses strategies of disguise and self-transformation that effectively perform the work of, and morph her into, the final girl. The fluidity or interchangeability highlights the shifting identificatory positions that are explored at length in Sherman's larger artistic oeuvre. In Sherman's hands, this fluidity of engaged perspective is not limited to the viewing audience but is also represented within the narrative of the film. As viewers shift from one character to another, so the protagonist's identificatory positionings shift from villain to final girl.

Perverse Pleasures

In some ways, Dorine fulfills the conventional qualities of a slasher killer. She is certainly an outsider, described by caustic coworker Kim Poole (Ringwald at her most petulant) as a "fucking freak." The narrative reveals, by way of flashbacks, that Dorine has a dark and psychologically troubling past, another key trait of the slasher's monster. As a child, Dorine was prey to her father's sexual advances. Fueled by a rage against her father and spurred on by her mother's insistence that her revelations of his abuse were lies, Dorine coolly causes the car accident that takes her father's life and leaves her mother physically impaired. Mousy Dorine, the film suggests, is capable of detached violence.

Like other horror and slasher villains, Dorine is a character dominated by the stranglehold of her mother. Dorine's mother constantly sings the praises of Dorine's father, a man who "ran a tight ship" and was able to "keep us girls under his thumb." As in other horror texts, such as *Psycho* (Alfred Hitchcock, 1960), a film named by Clover as the first slasher, or *Carrie* (Brian de Palma, 1976), the maternal figure is constructed as monstrous. Dorine's mother can be described as what Barbara Creed calls "the monstrous-feminine," not only because she attempts to control her adult daughter whom she failed to protect as a child, but also because in refusing to "relinquish her hold" on Dorine, she prevents her from taking up her "proper place in relation to the symbolic."[19] Although Dorine was capable of murdering her father, she is capable of little more than small rebellions against her mother. By the time her mother dies, Dorine has begun to murder and to transform, but it is her mother's death that marks a turning point in her murderous career toward a macabre lack of affect.

The slasher, whose goal is to arouse bodily sensations (especially disgust), requires that killers take a hands-on approach to their tasks, as Clover points out. Dorine's murders bring her and the viewer into close contact with her victims, and her affectless reactions arouse disgust. Creed argues that the arousal of disgust is absolutely central to the goals of slasher films. Moreover, it is central to the success of the slasher because it offers audiences a safe encounter with both the danger and perverse pleasure of the abject.[20] In *Office Killer,* Dorine's hands-on violence leads to a tactile, physical relationship with dead bodies, providing ample opportunity for the representation of abjection and the arousal of disgust. Dorine's weapons include knives, crowbars, and a gas canister inserted into an inhaler. In a particularly gory scene, she uses an industrial tape dispenser to kill an unnamed office worker, a young man she discovers flipping through a pornographic magazine in a storage room. The camera brings the viewer close to the wound as Dorine calmly pulls the weapon from his bloodied neck. Noticing the large bloody wound in Gary's chest, she exclaims, "Goodness, what happened to you?" After attempts to seal his wound with packing tape, she wipes him down with Windex, asking, "Doesn't that feel better?" Later, Dorine plucks away at Virginia's long black acrylic nails, explaining that they'll just get in the way of her typing. Virginia's hands are eventually removed altogether so that Dorine can use them as playthings to amuse her cats.

Like other slasher films, *Office Killer* invokes the abject in order to arouse what Creed calls the "pleasure in breaking the taboo on filth."[21] A disoriented Norah will eventually fall into Gary's rotting chest and scream out in horror. Contact with decaying corpses, which signifies a basic form of pollution, provides the opportunity for audiences to "eject the abject and re-draw the boundaries between human and non-human."[22] Dorine's intimate contact with dead bodies pollutes her; she is abject by association. As a figure of abjection, Dorine ought to be symbolically expelled from the film narrative, ideally by the final girl, the would-be victim whose struggle against the killer occupies a significant portion of the film. In *Office Killer,* however, the functions of the final girl are spread out amongst three figures: Kim, Norah, and Dorine herself. Kim is the only character in the film to harbor suspicions against Dorine. Norah is the only victim who has an opportunity to struggle against Dorine; she pleads with Dorine and comes close to overcoming her.

Yet it is Dorine, finally, who performs (in a roundabout way) the function of expelling the villain, the office killer who has been polluted by association with decaying corpses, blood, ooze, and body parts. Serving the function of the final girl, Dorine expels, or at least manages to conceal, the villain she has become through strategies of disguise and dissimulation. The complexity of Dorine's character—the multiple roles she plays as well as the many functions she fulfills (villain, victim, heroine, final girl)—echoes and contributes to Sherman's ongoing concern to explore identification as multiple, shifting, and fluid.

Notes

1. Qtd. in Jason Edward Kaufman, "Lens Life: Unmasking Iconic Photographer Cindy Sherman," *Art and Antiques* 28, no. 9 (2005): 50.

2. Catherine Morris, *The Essential Cindy Sherman* (New York: Harry N. Abrams, 1999).

3. Ibid., 104.

4. See Cindy Sherman, *Cindy Sherman* (Paris: Flammarion and Jeu de Paume, 2006).

5. See Cindy Sherman, *The Complete Untitled Film Stills* (New York: Museum of Modern Art, 2003).

6. Juergen Teller and Cindy Sherman, *Juergen Teller, Cindy Sherman, Marc Jacobs* (New York: Rizzoli, 2006).

7. Lisa Bloom, *With Other Eyes: Looking at Race and Gender in Visual Culture* (Minneapolis: University of Minnesota Press, 1999), 6.

8. Carol J. Clover, "Her Body, Himself: Gender in the Slasher Film," in *Screening Violence,* ed. Stephen Prince (New Brunswick, NJ: Rutgers University Press, 2000), 138–39.

9. Cindy Sherman with Graham Fuller, "The Real Scream Queen: Interview with Cindy Sherman," *Interview* (December 1997), n.p.

10. Rochelle Steiner, *Cindy Sherman* (London: Serpentine Gallery 2003), 23.

11. Kaja Silverman, *Threshold of the Visible World* (New York: Routledge, 1996), 11.

12. Clover, "Her Body," 125

13. Ibid.

14. Ibid., 130–31.

15. Ibid., 130.

16. Ibid., 154.

17. Ibid., 168.

18. Sherman, "The Real Scream Queen," n.p.

19. Barbara Creed, *The Monstrous-Feminine: Film, Feminism, Psychoanalysis* (London: Routledge, 1993), 12.

20. Ibid., 10.

21. Ibid., 13.

22. Ibid., 14.

Corinn Columpar   Chapter 10

At the Limits of Visual Representation
Tracey Moffatt's Still and Moving Images

From October 1997 to June 1998, the Dia Center in New York City introduced audiences to a wide array of works by Australian artist Tracey Moffatt
with a show titled *Free-Falling,* her first major exhibition in North America.
As is typical of most shows featuring multiple pieces by Moffatt, it included
examples of her work in a variety of media: still photography, video, and
film. And, as is typical of catalog essays produced for such shows, Lynne
Cooke's survey of the work attested adeptly, albeit briefly, to the various stylistic and thematic continuities that run through her corpus as a whole: an
embrace of artifice and intertextuality, the generation of imagery with both
autobiographical significance and universal legibility, and, finally, an engagement with narrative but refusal of closure. In contrast, academic analyses of
Moffatt's output produced by scholars working within the field of cinema
studies have tended to be far more focused, singling out for scrutiny her
film texts *Nice Coloured Girls* (1987), *Night Cries: A Rural Tragedy* (1989),
and *beDevil* (1993) while relegating her work in still photography (and to
a lesser extent, video) to a footnote or biographical preamble at best. Of
course, this narrowing of concerns is, in part, a function of the conventions of academic writing in general and the regulatory nature of disciplinary boundaries more specifically. Yet it is also, I would argue, related to the
way that "the cinematic" circulates as a privileged term within the discourse
surrounding Moffatt, denoting the legacy inherited, the tradition engaged,
and the character exhibited by her work, no matter the medium. The language of critic Stephan Berg is typical on this count; in discussing Moffatt's
photographic output he writes, "It almost seems as if the photos hungered
to be transposed into a moving, cinematographic context, as if they were liv-

ing only a shadow existence here as mere representatives of what they could otherwise become."[1]

Yet rather than reproducing a type of analysis that is quite commonplace in the critical discussion of Moffatt's work—one in which her photography is measured against a cinematic yardstick—Berg is, with this statement, starting to make an intervention in such an analysis, for he continues:

Yet, [that] impression is misleading. In reality—and they share this quality with Cindy [Sherman's] *Untitled Film Stills*—they only simulate an apparent dependence on film. It is a disguise behind which their photographic versions assert their independence. These are not film stills at all but pure photographs which work only in this medium. The fact that we think we see a film running behind and amongst them is simply a reminder of the great power of Moffatt's stage-crafting, which encourages us to spin threads and forge links where there is actually nothing but gaps and emptiness.[2]

Interestingly, in making a case for the medium specificity of Moffatt's photographic output, Berg speaks persuasively to the project in which both her still and moving images participate: the forging of a productive tension between, as he puts it, threads and links, on the one hand, and gaps and emptiness, on the other. Yet this perhaps unintended point does not invalidate his larger argument. While neither still nor moving images can lay exclusive claim to presence or absence, connectivity or atomization, the manner in which the aforementioned productive tension is created and the effects it produces vary between Moffatt's photography and her cinema and video due to key differences between these representational forms. Thus I initiate a reading of Moffatt's work in film, specifically her feature film *beDevil,* through her ongoing experiments with the still image with the goal of throwing into fresh relief both the fluidity that marks Moffatt's oeuvre as well as the role that medium specificity plays therein.

Moffatt's Cinematic Photography

In an interview she gave to Gerald Matt, Moffatt explains her approach to photography thus: "I have never just produced a single photograph and tried to make it stand alone as an artistic statement. . . . For me it is the narrative. It is difficult for me to say anything in one single image. With working in a photographic serial I can expand one idea—give it further possibilities. It makes photography close to film in its possibilities."[3] A survey of Moffatt's photographic output reveals the two primary ways in which she expands her idea: along the paradigmatic and syntagmatic axes of (visual) language. In her paradigmatic series she offers up multiple iterations of the same moment in parallel narratives. For example, *Scarred for Life* (1994) and *Scarred for Life II* (2000) contain nine and ten works, respectively, each of which presents a single image that resists facile interpretation on its own. Yet paired with a caption that provides background information about the event on display, a series title that points to that event's enduring effects, and a collection of other images that are similarly fraught, it comes to assume traumatic proportion and dramatic dimension. In another such series, *Fourth* (2001), no caption is needed, for the discrete images of Olympian athletes immediately after placing fourth in their event evoke well-established cultural narratives; therein they function as denouement to a climactic contest, the moment of realization and then resignation when determination yields to disappointment.

As much as Moffatt's paradigmatic series are invested in narrativity, it is more frequently her syntagmatic series that qualify her photography as cinematic in the eyes of her critics. For in these series, including *Something More* (1989), *GUAPA* (*Goodlooking*, 1995), *Up in the Sky* (1998), and *Laudanum* (1999), seriality produces a sense of succession such that a single story seems to play itself out across a series of images. Writing about *Up in the Sky*, Lynne Cooke describes the effect of all of Moffatt's syntagmatic series well: "however elusive the narrative, [the pictures'] unfolding is more important than the link each has to its referent, whereas the opposite is the case with still photography, in which the individual representation typically appears more tightly tied indexically to its source, to what was but no longer is."[4] In other words, Cooke ascribes a cinematic quality to Moffatt's photographs because of the extent to which they imply a correspondence between multiple signifiers and a single signified, namely, a multi-faceted yet internally coherent world that both derives from and exceeds its piecemeal representation. In part the ties that bind the photographs in any given series to one another over and beyond the real they represent are stylistic and, in turn, locational in nature. For example, the nine photos comprising *Something More* are characterized by blatantly artificial sets, saturated colors, and high-key lighting, all of which construct a highly stylized and self-consciously dramatic rendition of the outback; in *GUAPA* the absence of any environs and the soft-focus photography produce a serene and surreal void where the laws of gravity do not apply; *Up in the Sky* combines harsh light, barren landscape, and sharp focus in the creation of a landscape that reverberates with the postapocalyptic world of Mad Max; and, finally, in *Laudanum* use of the photogravure technique in conjunction with selective scratching, blurring, and masking transform the Victorian setting into a set piece of gothic horror.

Yet the photos in any of these series have a temporal relationship to one another as well as a spatial one, and it is precisely for this reason that they can be said to be narrative rather than merely descriptive. Indeed, Moffat also lends her work a temporal dimension and thereby generates dramatic momentum—that which compels Cooke to use the word "unfolding"—by staging a dynamic of interpersonal exchange and affective relations within that coherent space. The dynamism of these scenarios is only heightened by the inclusion of characters that are visibly different from one another due to race (signified by skin color and facial features) and social type (clearly connoted by costuming). Of all Moffatt's series, *Laudanum* is the most explicit in its use of such differences to produce the disequilibrium that fuels (Western) narrative. In it the power differential between an Asian maid and her white mistress is played out in not only a division of domestic labor but also a sexual relationship that smacks of sadism.

While such qualities may make Moffatt's photographic output "close to" film, it is nonetheless still governed by its own logic, which is partial and subject to continual revision. Not only do her individual photographs prove more evocative than descriptive, as if circling around rather than zeroing in on a central event, but Moffatt encourages her various curators and collectors to order the series as they see fit, save the first and last images therein, which remain consistent from one exhibition to the next. In *Something More*, for instance, Moffatt starts her narrative by introducing its protagonist, a small-town girl with big dreams of getting "something more" out of life, as well as a cast of supporting players, and, in turn, she concludes it with an image of tragic defeat, in which the girl is shown literally felled short of her goal, Brisbane, by three hundred kilometers. Lying between these two framing images are seven more, each of which features, in fragmented form, the girl in a state of (inter)action—be it with a boy who turns to her for comfort, a suitcase into which she piles her possessions, or a dominatrix to whom she bows in supplication.

Moffatt's Photographic Cinema

Much of Moffatt's work with moving images follows directly from the two impulses evident in her photographic series. On the one hand, there are the compilation videos she has created in collaboration with editor Gary Hillberg, each of which comprises a succession of clips from Hollywood films that all feature the same subject matter, be it tortured artists (*Artist* [1999]), black maids (*Lip* [1999]), romantic liaisons (*Love* [2003]), or apocalyptic scenarios (*Doomed* [2007]). In all four of these cases, montage functions as a means of encouraging meditation on dominant representational conventions as well as the popular narratives and ideological structures those conventions undergird; in some cases it also performs a task of revisioning as well. For example, *Lip,* which shares with *Fourth* an interest in those whom the limelight does not illuminate, not only lays bare the historically entrenched associations between black women and domestic servitude but also accords the black performers a centrality that they are typically denied in their capacity as supporting players and sassy stooges.

On the other hand, *Nice Coloured Girls* and *Night Cries* are more properly "cinematic" (and less metacinematic) insofar as they are structured around stories that exhibit some degree of spatial, temporal, and causal continuity. Although narrative, they nonetheless are exceptional in whose stories they tell and how they tell them; indeed, it was these factors that caught the attention of critics soon after the films' release at the end of the 1980s and thus recommended Moffatt as an object of scholarly attention within cinema studies. First, both feature Aboriginal women in roles other than those of ethnographic object and passive victim: *Nice Coloured Girls* follows the exploits of three young women who take advantage of a predatory white man by enjoying a night on the town at his expense, while *Night Cries* takes as its subject an Aboriginal woman whose ambivalence for her adoptive white mother is made manifest as she plays the roles of dutiful daughter and nursemaid with a combination of compassion and contempt. Second, Moffatt imbues those narratives with historical and political dimension by relying on a variety of anti-illusionistic strategies, including the generation of a highly stylized mise-en-scène, a refusal of the conventions of continuity editing in favor of intellectual montage, and the staging of provocative juxtapositions between soundtrack and image track. In so doing, Moffatt constructs for herself an identity as unconventional as that of her characters; boldly claiming, as she puts it, "the right to be avant-garde like any white artist," she defies popular expectations of the "ethnic" artist as native informant.[5] In light of the representational strategies she employs, viewers must engage with Moffatt's films much as they would with her photographs. As Cynthia Baron notes, "the mise-en-scène elements, sound-image combinations, and sequence-to-sequence combinations are so dense with meaning that they invite, require, and reward the kind of contemplation often reserved for one's leisurely or studied encounter with art gallery exhibitions."[6]

Yet even when screened in the context of an art gallery exhibition, as

Moffatt's short films frequently have been, a leisurely encounter, if not a studied one, is difficult to achieve since the ability to pause or slow the film's flow is out of the spectator's control. As Christian Metz notes, it is those attributes that distinguish film from photography—movement, plurality, phonic sound, nonphonic sound, and musical sound—that "challeng[e] the powers of silence and immobility which belong to and define all photography, immersing film in a stream of temporality where nothing can be *kept*, nothing stopped."[7] Moreover, those attributes also deprive film of "photographic authority," that quality which allows the photo to function as a fetish object, successfully arresting the spectator's gaze and proving a satisfying substitute for the reality it represents. Film, Metz contends, can lay claim to no such authority since it continuously points beyond the boundaries of its images to an offscreen space that is both signified and significant, even in its absence. As a result, film is instead "an extraordinary activator of fetishism [the process]. It endlessly mimes the primal displacement of the look between the seen absence and the presence nearby."[8] For this reason, specifically cinematic authority is a result of those techniques that produce a suturing effect, directing the spectator's attention away from the limits of the frame and all that they reveal: the circumscribed nature of the image and hence its status as produced rather than natural, spoken as well as speaking. Among the most salient of such techniques, according to Jean-Pierre Oudart and, in turn, Daniel Dayan, is shot-reverse shot editing. By making offscreen space present before its absence proves disconcerting, it constructs an all-enveloping illusion that evokes abundance rather than deprivation; by assigning its view of the world to an onscreen character, it constructs the film as "a product without a producer, a discourse without an origin" at the same time.[9]

What makes Moffatt's photographic work cinematic is her embrace of one of the five attributes Metz ascribes to film over photography—plurality—which, in turn, produces a sense of physical and narrative movement, if not an exact simulation of it. In expanding her ideas thus, Moffatt produces her photographs both as bounded, centripetal, and autonomous units and as parts of a larger whole in which "gaps and emptiness"—that is, lack—play a blatant role. Thus it is their cinematic qualities that compromise the "photographic authority" of Moffatt's series. Likewise, her films have little purchase on cinematic authority insofar as they refuse to absorb the spectator in any thoroughgoing way. Certainly a viewer of *Nice Coloured Girls* or *Night Cries* gets caught up in the film by way of its temporal flow. As Vivian Sobchack observes, the stream of temporality that Metz identifies is precisely what endows film with the capacity to construct an inhabitable space, one that accommodates lived bodies and invites the spectator into the scene on offer, whereas photography only "invites contemplation *of* the scene."[10] Nonetheless, that same viewer will rarely find him/herself stitched into the film, or the gaps in the film stitched over, through those devices that allow for, as Dayan puts it, possession of the image and, in turn, possession by the dominant ideology for which the film is a ventriloquist.[11] Moffatt's reliance on staged tableaux as the primary vehicle of narration (*Night Cries*) or discursive interludes within a larger work wherein point of view shots are in fact a structuring element (*Nice Coloured Girls*) ensures as much. Interested in the frame of the image as much as that which lies within it, Moffatt regularly plays both with and at the limits of visual representation.

Cue Sound

In his book *Re-Takes: Postcoloniality and Foreign Film Languages* John Mowitt make a persuasive case for a return to the study of enunciation in cinema, an endeavor that has fallen out of scholarly favor in the last two decades. In so doing, he develops a critical practice that builds upon the tradition forged by the likes of Metz and Dayan but refuses the ocularcentrism that tradition shares with the neoformalist work of its most vocal critics—namely, David Bordwell and Noël Carroll, for whom enunciation is tainted by its association with Grand Theory. Compelled less by a desire to adapt paradigms derived from linguistics to an analysis of the means by which film communicates visually than by an interest in the mutual interaction between language and film form, Mowitt pays particular attention to phonic sound. Explaining the assumptions dictating the critical practice against which he defines his own, he writes:

Instead of language, whether as concept or metaphor, having any relation either to the design or the construction of [filmic narration], it is surrendered, as Derrida would doubtless insist, to the paradigm of speech and regarded as essentially irrelevant to any conception of the codes of cinema, but certainly irrelevant to any conception of the codes operating to stitch the dialogue into the soundtrack and to cement the soundtrack and the image track together.[12]

While Mowitt's interest in the extent to which language and, moreover, linguistic differences influence film form is borne out in case studies of films that are bilingual, his approach also has implications for Moffatt's cinematic work, where differentiation is achieved through other means. In *Nice Coloured Girls,* for example, what distinguishes the voices of colonizer and colonized is not the language each speaks but the means by which their voices are represented. While a man with a British accent provides voice-over narration to the film by reading excerpts from the journal of Lieutenant William Bradley, a participant in Australia's "settlement" in the late eighteenth century, the three protagonists describe their interaction with a present-day "Captain" by way of subtitles. The result is a revealing dramatization of power and resistance: as is the case with their actions, the narration of the "nice coloured girls" slyly undercuts rather than directly confronts the presumption of authority and knowledge that the accented male voice bespeaks.

Yet it is with *beDevil,* her first—and only, to date—feature-length film that Moffatt most fully realizes what Mowitt refers to as the poetics of postcoloniality, an operation he associates with films that "give content to [the self-reflexivity that] might otherwise strike us as a blank or so-called purely formal process" and "make the question of enunciation, the who-sent-this-from-where-and-to-whom, belong to the statements put in circulation by the film text."[13] Explicitly attending to issues of narration—both within and by the film—Moffatt creates a text that exemplifies the multivocality Hamid Naficy associates with accented cinema, one wherein a profusion of speaking styles gives voice to diverse social identities and discrepant versions of history.[14] In so doing, she foregrounds enunciation as a politicized process by which characters differentiate themselves along lines of culture, race, gender, and generation.

Between the size of its budget and production crew and the scope of its vision, *beDevil* is the most ambitious project Moffatt has ever undertaken. Moreover, it serves as a career capstone insofar as it synthesizes so many of the concerns, both thematic and formal, that animate Moffatt's entire oeuvre. In the broadest of terms, the film is about ghosts and the multicultural communities that they haunt, but given the way it is constructed, it is also a nuanced examination of the act of narration that takes a step further the self-reflexive strategies that Moffatt typically employs. In her work with both still and moving images, Moffatt regularly creates assemblages of narrative units, be they photographs, shots, or scenes, that are either substitutable (*Fourth, Lip*) or sequential (*Something More, Night Cries*); with *beDevil* she combines these two strategies, extending her ideas both syntagmatically and paradigmatically by presenting in succession three discrete ghost stories with only a thematic thread to tie them. Moreover, within each of the three segments, Moffatt employs the conventions of continuity editing selectively, tending instead to create textual gaps by cutting regularly between multiple lines of action, characters, narrative modes, historical moments, and milieus in order to forge associative and affective relationships rather than ones based on causality or chronology. The result is a film that is perfectly in keeping with Moffatt's other work insofar as it draws attention to its own construction and demands that viewers be actively involved in making sense of their experience.

Yet this formal play is made even more poignant by the fact that *beDevil* explicitly thematizes the process of narration as well, calling attention to the means by which (hi)stories are recounted and knowledge is produced. At the center of the first section, titled "Mr. Chuck," is an encounter between Rick, a young Aboriginal boy, and the spirit of an American GI who haunts the swamp in which he drowned while stationed in Australia during World War II. Narrating this encounter in the present day are Rick as an adult (Jack Charles) and a local white woman named Shelley (Diana Davidson), who had taken young Rick under her wing after learning of the abuse he suffered at the hands of his family. The second section, "Choo Choo Choo Choo," has at its center a variety of supernatural phenomena including an invisible train driven by a mute conductor and the ghost of a blind girl whom that same train has struck and killed. In this section three narrators figure prominently: Ruby (Auriel Andrews), an Aboriginal woman who had multiple experiences with both the train and the girl when she was living in a house next to a set of train tracks; Mickey (Lex Foxcroft), an alcoholic white man who reports his take on the ghosts in a drunken slur; and Bob (Cecil Parkee), a Chinese Australian man who has converted an old train station into a local museum full of memorabilia from the past. Finally "Lovin' the Spin I'm In," the third section of the film, has a Greek couple, Dimitri (Lex Marinos) and Voula (Dina Panozzo), recounting to their son, Spiro (Ricardo Natoli), the story of a young Aboriginal couple to whom they used to rent the warehouse space next to their own living quarters. Having died a mysterious death twelve years earlier, the two lovers now haunt their former place of residence, appearing on occasion to Spiro and his family as well as to the current tenants of the warehouse.

In an astute reading of *beDevil*, Glen Masato Mimura demonstrates how the ghost stories therein function effectively as trope, allowing for the materialization of memories on the part of those Aboriginal Australians and Torres Strait Islanders who have suffered displacement at the hands of land developers spurred on by suburban sprawl and tourist trade. As a result, he concludes, Moffatt's film has a profound affinity with the ghosts at its center: it "critically haunts Australian and global cinema in their national and international contexts, lingering like a bad memory to phantasmatically repeat the ghostly histories and geographies that the mainstream cinemas seek to evict."[15] An additional way in which the spectral serves symbolic and, in turn, ideological purposes, however, is by dramatizing issues of presence and absence, seeing and telling. Indeed, the project in which both the film and its sprawling cast of eclectic characters are engaged is that of giving presence to an essentially intangible phenomenon, be it through the stories told about that phenomenon by people in the present bearing witness to the past or the flashbacks wherein it assumes spectral form through specifically cinematic means (superimposition, dream sequence). That those doing the representing in and through *beDevil* are individuals typically denied discursive authority in accordance with their deviation from Audre Lorde's "mythical norm" only lends this aspect of Moffatt's work more gravitas.[16]

Cinematic Pedagogy

The first section of *beDevil*, "Mr. Chuck," functions as a primer on Moffatt's vision by laying bare the fundamental importance of thread and links, gaps and emptiness. In it, Shelley and Rick serve as narrators, both addressing the camera directly as if participating in a documentary about the American GI that haunts their local swamp. While Rick's narration is typically limited to the visceral details of his ghostly encounter (the smell of the swamp, the feel of the GI's touch), Shelley speaks to a number of additional topics, including her relationship with Rick as a child. In a sequence dedicated to this matter, the film cuts back and forth between Shelley in the present and flashbacks of the events she describes: Rick's attempts to steal from her shop, her thwarting of those attempts, and their cultivation of a familiar relationship. During this sequence, Moffatt relies heavily on the visual approach that characterizes her entire body of work, circumscribing the viewer's vantage in such a manner as to draw attention to the edges of the image and beyond and thus to the fact of (cinematic) enunciation; at the same time she also signals a number of representational strategies that she will rely on frequently throughout *beDevil*. For example, during the flashback scenes she depicts the discovery of Rick's thievery through a type of shadow play, and she represents Shelley metonymically by isolating details of her appearance: her manicured hands and coiffed hair, the neckline of her dress and a well-heeled foot tapping in disapproval. In the present, moreover, she offers up a shot of Shelley reacting in shock to some stimulus without a corresponding reverse shot.

Whereas such an approach to visual representation is typical of Moffatt's work in photography and moving images, *beDevil* seizes upon the way "the cinematic brings the existential activity of vision into visibility" by incorporating gaps and emptiness into the film's soundtrack as well.[17] A case in point is Shelley's selective narration in the sequence described earlier. At one point she mouths her age—"seventy"—rather than speaking it aloud, thereby playfully drawing attention to her ability to refuse to speak and thus, at least potentially, to withhold information. On two other occasions, however, her falling silent has more serious repercussions. In the first of these, she concludes a suggestion that Rick suffered at the hands of his step-uncles in a decidedly incomplete and inconclusive manner: "I shouldn't say it, but I don't think his homelife was . . ." Exemplifying the connection between sight and sound to which Mowitt refers, Shelley's silence dictates the occlusion of anything but hints of such abuse from the film's image track as well, thereby risking its invisibility within his-story at large. The second time she trails off is when she discusses her awareness of Rick's situation: "Yes, I knew what was going on. We on the island all knew. We could've helped that child. We could've . . ." In this instance she implicates herself and her community in Rick's fate in an ambiguous manner, both performing her emotional investment and simultaneously raising the specter of, but still distancing herself from, unspeakable historical practices, such as state-mandated internment and adoption.

Rather than foregrounding the gaps within any one individual's speech, the second section of *beDevil*, "Choo Choo Choo Choo," concerns itself with the gaps between various people and their stories. "Mr. Chuck" prepares the ground for such a focus by laying bare the extent to which Shelley's social location and her speech acts mutually condition each other: as noted, her narration is relatively wide-ranging, bespeaking those things in which she, more than Rick, has a vested interest, including not only her affection for Rick but also her association with the American soldier that died and her father's involvement in developing the island that she and Rick both call home. "Choo Choo Choo Chooo," in comparison, offers up many more voices, all of which prove necessarily personal and partial. In addition to the three characters singled out to provide testimonials in direct address, as did Shelley and Rick before them, the entire surrounding community becomes complicit in the act of narration as well when random members are shown singing a song and performing a choreographed series of gestures inspired by local lore of the phantom train. Moreover, there is little overlap in the phenomena being described from these multiple points of view. Ruby begins her narration with mention of the ghost that eventually takes shape onscreen—a blind girl who walks the train tracks—but she subsequently broaches a wide variety of other mysterious phenomena as well; Bob relays the story that the townspeople pantomime, one involving a train conductor who hanged himself and his ghostly voyages; and, finally, the alcoholic Mickey describes a female spirit that visits him, but stresses that she is not the blind girl to whom Ruby refers. The sum result of this is a series of narrative fragments, both aural and visual, that never quite coheres. Rather than offering multiple perspectives on the same phenomenon, "Choo Choo Choo Choo" refracts the viewer's field of sight such that the acts of telling assume far greater dimension than the stories told.

When compared to the first two sections, the film's final one, "Lovin' the Spin I'm In," proves almost conventional in form. To be sure, Moffatt's touch is evident in the stylized mise-en-scène, the non-naturalistic use of dance to communicate certain interpersonal dynamics, and the refusal to reveal select sights to the viewer. Nonetheless, the fourth wall remains intact, since no one speaks to or acknowledges the camera in any way, and both the segment's narrative and narration are relatively straightforward, with Voula alone recounting the story of the couple that haunts the area. Even its editing is more exemplary of a classical paradigm. In fact, "Lovin' the Spin I'm In" replicates the situation at the heart of *Rear Window* (Alfred Hitchcock, 1954), a film in which shot–reverse shot editing plays such a central structuring role that it exemplifies the workings of suture better than any other: Spiro's bedroom window looks out on the haunted warehouse, providing him with an unobstructed view of the tenants therein. In the scene in which Voula describes to her son the events that ended tragically years ago and led to the present hauntings, the two of them sit side by side, assuming the position of rear window voyeurs. In a later scene, Spiro even tracks his father's movement through the warehouse, as Jeffries (James Stewart) does with Thorwald (Raymond Burr), by watching him pass from one window to the next.

Yet in light of the two segments that precede this final one, *beDevil* calls into question that which *Rear Window* shores up. When Jeffries's perspective is seemingly validated by the latter film's end, the fallibility of his vision (which is most clearly demonstrated when he falls asleep on the job) and the holes in his—and Hitchcock's—story (the identity of the woman with Thorwald that same night) comes to matter little to the sutured spectator. In *beDevil,* however, it is the gaps—those events, ideas, and vantages that escape, even defy, description—that demand recognition and haunt the text, even in the section with the fewest visible seams: necessarily circumscribed by her own social location, Voula's version of events is not the whole story. In making absence present, *beDevil* calls into question the completeness of an historical record and visual arts tradition that regularly marginalizes certain voices. It thus exemplifies the poetics of cinematic postcoloniality, giving

As she and Spiro look out their (rear) window (*above*), Voula says,
"Let me tell you about Immelda" (*below*). (Courtesy of Women
Make Movies.)

expression to the concerns that flow through Moffatt's corpus as a whole: the stakes of narration, both aesthetic and political, both pleasurable and perilous.

Notes

1. Stephan Berg, "Somewhere," in *Tracey Moffatt: Laudanum,* ed. Brigitte Reinhardt (Ostfildern: Hatje Cantz, 1999), 38.

2. Ibid.

3. Gerald Matt, "An Interview with Tracey Moffatt," in *Tracey Moffatt,* ed. Paula Savage and Lara Strongman (Wellington, New Zealand: City Gallery Wellington, 2002), 35.

4. Lynne Cooke, "A Proto-Filmic Odyssey," in *Tracey Moffatt: Free-Falling* (New York: Dia Center for the Arts, 1998), 39.

5. Scott Murray, "Tracey Moffatt," *Cinema Papers* 79 (May 1990): 21.

6. Cynthia Baron, "Films by Tracey Moffatt: Reclaiming First Australians' Rights, Celebrating Women's Rites," *Women's Studies Quarterly* 30, nos. 1–2 (2002): 153.

7. Christian Metz, "Photography and Fetish," *October* 34 (Autumn 1985): 83.

8. Ibid., 87.

9. Daniel Dayan, "The Tutor-Code of Classical Cinema," in *The Film Studies Reader,* ed. Joanne Hollows, Peter Hutchings, and Mark Jancovich (New York: Oxford University Press, 2000), 224.

10. Vivian Sobchack, "The Scene of the Screen: Envisioning Photographic, Cinematic, and Electronic 'Presence,'" in *Carnal Thoughts: Embodiment and Moving Image Culture* (Berkeley: University of California Press, 2004), 144.

11. Dayan, "The Tutor-Code," 223–24.

12. John Mowitt, *Re-Takes: Postcoloniality and Foreign Film Languages* (Minneapolis: University of Minnesota Press, 2005), 63–64.

13. Ibid., 89–90.

14. Hamid Naficy, *An Accented Cinema: Exilic and Diasporic Filmmaking* (Princeton, NJ: Princeton University Press, 2001).

15. Glen Masato Mimura, "Black Memories: Allegorizing the Colonial Encounter in Tracey Moffatt's *beDevil* (1993)," *Quarterly Review of Film and Video* 20 (2003): 122.

16. Lorde coined this term in "Age, Race, Class, and Sex: Women Redefining Difference," where she defines it as "white, thin, male, young, heterosexual, Christian, and financially secure." *Sister Outsider* (Freedom, CA: Crossing Press, 1984), 116.

17. Sobchack, "Scene of the Screen," 147.

Becomings

"This Girl Behaves against It"

An Interview with Samira Makhmalbaf

Samira Makhmalbaf was just seventeen when she made her first feature film, *The Apple* (Sib, 1998). It was one of the most remarkable debuts of that decade. Set in the back streets of her hometown, Tehran, it told the true story of Zahra and Massoumeh Naderi, twin girls who were locked up at home until the age of twelve by their blind mother and unemployed father. Only when neighbors reported the case to Social Services were the twins released into daylight for the first time, barely able to communicate and entirely innocent of the world.

Makhmalbaf somehow persuaded everyone involved in this case—the twins, their parents, even the social worker—to reenact the story for her camera, just days after it came to light. With emotions still palpably raw, the acting had extraordinary conviction; there was no doubt that this was a film grounded in reality. It was her precocious command of directorial styles that made the film so distinctive. *The Apple* sometimes feels like a documentary, with grainy pictures and chaotic sound, but in moments of stillness it resembles a tapestry of symbols plucked straight from the unconscious: a flower, a watering can, a hand-mark on a wall. These many textures suggest multiple layers of meaning. The film can be read as a psychological inquiry into communication, a political parable about ignorance and repression, a treatise on gender in the Islamic world. Yet it is the thread of humor, compassion, and warmth binding it all together that makes this film so extraordinary. The director refuses to judge her subjects. All the characters have reasons for their actions, and we are encouraged to understand them on their own terms.

Makhmalbaf's achievement did not come out of nowhere. She was part of an explosion of new Iranian cinema in the 1990s, a decade when directors such as her father, Mohsen Makhmalbaf (*Gabbeh* [1996], *A Moment of Innocence* [*Nun va Goldoon,* 1996]), and Abbas Kiarostami (*Close Up* [*Nema-ye Nazdik,* 1990], *The Taste of Cherry* [*Ta'm e guilass,* 1997]) won previously unimaginable acclaim on the international art cinema circuit. But with *The Apple,* the Iranian New Wave gained a charismatic poster child. She went one better with her follow-up, *Blackboards* (*Takhté siah,* 2000), which was set in the mountains of the Iran-Iraq border among the Kurds of that region. It won the Jury Prize at Cannes, and when she accepted the prize "on behalf of the new, young generation who struggle for democracy and a better life in Iran," the world's media went wild. Style magazines fell over themselves to cover this precocious woman in the black chador; veteran auteurs such as Jean-Luc Godard paid homage to her. In 2002 she contributed a segment to the portmanteau film *11'09"01—September 11,* alongside world-renowned directors such as Youssef Chahine, Mira Nair, and Ken Loach. "God, Construction, and Destruction" edged between documentary and fable, as it observed a teacher in a refugee camp on the Iranian border attempting to explain the scale and terror of the World Trade Center attack to her young pupils.

For her third full-length film, *At Five in the Afternoon* (*Panj é asr,* 2003), Makhmalbaf traveled to Afghanistan. The focus this time was on Noqreh, a twenty-three-year-old Afghan woman who dreams of becoming president of her country. Though she is from the generation excluded from school by the Taliban, and although her father still supports the deposed regime, she and her friends are far from passive. Makhmalbaf shows their passionate debates about what it means to be a Muslim woman. While she does not flinch from showing the hard realities of life in contemporary Afghanistan, she emphatically rejects any simplistic notion of Muslim women as oppressed victims. Though the film is full of images of destruction and sterility—milk run dry in mothers' breasts, families squatting in shattered aircraft fuselages—there are also moments of serene, surreal beauty that speak of movement and possibility. Amid the rippling sea of bright blue burqas and rows of umbrellas flapping open in the sun, there is a sense of fluidity, of human potential unbroken even under tragic circumstances.

"A brave and intelligent girl can make her own decisions," argues one character in the film, a statement given force by the director's own achievements. For if it seems improbable that a woman could be president of Afghanistan, how likely is it that a teenage girl from Tehran could emerge as one of the world's great filmmakers? She demonstrated her resilience and courage in making her most recent film, *Two Legged Horse* (screened in 2008–9 at Toronto, San Sebastian, Montreal, Belgium, Middle East, Women's World, São Paolo, Pusan, AFI in America, Rome's Asian Films, Estonia, and India's

Kerala film festivals). Refused permission to shoot the tale of a wealthy boy who hires a poor boy to carry him around like a horse in Iran, she returned to Afghanistan. The set was bombed, causing severe injuries to six people, but Makhmalbaf stayed the course to complete the shoot.

She also paved the way for her sister, Hana, who exhibited a short film at the 1997 Locarno film festival when she was only nine. *Buddha Collapsed out of Shame* (*Budha as sharm foru rikht,* 2007), Hana's debut feature, was shot in Bamiyan, Afghanistan, when she was eighteen, and received accolades and awards at film festivals in Berlin, San Sebastian, Thessaloniki, and Hong Kong. Samira, who was selected as one of the forty best directors in the world by the *Guardian* newspaper in 2004, has become a regular festival jurist and one of the most iconic stars of the international film festival circuit. *At Five in the Afternoon* received the Jury's Special Award at the Cannes Film Festival, where the film premiered. We met then to speak about her work.

SF Said: Tell me about making your first film, *The Apple.* What made you choose that subject, and those girls?

Samira Makhmalbaf: A lot of sadness made me do that. I saw this report about the girls on TV, and I was thinking, "What makes a father put his daughters in jail? What? What?" It was so sad for me, and I felt sympathy, maybe because I was a girl, I was Iranian, I was from that culture. So I was thinking, "It could be me." And I couldn't get rid of it. When I don't know how to get rid of a hard thing, I go through it, and I wanted to go through it; I wanted to do something.

SFS: How did you get them to act their story out in the film?

SM: It was very difficult. I always try to work with nonprofessional actors, and they're different human beings, with a different culture, different way of life, different experience, different belief: sometimes I don't believe in what they believe. The only thing I try to do, which is the hardest thing I think in our lives, is not to judge. Always I try to remember not to judge, not to think that you know everything, and not to decide before seeing someone. Try to love. For me it's a challenge any time to make a movie. I don't make a movie with just things I know: I have a lot of questions, I go and experience, I see. So I went to see the father. Not to judge him; I went to see who he was. And I saw: he loves his children! What makes him do what he does is what he believes; he's not a selfish man or a cruel man.

SFS: How about the girls?

SM: It was very hard to communicate with them. They didn't know how to speak at all. They looked at me as if I was a chair, not a human being. And I thought, "How can I communicate with them?" Then I thought, "I have to love them. If you love, it will come to you." So I went to them, and I saw how important communication is for being a complete human being. These two girls, in eleven days, they changed a lot; you see it in the movie. From the beginning to the end, it was eleven days. For me, nowadays, I always think that to be a complete human being, you need more communication. And sometimes I think—for example in Iran—women have less communication, compared to men.

SFS: Are you still in touch with the girls?

SM: Yes, of course.

SFS: What are they like now?

SM: They are not exactly like other people, but let's say, 95 percent, because they didn't have mental problems, nothing wrong physically. So they changed a lot, very very fast, and they lived with another family, because their father couldn't take care of them, and their mother died very soon after. Now they go to school and they grow up.

SFS: What do they think of the film?

SM: [laughing] At the beginning they were a little bit ashamed! They were ashamed that they behaved like that, because now they came into society, they have friends, they go to school. They loved the movie in a way, and in a way they didn't, because they were ashamed.

SFS: I'm interested in the conversations that women have in your films. In *At Five in the Afternoon,* the girls in the school have many debates about what a Muslim woman can do. It's amazing to see this on screen, because Muslim women are so often portrayed as passive victims, but you've given them a voice.

SM: The first day I went to Afghanistan, I didn't have any idea about Afghan women. I was walking in the street, and they were under burqas. It was after the Taliban, but still more than 90 percent were under burqas, and I thought they were just victims. But then I started talking to them. They have big desires, they are full of hope. And so many of them also spoke English! I thought, "Where did they learn?" It was great. I wanted to cry, because I thought they were the unfortunate ones in the war, but they could still have hope and ideas and desires, and I didn't imagine that. Then I went to a school, and I started to talk to the girls. I asked them, "What are you going to do in the future?" And they started to say, "Engineer, doctor, teacher." I wanted to know, What do they think about the difference between men and women? So I asked them if there was anybody who wanted to be president of Afghanistan; or do you think if a woman ran instead of Mr. Karzai, would you vote for her? And they started to say no—but after one hour of talking, all of the class wanted to be president, and they all said yes!

SFS: Your films feel very open. It feels like you're not just trying to make one point but to show many different points of view. You even show an old man who supports the Taliban, and it seems like you're trying to understand him.

SM: You're right. In this film, I tried to behave like I did with *The Apple:* no judgment. It's like all the mass media say, "OK, the problem of Afghanistan is because of the Taliban; they're gone now, so they've got no more problems there!" But I thought, "I have to understand the Taliban ideas also." When I went to Afghanistan, I saw an old man in the road; he closed his face and turned his back on me and faced the wall. I really felt sympathetic to him. Before, he had power, but now he doesn't have any. Before, he could put a burqa on me, but now he must close his eyes. The father in the film was representative of past generations like that. I tried to make no judgment, tried to understand the man who supports the Taliban, and also at the same time, the girl who doesn't want that idea.

SFS: The film features a number of direct quotes from the Koran about the status of women in society. When you hear these quotes in the film, against the story we're seeing, it feels rather critical of Islamic tradition.

SM: I wanted to go directly to the thing that the Koran says because it is something that they believe in. And there is a contrast in the scene of reading the Koran. I think the form is really beautiful, it's very artistic, and maybe because I'm from a Muslim country, it goes to my heart, it touches me. But at the same time, when I see what it says about women, you don't know what kind of feeling you have! But I didn't try to say something about the Koran or Islam; it's the thing that they believe in, it's the book that they read, so it says that. But this girl behaves against it.

SFS: You've become a very well known filmmaker now, particularly in Iran. Is it difficult for you to lead a normal life?

SM: It's a little bit hard when you're famous and when you are a film-maker, because you have to be able to look and see, and not to be seen so much. But when I go back to Iran, I'm like all the other girls, I lead the same life, and it's good. And in Afghanistan, people don't know me in that way, who I am.

SFS: Is it true that you stopped going to school at fourteen because you wanted to learn how to make films?

SM: Yes. I would say I was a good student, and I really believed in studies, because I thought it's the only way to learn something, to change. But there were some years I was thinking that I'm not learning so much. I was thinking that the way they teach us, they make you not think more, not have questions. As soon as I lost my faith in that school, I just left it. Nobody could believe it, because I was a good student. They thought, "What happened?" Some of them thought I must be getting married!

SFS: But you were studying filmmaking with your father. Tell me about the school your father started, to teach you.

SM: It's not that he built some school; it was our house. Some of my friends came, some of my father's friends came, and they started to teach us. For example, they brought some pictures to show us, or they brought a camera and started to teach us how to work with it technically. They would give this camera to me, I took pictures, and we would analyze them. It was like this: practical, theoretical.

SFS: People sometimes compare your family to the Coppolas: your sister Hana and your brother Maysam are also making films. What do you think of this comparison?

SM: We were the first ones! We were before them! So they are like us! But it's good; at least there's one other family like us. Because people sometimes think you are guilty; that we are making films, all the family. They say, "Why? Why you do this?!" And I think maybe it's because of the love of cinema my father gave us. He could give the love of cinema, he could teach us, and at the same time, he could believe in us, he could trust us, he could let us believe in ourselves. We were beginners, and younger, but we could go our own way. He believed that as much as he can have points of view which are beautiful and good, we can also have a point of view. And nowadays, I believe so too.

SFS: At the beginning of your career, critics sometimes said that your films must really be your father's work; they didn't seem to believe that you could have made them yourself. No one says that any more. Did that ever annoy you?

SM: I don't know why that was. One of the reasons was maybe because they didn't believe that young people could make films. But what do they think cinema is? Cinema's just like a window, a point of view. Nowadays, it's digital, it's going to be like a pen: anybody can write and have their own point of view. I think you can be ten years old and have your own point of view; you just have to believe what you're saying. Maybe they think you need to have experience to have an idea. But anybody can have experiences. What does it mean, to be experienced? Which age is experienced? Forty, fifty, sixty? I don't know. At any age, you have your own point of view!

SFS: Your films take real situations, real people, and are very specific in their settings, yet there's also a sense that they're about something wider. They feel universal.

SM: Yes, that's something that I think about. To me, something can be also the symbol of something else at the same time. For example, the situation of Afghan people: it's very much for them and specially for their situation and at the same time I think it's not only about Afghanistan. It's about also Iran. I could do this film to say something that I can't talk about in the situation of Iran nowadays; or it can be the story of so many Eastern countries. So yes, you're right, I try to be like that. Because I think, before anything, most of the problems of humanity belong to all humanity. So I think, before being Iranian or being a woman or being young or whatever, I'm a human, OK? So I try to make a film for humanity. And I try to go through the reality; but it's not a documentary, it's fiction.

SFS: How are things in Iran now [May 2003]?

SM: Compared to before Mr. Khatami, so many things are better, very much better, especially for the movies. It's better, but I don't know.

SFS: Reform has slowed down?

SM: Yes, it's slowed down a lot. I have to say, some part of our problem comes from the written law, but some part comes from the unwritten law: it's in the culture of the people. And democracy is not just saying, "OK, from now on we are going to have democracy!" It takes time. In Afghanistan, I think the problem is deeper. It's like a cancer; it gives a kind of internal deformation. It takes time.

SFS: Could a woman be president of Iran?

SM: In Iran? [Long pause.] It's hard. No, it's very hard, because of the written law and the unwritten. Even in Europe or America, you don't have that many women presidents, so it means that something is the problem of humanity, all the world.

SFS: OK, but there used to be very few female filmmakers, and now there are many.

SM: In the world. And also in Iran we have! Sometimes you need to break a cliché.

SFS: So you, as a young woman making films like this, can make people think that anything is possible.

SM: I'm happy for that. At the beginning, people don't believe, they don't believe, but little by little, they get used to it, and nowadays in Iran, we have so many young female filmmakers. So when we have one president in an Eastern country, some other women will start thinking about it: "I can also be a president. . . ."

Chloé Hope Johnson

Chapter 12

Becoming-Grrrl

The Voice and Videos of Sadie Benning

Artist Sadie Benning uses cross-media forms to explore topical sociocultural issues, creating fluid connections across genres, audiences, and expressive modes. Benning's filmic oeuvre ranges from experimental four-minute videos (*New Year* and *Living Inside,* 1989) to more accessible shorts such as *The Judy Spots* (1995) for MTV to a full-length art video, *Flat Is Beautiful* (1998). Most of Benning's early video works have had minimal distribution: her videos are usually screened at independent film festivals or in gallery spaces. Despite this limited exposure, she has found effective ways of circulating her works in more popular media without compromising her artistic edge or transgressive vision. More recently she worked on a music project with the band Le Tigre and the video clip "Aerobicide" (1998) for Julie Ruin (aka Kathleen Hanna). Through her use of different media, Benning creates multiple identity spaces that traverse one another, as she moves within and between alternative and mainstream music and video practices. Making her audience complicit in the creative process, she assigns to them a collaborative agency that generates multiple meanings in and beyond the work. In so doing, she opens up affective trajectories that connect to wider, more diverse communities.

Benning's audio-visual works exist outside of those boundaries that function to fix identity formation to heteronormative representations. Difference, sexual or otherwise, is the thematic thread flowing through each video, song, or film, expressed through the displacement and incorporation of mainstream, popular, and iconic images that Benning removes from their initial context and then drops into unfamiliar terrain. As she blends media within individual texts and crosses over into a variety of artistic and social

172

milieus, she demonstrates the fluid potential for meaningful identity construction on the edge of and counter to dominant sociocultural perceptions and attitudes.

Benning's practice of examining difference through creative methods of generating alternative subjectivities can be read through Gilles Deleuze and Félix Guattari's concept of becoming-woman, which they define as a process that every individual, irrespective of sexuality or gender, must embark on before any other mode of becoming can occur.[1] Knowing no conceptual or practical limits, becoming-woman opens up perception and makes visible everybody's potential for change, freedom, and transformation. Art, with its ability to alter dominant perceptions and hegemonic power relations, is fundamental to the process of becoming. Artists, claim Deleuze and Guattari, are not only the creators and inventors of affects through their work but also those who "give [affects] to us and make us become with them, they draw us into the compound."[2] As a transmission of thought and vision takes place between artist and audience, individuals are able to cultivate a space in which to develop a greater understanding of the world they inhabit and thereby effect actual conceptual shifts, not purely metaphorical ones.[3] Benning ranks among those whose "ultimate political goal as film-makers is to go beyond current identities and create the images and voices of a people to come."[4]

As a mode of "go[ing] beyond," becoming-girl is a process in which movement and speed within physical and cognitive environments are far more rapid and intense than becoming-woman.[5] When Benning calls in her videos for "girl power" and a "revolution, girl style, now!" she speaks of a future in which girls are able to exercise agency in the world; construct their own identities outside of dominant culture's rigid structures, which limit corporeal, intellectual, and sexual expression; and, finally, engage with difference and desire both actively and productively. Telling an autobiographical tale through a portrayal of multiple identities, Benning actively challenges stereotypes and raises questions by pushing her own experiences beyond the personal and out into a public sphere.

Becoming-Girl (in the Bedroom): Benning's Pursuit of the Fluid Image

From the safe remove of her bedroom, Benning finds the freedom to play with and challenge the stereotypical gendered representations in popular culture. Benning approaches these stereotypes in her work with an outsider's status based not solely on her sexuality (her self-proclaimed queerness in a heteronormative world) but rather more as an adolescent girl articulating feelings of estrangement within her own culture. Guattari claims that although adolescents "are mentally manipulated through the production of a collective, mass-media subjectivity, they are nevertheless developing their own methods of distancing themselves from normalized subjectivity through singularization."[6]

The singular and personal elements that mark Benning's work are blended with "impersonal" images of classical Hollywood movie stars, pop icons, and other ideologically entrenched archetypes, which she brings into her own private space. Incorporating popular representations into domestic space, and moving across media, Benning works to break down, negate, and challenge these divisive categories to formulate the becoming-girl. Through her loose narrative trajectories, in particular the video *It Wasn't Love* (1992), her "love-on-the-run story" inspired by *Bonnie and Clyde* (Arthur Penn, 1967), Benning distances herself from mass-media subjectivity by remediating pop cultural icons, associated with 1960s rebellion, within private space to articulate feelings of difference, alienation, and detachment in a world of exclusion that willfully fails to understand her. In *It Wasn't Love*, Benning depicts a fleeting, yet physically intense and emotionally charged, moment that she shares with a "bad" girl who promises to take her to Hollywood. They get only as far as a fried chicken restaurant parking lot.

As Benning is remembering this incident, she is describing her in-between status as a becoming-girl: feeling lost in an environment at once disturbing and exciting, she is torn between the innocent glamour of romantic love and the fugitive nature of passionate physical and emotional intimacy. Becoming reveals the hard realities of suffering and angst that come with desires, both realized and crushed. In learning to reconcile ingenuous hope and trust with disillusionment and the empty promises of the "adult" world, Benning negotiates these complex feelings by observing that "it wasn't love, but it was something." That "something" is a becoming inhabited by the adolescent girl, a state in between polarized modes of being. The mere presence of adolescence as a social grouping challenges and subverts any fixed social category or representation.[7] The adolescent girl becomes a smooth surface where image and identity projection are fluid and transformative.

In a scene from *Girl Power* (1992), Benning's voice-over tells us how she would "wag" school and run away to be on her own. She talks of escaping to places where she could be herself, be free, if only for a short time. Opening the film with a close-up of her own mouth, before the image cuts to footage of a young girl, Benning tells her audience in voice-over, in a low-key, matter of fact tone:

So, ah, today, that's right, I skipped school. But, ah, whatcha gonna do about it? Nothin'! Just like I thought. I went down to a river 'cause no-one can find me there, not even the cops. Sometimes, they catch me wandering around. They try to take me back, "to where you belong" they said. But they know nothin' 'bout where I belonged. So I did it every day . . . went on journeys for hours, miles. I knew that's where I belonged. 'Cos that's where I wanted to be.

This is spoken from the perspective, and in the tone, of an adolescent girl rebelling against institutionalized forces that would deny her life experience. Yet the image onscreen is of a girl no older than eight years, wandering aimlessly through desolate parklands or along lonely train tracks toward an unknown destination. At random moments the girl acknowledges her awareness of being filmed by gesturing rudely toward the camera and defiantly poking out her tongue.

By playing around with the concept of age and physical maturity, which she does consistently in her work, Benning reveals the indeterminacy of chronologically prescribed categories and labels. In these moments, embodied identity becomes unfixed and fluid. Later, in *Girl Power*, Benning films a physiological chart, like those one might see in a family physician's waiting room or a child's anatomy book, which begins with a drawing of a baby girl and moves along from figure to figure, mapping the physical development and transformation of the female body from prepubescence to adulthood. The juxtaposition of the empirical image of the chart with the instances of deliberate inconsistency between image and voice-tracks enables Benning to comment on the transformative nature of femininity in a way that exceeds the corporeal and material. Counter to dominant chronological demarcations of childhood and adulthood, the becoming-girl renders visible the multiplicities that exist within the individual and posits that the physical (female) body, regardless of age, is not essentially representative of subjectivity and identity formation.

Rather than rejecting feminist history and theory, Benning's videos acknowledge select elements therein to undermine, critique, and subvert conventional inscriptions. She is seeking alternative representation through a disruption of dominant history from the perspective of a minor figure, in Deleuze's sense. Although dialectical shifts between major and minor, or mainstream and alternative, cultures are becoming increasingly blurred due to the media's expanding technological power to infiltrate all social spheres, there are creative methods and artistic spaces that elude complete absorption by dominant culture. Certain creative and social elements find fluidity through the ambiguous existence of bodies becoming. Benning's videos demonstrate a minor articulation of becoming through her depiction of a corporeal materiality and subjectivity, both lived and virtual, mediated through unconventional, multiple, and alternative praxes. As both artist and subject, Benning's active and embodied aural and visual communication show what it is to become minor.

Explaining her feelings of isolation and detachment from the world around her, Benning's voice-over in *Girl Power* says that "in the world in [her] head, [she] is never alone." While she says this, the words "ashamed," "ridiculed," "denied," "fucked with," "fuck you man," and "hear me or die" drift across the frame. The text is superceded by news footage of race riots, as Benning's voice-over continues, "It was at school, with my father, in my own culture, when I felt most alone." The emotional battering she feels on a daily basis is paralleled with—and expressed analogically by—the violence depicted in a news loop of war, death, and destruction. The comparison she draws between the violence she experiences and contains as adolescent girl and the media representation of political violence positions adolescence as a category subject to violence. Her message that the adolescent girl is as much an outsider as those victimized by racist, homophobic, political, and religious prejudice (albeit in more subtle and subliminal ways) is presented through the merging of private and public spheres.

Becoming-Brando: Reconstructing Gendered Iconography

Benning pushes her marginalization further by queering her white, middle-class, adolescent subjectivity. Benning's deconstructions of gendered and cultural norms generate potential viewing positions as both outsider and confidante, guiding spectators into affective, intimate, and exploratory spaces. The spectators are made acutely aware of their own existence, feeling themselves strangers in their own environment as images, sounds, representations, and texts familiar to them are called into question. Benning's references to famous teen icons of the 1980s and 1990s, such as Matt Dillon and Luke Perry, highlight her alternative engagement with adolescent popular culture as she mobilizes these icons through an open acknowledgement and exploration of her queer identity. Unlike adolescent girls who display posters of male television and film stars on their bedroom walls in order to imagine themselves as the stars' girlfriends, Benning's admiration for these male pop idols is suggestive of *becoming* the hero.

By refusing both normative subject positions and aesthetic boundaries, Benning formulates a highly personalized sociocultural and aesthetic history. The "impersonal" images she selects from various media, such as news footage, current affair programs, MTV, teen magazines, and movie posters, are filtered through the interstices of television, where they find a new outlet in the intimate and private space of her bedroom. Looking at the enormous effect television has on everyday life, Catherine Elwes suggests: "With television now one of the major vehicles for the dissemination of cultural images of women, video was an obvious medium with which to begin dismantling stereotypical representations and assert the political, psychic, and aesthetic evolution of women's newly raised consciousness."[8] Using video to intercept and recontextualize images, particularly from television, Benning finds her voice by *blending* expressive media and artistic forms.

Benning's video *It Wasn't Love* makes reference to a range of Hollywood genres made famous in the classical period of the 1940s and 1950s, when celebrities such as Humphrey Bogart, Cary Grant, Frank Sinatra, and Marlon Brando dominated the silver screen. As her own protagonist, Benning shifts between stereotypical character roles. She plays the tough guy hero, flaunting many of the generic signifiers of classical Hollywood. She dresses in a leather jacket one moment, a bowler hat and cane the next, smoking a cigar or sporting side-burns and fake tattoo. She mimics Bogart in *Casablanca* (Michael Curtiz, 1942) and Brando in *The Wild One* (László Benedek, 1953) before turning her attention to the iconic female characters. Her 1940s film noir femme fatale, in platinum blonde wig and heavy make-up, flourishing a cigarette, parodies the archetype paradigmatically portrayed by Barbara Stanwyck in *Double Indemnity* (Billy Wilder, 1944). Benning's use of classical Hollywood characters and their costume and make-up signifiers undermines existing gendered limitations and their rigid meanings. These transformations are less specifically an articulation of gendered cross-dressing within the butch/femme binary and more generally a comment on the power of the image and the role of the performer. By co-opting mainstream film's symbols and star personae within her makeshift bedroom mise-en-scène, Benning deconstructs the Hollywood myth so that its iconography reveals the multigenerative potential of the image.

Benning's overall critique and subsequent subversion of classical Hollywood generic codes and, in turn, of the ideologically prescribed sociosexual categories they maintain(ed) is supported by the meticulously chosen soundtracks used throughout her videos. The image track is used to destabilize the popular and standard meaning of a classic song, such as Frank Sinatra's rendition of "My Funny Valentine," while the soundtrack simultaneously subverts that image. In a witty parody of masculinity, Benning lip-synchs to Fats Domino's "Blueberry Hill" in *It Wasn't Love,* while dressed like one of Sinatra's Rat Pack. She later mimes along to Peggy Lee's "Fever" in the guise of a Hollywood screen starlet. Setting up a conventional binary division between Hollywood hero and starlet, and more generally between man and woman, Benning makes clear that she neither fits, nor conforms to, either of these cultural stereotypes. Using Prince's "I Wanna Be Your Lover" over a clip from *The Bad Seed* (Mervyn LeRoy, 1956) she twists the film's relationship between mother and daughter into something entirely unexpected. Through her eclectic mix of various artistic and everyday forms in her videos, Benning plays with and on our expectations of gendered representations in relation to generic conventions and our subsequent perceptions of our own realities. She takes a seemingly static image or song and mobilizes its potential multiplicity of meanings and translations. In doing so, she grants agency to herself and her viewer, affording both artist and audience entrée into a world of multiple realities generated through alternative ideologies and modes of expression.

Benning's individualized mode of expression opens up affective connections where images, music, text, and sound mix and flow at multiple points within and beyond a specific video, film, or song. In doing so, her works engage that shared point between artist and audience, creating connective lines that merge in a crystalline moment where identification, expression, affection, and memory entwine to form a representation that shatters preexisting referents and models. Particularly within video, where meaning extends beyond the image and bleeds from one milieu into another, this moment generates a contiguous mass of affective points, connected by a web of lines leading to unknown territories. With no prescribed way of being in the world, the primary concern becomes finding ways of realizing and creating new sensations, experiences, and meanings that resist established binaristic categories. It is at this point where bodies embark on a process of becoming, not merely an enhanced understanding of being.

(Be)Coming Out: Screening Sound, Staging Affect

After years of examining her own body and subjectivity closely under the microscope that is her camera, and appearing to her audience as an abstracted and fragmented two-dimensional image, Benning stepped out of the cinematic frame and became involved in a music scene with its roots in the riot grrrl movement. Emerging from underground subcultures in Seattle, Portland, and Olympia during the 1990s, riot grrrl was started by a group of musicians, artists, and writers determined to create a musically based sociopolitical scene for women that was as aggressive, angry, and defiant as the hardcore scene. It was one of the first sociomusical movements to embrace adolescence as the cornerstone of its subcultural formation, by acknowledging adolescent girls as highly politicized and active members of society.[9] Engaging with the punk ethos, riot grrrl was an antidote to punk's growing misogyny and gender exclusion. Punk, in all its manifestations, whether musical, political, theoretical, aesthetic, or cultural, rests on its faith in the anarchic to provide an outlet for counter-cultural expression and response. Women were drawn to punk because it attempted to give voice to minorities by destabilizing dominant culture.

Riot grrrl was originally used as a name for a zine started by Bratmobile's Molly Neuman and Allison Wolfe. Gerri Hirshey explains that the riot grrrls were "papering the country with militant fanzines like *RiotGrrrl, Girl Germs,* and *Bikini Kill.* They offered one another support in networks, concerts, and other femtastic forums."[10] Riot grrrls focused on punk's call for a democratization of music production, including performance, recording, distribution, and musicianship, in line with punk's DIY ethic. The grrrl bands appropriated the sounds and styles of punk and reinterpreted every element in a feminist vein, pushing a grrrl agenda and vision. Riot grrrls' primary concern was to challenge patriarchal assumptions regarding gender and sexuality through music and its attendant fan culture. Benning began making videos as an adolescent girl in the era of riot grrrl, so it seems a logical progression that she should join forces with Kathleen Hanna (formerly lead singer of Bikini Kill, arguably the most influential band of the first wave of riot grrrls) and Johanna Fateman (creator of zines such as *Artaudmania,* 1997) to engage with the riot grrrl ethos directly through the formation of their band Le Tigre.[11]

Having cited Bikini Kill's influence in *Girl Power*'s end credits, Benning embraced the opportunity to collaborate with Hanna by making the video for the song "Aerobicide," the single for Hanna's first solo project, *Julie Ruin* (1998).[12] On completion of the "Aerobicide" video, Benning expressed an interest in helping with visuals and music for the live show that Hanna was devising in an attempt to develop her alter-ego. Hanna and Fateman met up in New York where, instead of using the existing songs from *Julie Ruin,* they began writing new material, which was subsequently sent to Benning in Chicago.[13] After hearing Hanna and Fateman's latest songs, Benning made the trip to New York, where they began working on the project that was to become Le Tigre.[14]

Through her work with Le Tigre, Benning moved beyond the cinematic apparatus, enhancing her means of self-expression and vocalizing her thoughts directly from the stage. With their extreme close-ups of her mouth, eyes, and hands, her videos disembody her voice and alienate the subject from itself; in the process they objectify and universalize her experiences and emotions, which would otherwise remain intensely individualized as part of an autobiographical text. Music, however, has the capacity to open up different audio-visual environments to multiple interpretations, interactions, and affective possibilities. Due to its sound, production, and associated social scenes, which are all part of its capacity to exceed sociocultural limitations and to create multiple networks, music can create an atmosphere that video alone cannot.

Live musical performances also allow artists to engage actively with their audience, forming immediate and interactive personal connections that work to construct virtual communities based on a shared ethos. An extension of her work in video, Benning's music-making allows her to use her actual and virtual presence to formulate collective identities based on their fluid potential to generate a "metamorphic zone between fixed identities."[15] Patricia Pisters argues, drawing on Deleuze and Guattari, that music remains irreducible to "man" or "woman."[16] Benning transforms vocal gender by moderating the sound of her voice electronically through synthesizers and microphones, producing a fluid mode of articulation.

In "Hot Topic," Benning sings the selected names of those culturally important to her, aligning herself with a group of artistic individuals regardless of their gender.[17] References to teen heartthrobs, female musicians, and movie stars that recurred in her videos are now sung in the same breath and context as significant feminist artists such as Yoko Ono and Carolee Schneemann, riot grrrl bands like the Butchies, Sleater Kinney, and the Slits; queer writers and theorists of alterity Gayatri Spivak, James Baldwin, Gertrude Stein, Jean Genet, and Dorothy Allison; and black singers and activists such as Aretha Franklin and Nina Simone. With every reference made to another artist, musician, or writer, Le Tigre interpellates audience members through differential shared appreciation for these figures' significance, generating multiple, interconnecting communities constituted through citation. During live performances of "Hot Topic," a video was projected onto screens behind the band, with images of each artist cited appearing alongside cartoon-style drawings of everyday objects, creating a scrapbook aesthetic similar to Benning's videos of pop star posters on her bedroom wall.

Le Tigre's live shows are a combination of electro-punk music, politicized and theory-informed lyrics, video projections composed of moving and still images, as well as choreographed dance moves and matching outfits. Discussing women artists' attraction to video art and live performance, Elwes writes, "Women were impatient to speak, to visualise and to become visible. They gravitate towards performance and video because of their confrontational nature and their ability to deliver an immediate message to an audience."[18] Both music and video are capable of forming a connection in an instant. Music invents a people and generates multiple levels of engagement and interactivity.[19] Benning's voice, once delinked from the image of her body, is now multiconnected in the recording studio she shares with her bandmates, and on the stage where they engage with their audiences. Music connects with its performer and audience on multiple levels of engagement, injecting each individual with an energy to move, both physically and cognitively. Through a combination of sound, rhythm, voice, and lyrics, a song moves and affects us, making our embodied subjectivity mobile and fluid.

Significantly, Benning returned symbolically to the adolescent space of the bedroom to imagine forms of feminist interactivity that merge public and private spheres. Le Tigre's song "Eau D'Bedroom Dancing" celebrates almost nostalgically the freedom of being in this private, insular space. The band sings:

> I'm in the sky when I'm on the floor
> The world's a mess and yr my only cure
> There's no time for me to act mature
> The only words I know are "more," "more," and "more"
>
> No one to criticize me then
> No one to criticize
>
> There's no fear when I'm in my room
> It's so clear and I know just what I want to do
> All day bedroom dancing
> To you I wanna say
> Yr my thing[20]

Alone in their bedrooms girls feel liberated, able to envision a world they want to be a part of—could be a part of—in a society that embraces rather than ridicules difference. Emboldened, they imagine affective public spaces that reflect minor cultures and make possible becoming-grrrl.

Notes

1. Patty Sotirin, "Becoming-Woman," in *Gilles Deleuze: Key Concepts,* ed. Charles Stivale (Chesham, UK: Acumen, 2005), 102.

2. Gilles Deleuze and Félix Guattari, *What Is Philosophy?* trans. Hugh Tomlinson

and Graham Burchell (New York: Columbia University Press, 1994), 175.

3. Alice Jardine, "Woman in Limbo: Deleuze and His Br(others)," in *Deleuze and Guattari: Critical Assessments of Leading Philosophers,* ed. Gary Genosko (London: Routledge, 2001), 1404.

4. Ronald Bogue, "The Minor," in Stivale, *Gilles Deleuze,* 118.

5. See Felicity J. Colman, "Hit Me Harder: The Transversality of Becoming-Adolescent," *Women: A Cultural Review* 16, no. 3 (2005): 356–71.

6. Félix Guattari, *The Three Ecologies,* trans. Ian Pindar and Paul Sutton (London: Continuum, 1989), 33.

7. Félix Guattari, *Soft Subversions,* ed. Sylvere Lotringer (New York: Semiotext(e), 1996), 64.

8. Catherine Elwes, *Video Art: A Guided Tour* (London: I. B. Tauris, 2005), 40.

9. Christie Milliken, "The Pixel Visions of Sadie Benning," in *Sugar, Spice, and Everything Nice: Cinemas of Girlhood,* ed. Frances Gateward and Murray Pomerance (Detroit: Wayne State University Press, 2002), 290.

10. Gerri Hirshey, *We Gotta Get Out of This Place: The True, Tough Story of Women in Rock* (New York: Grove Press, 2001), 159.

11. Bikini Kill's songs include "Rebel Girl," "Reject All American," "Suck My Left One," "White Boy," "Anti-Pleasure Dissertation," and "I Like Fucking." The band recorded on the independent label Kill Rock Stars, which gave them complete artistic freedom and helped to maintain their authenticity as a punk band retaining the DIY ethic. See Maria Raha, "Hot Topic: Le Tigre," in *Cinderella's Big Score: Women of the Punk and Indie Underground* (Emeryville, CA: Seal Press, 2005), 203–8 and 243–46; Andrea Juno, *Angry Women in Rock: Volume One, Re/Search* (New York: Juno Books, 1996), 82–103; and Gillian G. Gaar, "Enjoy Being a Grrrl," in *She's a Rebel: The History of Women in Rock & Roll* (New York: Seal Press, 2002), 365–400.

12. The video can be viewed in part through the Video Data Bank at http://www.vdb.org/smackn.acgi$tapedetail?AEROBICIDE_002.

13. Raha, "Hot Topic," 244.

14. All of Le Tigre's details can be found on their website at http://www.letigreworld.com.

15. Ronald Bogue, *Deleuze on Music, Painting, and the Arts* (New York: Routledge, 2003), 35.

16. Patricia Pisters, *The Matrix of Visual Culture: Working with Deleuze and Film Theory* (Palo Alto, CA: Stanford University Press, 2003), 200.

17. This song is from Le Tigre's self-titled first album, which was the only full album Benning participated in before leaving the band. The lyrics for the song can be viewed at http://www.letigreworld.com/sweepstakes/html_site/song/hotopic.html.

18. Elwes, *Video Art,* 41.

19. Bogue, *Deleuze on Music,* 52.

20. Le Tigre, "Eau D'Bedroom Dancing," *Le Tigre* (Mr. Lady Records, 1999).

Surfacings

Translating Orientalism

Leslie Thornton's *Adynata*

The title of Leslie Thornton's 1983 experimental film *Adynata* refers to a rhetorical trope meaning a declaration of impossibility, often the impossibility of expression itself. It can also take the form of a confession that words fail us or "a stringing together of impossibilities."[1] The phrases "I'm speechless" or "words cannot express" are familiar examples of this trope. Etymologically, "adynata" refers to a state of powerlessness: its Greek root words contain an analog of the phrase "without dynasty" (*a dynasthai*), in which we may hear an echo of China's imperial past. *Adynata*'s title thereby alerts us to the fact that the film will be in some way about the impossibility of representing the East and the power dynamics that have historically attended the circulation of Orientalist images, although it is unclear at first how precisely the film will address these issues. Does "adynata" refer to the powerlessness of the East to represent itself, that is, to the West's usurpation of this privilege, as per Edward Said's argument? Or is it the filmmaker's good-faith declaration of her own powerlessness to represent a place that differs so radically from her own, a confession that words and images fail her in the attempt to depict alterity? Or is it perhaps a caveat about the collection of images we are about to view, a warning that we are to read them as provisional signs, rather than images that aspire to an accurate representation of the East?

The Orient as Enigma

While *Adynata* in fact supports all these possible readings, I prefer to resist reading it as a comment on the impossibility of cross-cultural representation. It is tempting to set up a contrast between Hollywood's fantastical, falsified version of the East on the one hand and indigenous, vernacular Asian national cinemas on the other. To do so would be to situate Thornton's film as a kind of corrective to the former, which, however, can never aspire to or compete with the latter in terms of authenticity. In my analysis of this film, I attempt to move away from these binary oppositions. Instead, I propose to undertake further exploration of how the very notions of authenticity and falseness, original and copy, have been mapped onto East and West in the cinematic imaginary. I ultimately read *Adynata* not simply as an avant-garde critique of the West's falsification of the East, where a declaration of the image's insufficiency suffices for political and ethical exoneration, but as a resistant film that churns through the material of Orientalist fantasy without precisely negating it. *Adynata*'s ethical move, in other words, is not simply to declare the impossibility, absurdity, or violence of Orientalism but to work and deal in good faith with its enigmas, to think about their possible sources, and to problematize the very possibility of locating some kernel of truth beneath them.

The Orient often serves as a metaphor for things enigmatic and unknown in twentieth-century American visual culture. This metaphor can be read through the work of psychoanalyst Jean Laplanche. In his book *Essays on Otherness,* Laplanche offers a re-reading of Freud's notion of the unconscious.[2] The unconscious, Laplanche claims, is a repository not only for taboo desires or repressed memories but also for signs—be they verbal, visual, or tactile—that the infant subject simply fails to comprehend. These "enigmatic signifiers," as Laplanche calls them, present a puzzle for their recipient. While the infant may understand that they are addressed to her and that they demand a response of some kind, their content is wholly unintelligible. To make matters worse, these communications are permeated with unconscious, often sexualized meanings of which even their senders are unaware. For Laplanche, these signs do not simply disappear with mature understanding but remain at the heart of human interaction. The originary scenario of the enigmatic signifier is retriggered throughout the subject's life whenever she is sent a mixed message, interpellated by an ambiguous address, or confronted with a sign that seems to invite and yet resist decoding. The response to this situation ranges from vain attempts at translation to paranoid aggression. The inscrutable alterity that they represent is not equivalent to the Freudian unconscious nor to the abstract big "Other" of the Symbolic in Lacan's work. Rather, it has its source in concrete, individual human beings and the messages they send. This aspect of Laplanche's theory makes him especially useful for thinking about race and other forms of social difference that psychoanalysis has frequently been accused of failing to address.

In Hollywood cinema, the Orient frequently occupies the place of the enigmatic signifier: the East becomes the primary emissary of that which is withheld from comprehension, impossible to decode, or vexingly unintelligible to the West. Films from D. W. Griffith's *Broken Blossoms* (1919) to Sofia Coppola's *Lost in Translation* (2003) have represented the Orient not simply as other, nor even simply as feminized, exoticized, and perilous, but as duplicitous and semiotically challenged. In the American cinematic imaginary, Asian cities appear to be populated by withholders of ambiguous and dangerous secrets that are irretrievably lost in translation. The Orient is figured as a paranoid space, filled with crowds of figures who move chaotically, layered planes of shadows and glass that make reflections indiscernible from their objects, and a whole jumble of mysterious signs. These signs are seductive and erotic insofar as they solicit the gaze of Orientalist knowledge with the promise of their decipherment; they are threatening to the extent that they turn away from and resist this gaze. Ultimately, the enigma is insoluble: it lies not in the East, but in an *internal* alterity that Laplanche situates at the foundations of subjectivity and that is projected outward in these films through a disorienting series of imagistic tropes.

The Chinese Theatre and Ideographic Myth

As Eric Lott, Kelly Benigno and Oliver Trigo, and others have shown, these tropes are apparent in films noir, such as *Murder, My Sweet* (Edward Dmytryk, 1944), *The Lady from Shanghai* (Orson Welles, 1947), and *Chinatown* (Roman Polanski, 1974).[3] The notion of the Orient as enigmatic is discernible not only in the narrative workings of particular films; it also informs the bases of film culture and form more broadly. An enigmatic East is also reproduced in movie palace architecture of the 1920s and 1930s. Grauman's Chinese Theatre, which is supremely famous and recognizable among movie theaters and the site of Hollywood's own pantheon of stars, imagines the Orient as a collection of duplicitous, bewildering, and hyper-codified signs.[4] In much the way that, according to Antonia Lant, Egyptian-inspired movie palace décor evokes the riddles of the Sphinx and attaches this enigmatic quality to the filmic image itself, so "The Chinese," as the theater is sometimes known, plays up the association between the Orient and indeterminacy.[5] The fire curtain was designed to look like a giant lacquered cabinet in peacock blue, with intricate gold and silver designs of birds and trees. The theater was always delicately perfumed so that guests could "easily imagine themselves in a Chinese palace."[6] The usherettes were costumed in copies of Chinese theatrical gowns, which were embroidered in gold and covered with tiny framed mirrors. The lobby of Grauman's Theatre also contained several automata, wax mannequins of Chinese people that moved mechanically to give the appearance of smoking opium or fanning. As an old tourist pamphlet describing the theater states, "These were indeed so realistic that people tried to talk to them."[7]

The simulacrum becomes yet more tangled, and the Chinese Theatre doubly removed from the "real" China, when we learn that its architecture and interior design were inspired not by actual buildings but by the Orientalist period of Chippendale.[8] The fantastical Orient that is reproduced in the theater is thus not simply a virtual copy of a preexisting "original" China but a reflection of a more pervasive fascination with and paranoia about the larger implications of Western copies of Asian originals, and how these relations map onto the medium of cinema more broadly. Grauman's Theatre has become, to some extent, a synecdoche for Hollywood; the theater is an emblem for a Californian West that is itself curiously Eastern. It thus reveals an Orientalist alterity at the heart of cinema culture, albeit one veiled by a series of mistranslations.

The fear of the Asian copy and its proliferation throughout the West is a prevalent theme in contemporary U.S. discourse about China and reflects an ambivalence about Chinese development, modernity, and entry into a global capitalist economy and marketplace. Concerns about pirated DVDs and music, the availability of counterfeit or "knock-off" designer objects, and other imitation versions of Western electronic and consumer goods dominate news coverage of the Chinese economy to a disproportionate extent. They represent the most recent development in a long history of Sino-American relations, which, throughout the nineteenth and early twentieth centuries, were dictated primarily by concerns about trade and a desire for unfettered access to ports and markets.[9] The verb "to shanghai," which, according to the Oxford English Dictionary, originated in 1871 as a colloquial term meaning "to transfer forcibly or abduct," also evokes this paranoia about exchanges between East and West. The many films from Hollywood's classical era that echo this theme in their titles—*Shanghai Express* (Josef von Sternberg, 1932), *The Shanghai Gesture* (Josef von Sternberg, 1941), and so on—are further examples of cinema's imbrication of things Eastern with concerns about copies, piracy, abduction, and appropriation.[10] But who has appropriated from whom? There is a sense in which fears about Eastern piracy represent the reversal of a Western Shanghai gesture.

Similar vestiges can be located at the foundations of film theory. A key example is to be found in Sergei Eisenstein's *Film Form,* in which Eisenstein characterizes formal elements that have frequently been thought of as part of a Western cinematic idiom as derivative of Asiatic linguistic models. In "The Cinematic Principle and the Ideogram," Eisenstein proposes to catalog "the cinematic traits of Japanese culture that lie outside the Japanese cinema."[11] The most pertinent of these is a trait that he attributes to the Japanese language, which he describes as "the combination of two hieroglyphs" to create a conceptual meaning that arises from their conjunction. Eisenstein likens this process to his own theory of cinematic montage and praises the way that "material," "representational" signs become the catalyst for political and intellectual meanings in Japanese linguistic and dramatic forms. Yet Eisenstein's characterizations of Asian language as "representational" or "hieroglyphic" rest upon a ruse. As John DeFrancis has pointed out in his writings on the ideographic myth, Chinese characters (from which both the Japanese and Korean systems of writing are derived) are not in fact pictographic but phonetic.[12] Like alphabetic writing, they are governed by codes of grammar and usage; even if their forms can be traced at their origins to pictorial ones, their function in the present is to signify verbally. As Rey Chow points out, it is not only Eisenstein but also Derrida who falls victim to this myth, in *Of Grammatology*. Chow writes, "The implications of DeFrancis' observation are staggering when we recall how Derrida's early work invokes Chinese 'ideographic' writing as *the* metaphor for difference from 'Western' phonocentrism."[13] In keeping with the logic of the enigmatic signifier, and through a misreading of Asian signs—that is, a mistranslation of language itself—the East comes to pervade the seemingly Western systems of both post-structuralist theory and cinema theory.

Adynata

The examples I have just given—Grauman's Chinese Theatre and Eisenstein's writings on the ideogram—are but a brief shorthand for indicating some of the ways one might detect an Orientalist impulse at the foundations of film culture and form. More specifically, these two examples demonstrate that this Orientalism involves not merely a fetishization of the exotic but a projection of difference at a more fundamental level, that of signification itself. "Oriental" signs are generally viewed in two ways: either as hieroglyphic, iconic, or representational and therefore closer to the primitive and the preverbal, and further away from the abstract and the Symbolic; or, in a related move, as duplicitous, enigmatic, and coalescing the virtual and the actual in indiscernible ways. Both these tropes are deployed with a difference in Thornton's *Adynata.*

Adynata begins with shots of two faded photographs from a Chinese wedding circa 1861 and proceeds to investigate images commonly associated with the East through an experimental collage of found footage, lush images of flower blossoms and silk fabrics, and restaged shots of Thornton herself posing as both the husband and the wife from the photograph, in the manner of (and anticipating by a few years) Cindy Sherman's *Untitled Film Stills.* In an avant-garde move, Thornton "detourns" each of these images. Exotic blossoms, slippers for bound feet, and the color red are all presented with metaphorical quotation marks around them. Likewise, she returns these images to sender. The flowers are not in Japan but in the Brooklyn Botanical Garden in New York; the music we hear on the soundtrack is not Chinese opera but a song from the Rodgers and Hammerstein musical *South Pacific* (Joshua Logan, 1958). A degraded image of people running, which we might assume to be documentary footage from World War II, is in fact a distorted and reshot version of the final scene from François Truffaut's *Shoot the Piano Player* (*Tirez sur le pianiste,* 1960). An image of an official-looking man listening intently to speech on an audio headset is overlain with sinister-sounding Korean dialogue, evocative of U.S. intelligence gathering activities from World War II, the Korean War, or the Vietnam War. The dialogue, however, is benign chatter from the soundtrack of a Korean soap opera, and the image is taken from a 1950s science fiction film. Thomas Zummer has written that these images form "an abyss of technical reproductions and appropriations."[14] Writing about the Chinese wedding photograph, Linda Peckham suggests that "all of the imitations and inventions deriving from it suspend authenticity, obscure the distinction between copy and original, fact and fiction."[15]

In *Femmes Fatales,* Mary Ann Doane suggests that these images are hyper-codified, layered with signifying excess. As Doane puts it, "readability is diminished through a surplus of codification."[16] The signs of the Orient, far from assumed to be natural or primitive, as they traditionally are in Orientalist discourse, are rendered in this film as fully worked-over by culture. In Doane's words, *Adynata* reveals "the absurdity of the Western desire to grasp . . . the Orient through representation, by creating an image of the Orient that flaunts its own inadequacy."[17] The film's Brechtian distanciation techniques—the use of slow-motion, refilming, a jarring soundtrack, and similar devices—work to render the images suspect and to expose them as quotation, projection, and the product of Western fantasy. One way that Thornton accomplishes this task is through her commentative use of appropriation. *Adynata*'s found and archival footage are not marked as separate from the original images. They are in fact rendered indistinguishable to an

Adynata (Leslie Thornton, 1983). (Courtesy of the filmmaker.)

extent through Thornton's serial form of montage, which relies on associative matches rather than the rules of discursive continuity. If the Truffaut clip and Korean soap opera are "pirated," Thornton seems to say, then so are the seemingly "original" images of herself masquerading in a Chinese wedding costume or the Japanese-inspired landscape shots from the botanical garden. Everything we see has been appropriated or "shanghaied" in some way. The film thereby exposes the fears about Asian piracy and theft that haunt Hollywood cinema.

As I suggested earlier, however, *Adynata* does more than simply reveal the "falseness" of Orientalist imagery and more than simply trace its projections back to their roots in a Western psyche. One could argue that *Adynata* is a film about the very notion of mimetic and iconic signs, or signs based on resemblance, and their persistent association with the Far East, as we have seen in Eisenstein's writings on Japan as well as in the examples of film noir that I cited earlier. The Brechtian alienation-effects Thornton employs, expressing the idea that these images are "just signs," is to some extent undone by the film's visual sumptuousness. These images have an almost tactile quality, rendered with all the immediacy and hyper-presence that cinema is capable of offering. Despite its semiotic layers, *Adynata* presents these ob-

Adynata (Leslie Thornton, 1983). (Courtesy of the filmmaker.)

jects not as thin, denuded signifiers but as richly saturated, colorful, sensual, and visually pleasurable.

Adynata's floral imagery, draping silk fabrics and embroidery, and even the photograph of the Chinese wedding, which is reshot in a number of aura-bestowing close-ups, thus seem to risk reproducing the very exoticism and fetishization of the East that they purport to deconstruct, which is the same exoticism that guests encountered in the simulacral world of Grauman's Chinese Theatre. By taking this risk, however, Thornton enables another kind of critique. With its sumptuous imagery, *Adynata* reminds us that if the bound foot is a primitive, mimetic imitation of nature, lacking in Western rationality, then so is the medium of film itself, to the extent that the West embraces its lure. If we believe that Western words and images fail to express the Orient, as the film's title initially leads us to believe, then perhaps that is because those words and images are less purely Western than we have presumed. That is, perhaps we have overlooked the kernel of alterity—or at least the intricate and lively fantasies that have crystallized around encounters with this alterity—that informs the very bases of the Western cinematic imaginary.

Notes

1. Richard A. Lanham, *A Handlist of Rhetorical Terms* (Berkeley: University of California Press, 1991), 3.

2. See Jean Laplanche, *Essays on Otherness* (New York: Routledge, 1999).

3. Eric Lott, "The Whiteness of Film Noir," *American Literary History* 9, no. 3 (1997): 542–66; Kelly Oliver and Benigno Trigo, *Noir Anxiety* (Minneapolis: University of Minnesota Press, 2003).

4. Grauman's Theatre opened on May 18, 1927, with Cecil B. DeMille's *King of Kings* and was designed by architect Raymond Kennedy for the firm of Meyer and Holler.

5. Antonia Lant analyzes Egyptian motifs in paracinematic culture in "The Curse of the Pharaohs, or How Cinema Contracted Egyptomania," *October* 59 (Winter 1992): 86–112.

6. Terry Helgesen, *Grauman's Chinese Theatre Hollywood* (A Console Feature, 1969), 6.

7. Ibid., 3.

8. Ibid., 24.

9. In 1899, the United States' desire to secure access to Chinese ports and markets culminated in the Open Door Policy, guaranteeing noninterference with treaty ports in the various national concessions. As Akbar Abbas has noted, two of these port cities, Shanghai and Hong Kong, have a curious status, for they are in a sense already Western creations. Shanghai's concessions and extraterritoriality laws and Hong Kong's colonial history suggest that a bewildering series of projections and appropriations that culminate in the notion of the East as "fantastical western construction." See Akbar Abbas, "Cosmopolitan De-scriptions: Shanghai and Hong Kong," *Public Culture* 12, no. 3 (2000): 769–86.

10. For one reading of cinematic Shanghai that addresses Orientalism's relation to gender and sexuality, see Amy Villarejo, "Archiving the Diaspora: A Lesbian Impression of Ulrike Ottinger's *Exile Shanghai,*" *New German Critique* 87 (Autumn 2002): 157–91.

11. Sergei Eisenstein, "The Cinematic Principle and the Ideogram," in *Film Form: Essays in Film Theory,* trans. Jay Leyda (New York: Harcourt Brace Jovanovich, 1977), 28.

12. John DeFrancis, *The Chinese Language: Fact and Fantasy* (Honolulu: University of Hawai'i Press, 1984). Another way of describing this would be to say that Asiatic languages are "symbolic" sign systems rather than "iconic" ones, in Charles Peirce's terms.

13. Rey Chow, "Introduction: On Chineseness as a Theoretical Problem," in *Modern Chinese Literary and Cultural Studies in the Age of Theory: Reimagining a Field,* ed. Rey Chow (Durham, NC: Duke University Press, 2000), 22.

14. Thomas Zummer, "Leslie Thornton," *Senses of Cinema* (November 2002) http://www.sensesofcinema.com/contents/directors/02/thornton.html.

15. Linda Peckham, "Not Speaking with Language/Speaking with No Language: Leslie Thornton's *Adynata,*" in *Psychoanalysis and Cinema,* ed. E. Ann Kaplan (New

York: Routledge, 1990), 182.

16. Mary Ann Doane, "The Retreat of Signs and the Failure of Words: Leslie Thornton's *Adynata*," in *Femmes Fatales: Feminism, Film Theory, Psychoanalysis* (New York: Routledge, 1991), 187.

17. Ibid., 180.

Elizabeth Watkins

Chapter 14

Color and Fluids

The (In)Visibility of *The Portrait of a Lady*

In her essay "Woman's Stake: Filming the Female Body," Mary Ann Doane argues that the production of meaning in cinema echoes the "crucial and complex relation between body and psychic processes, that is, processes of signification," which necessarily engage issues of sexual difference.[1] Just as subjectivity depends on maintaining a fissure between the psyche and the (mother's) body, so cinematic representation depends on a sublimation of the female body into an image or symbol. Thus, even though woman is the quintessential cinematic subject, "there are no images either for her or of her."[2]

In an attempt to reframe the production of meaning in cinema, Doane engages with the work of Luce Irigaray, who grounds a claim for a specifically feminine relation to language in the diffuse sensuousness and multiplicitous eroticism of the female body. Such feminine specificity in, and in excess of, the phallogocentric structure of representation presses upon the formation of meaning in cinematic theories that center on the image of woman. In "The 'Mechanics' of Fluids," Irigaray evokes the fluid to contest the privileging of the scopic.[3] For her, fluids are a residual trace of primary relations to the maternal within the inscription of desire that formulates and organizes the subject's being in and of the visible world. An attention to the body attuned to touch, sound, and sensation as facets of perception integral to vision disturbs the structural linguistic basis of theories of the cinema. Thus Irigaray's work, with its theorization of fluids as the forgotten maternal ground of philosophical and psychoanalytic discourse, opens a space in which to imagine a cinematic theory of female subjectivity.

Becoming a Portrait

In Jane Campion's *The Portrait of a Lady* (1996), the emotional and intellectual intensity of the female characters, and of femininity, is conceived formally in relation to Henry James's novel, whose influence can be traced through screenwriter Laura Jones's visual reworking of his themes and metaphors.[4] An attention to the specificities of James's text reveals its potential for cinematic adaptation; the film's fluidity in movement, constituted through variations in color, shadow, saturation, and transparency, both reflects and refracts Jamesian discourse. Literary theorists have argued for James's elemental imagery of water, light, air, and architecture in *Portrait* as a "making visible" of his character's internal subjective and moral dilemmas.[5] Sarah B. Daugherty, in particular, has suggested that the "instability" of James's metaphors lies in his own conception of the creative process as elemental, in his "reverie of the germ, counseling aspiring authors to be receptive to 'every airborne particle' and to convert the 'very pulses of air into revelations.'"[6]

Daugherty maps James's association of literal and metaphorical inspiration onto protagonist Isabel Archer's journey into Gilbert Osmond's "house of suffocation," identifying imagery evocative of the physical sensations of drowning as a struggle between the vibrant physicality of her body and the risk of becoming the (disembodied) portrait of a lady.[7] A residual trace of this theme can be seen in Campion's film as the fluid movements of the camera follow Isabel's (Nicole Kidman) attentive sorrow for the dying breaths of her uncle, Mr. Touchett (John Gielgud), and the consumptive dissolve of her cousin Ralph Touchett's (Martin Donovan) death. A haze of blue light suggestively connects their illnesses to smoking, registering the sensation of inhalation and exhalation to reinforce a metaphor of suffocation. An analysis of the film's imagery of deliquescence, suffocation, and decay thus engages with the affectivity of cinematographic matter and form in order to discern both the potential and significance of the material fragility of the photographic medium that underlies it.

The visual aspects of James's metaphors, such as the contrasts in light and darkness that mark the ethical and moral dilemmas of his characters, are reflected in Stuart Dryburgh's cinematography. In one sequence, Osmond's daughter Pansy (Valentina Cervi) walks with Isabel in the courtyard, only to stop and observe the edges of the shadow cast by her father's house, which she has been forbidden to cross. A medium close-up of her shoes pressed against the shadow's edge is scored by the disembodied voices of the two young women discussing the interdiction. The distance of her journey is marked by the shadow, but the boundary created by her father's will is internalized and invisible. This sequence emphasizes the effect through contrast: detail is bleached from sections of the image by an excess of light, while shadow and grayscale consume the darker periphery. The film's shallow depth of field creates an allusion to Rembrandt's portraits, in which a recognizable pattern of color and light emerges from, and is conversely constituted by, a pool of darkness.[8] The complex chiaroscuro belies the delineation of the shadow line. The materiality of the film registers the "unseen," operating as a trace of the characters' psychical and somatic processes within and in excess of James's metaphorical boundaries to examine theories of subjectivity and difference in cinema.

While James's novel introduces Isabel through Ralph Touchett's "conscious observation of a lovely woman," Campion's film moves from the prologue, which features young women who appear contemporary to the film's making describing the hopes and encounters of first kisses, to an extreme close-up of Isabel's eyes, reflecting Laura Jones's insistence on Isabel as "the [film's] centre of consciousness."[9] Isabel then traverses an expanse of lawn at the Touchetts' house, Gardencourt. A shot-reverse shot suggests Ralph's observation of Isabel, but as the camera lingers on the image of him, the speed of the film slows, remarking his presence. The slowing of this shot appears to prioritize gendered "to-be-looked-at-ness" only to disturb it. The following shots show Mr. Touchett briefly catching Ralph's act of looking followed by an unexpectedly sharp angle that details Isabel's actions as she lifts a small dog from the ground high into the air. The juxtaposition of these shots returns the point of view to Isabel.

The formal imagery of *Portrait* may be a residue of its literary source, but the staid surface of the film's generic costume drama codes is inflected by distractions. It is permeated by a myriad of reflections and fleeting impressions: the speed of the film varies, a precise schema of color temperature undulates across sequences to demarcate Isabel's progress, while the musical score is threaded with tiny sounds and fragments, of leaves rustling, of the inhalation of breath, of fingers drumming.[10] The complex interrelations of these layers are at first barely perceptible, but a closer, more detailed viewing reveals Campion's intervention in both the narrative of James's novel and also the patterns of representation that are conventional in mainstream cinema.

Refracting Femininity

Portrait is threaded with manifestations of liquids at the level of film image, sound, text, and material, which particularly mark Isabel's relationship with Madame Merle (Barbara Hershey). Throughout the film, Isabel's meetings with Madame Merle are permeated by images of liquids, themes associated with water, fluid movements of the camera, and a sense of fluidity brought about by the special effects that blur subject and object. The configuration of lighting and prisms used during filming to reflect and refract the images produces a liquidity of movement. In certain sequences these effects interact with the residual marks of processing to affect visual clarity. In the sequence where Madame Merle first learns of Isabel's newly inherited wealth from Mrs. Touchett (Shelley Winters), a visual anomaly that "appears to be either a watermark or print damage—traverses down the right side of Hershey's face."[11] This anomaly, occurring at the level of the photographic emulsion and celluloid, manifests, when the DVD is viewed in slow motion, as a series of watermarks, like droplets of fluid on the screened image. In this sequence a horizontal line of distortion also rolls down a close-up shot of Merle. These distortions may occur without design and are specific to the print from which the DVD was taken, but they are synchronous with the moment in the film's narrative when Isabel's wealth instigates Merle's surreptitious intent to influence her future, operating as another facet of the fluidity and movement through which their relationship can be traced.[12] Echoing the viscosity of images of liquids, dust, and smoke prioritized in the visual field by the use of slow-motion sequences of film, the celluloid reveals the touch of the film processing liquids as a visual metaphor.

Toward the end of the film, when Isabel is newly aware of Madame Merle's deceit in seducing her to marry Osmond (John Malkovich), with whom Merle conceived Pansy, the two "mothers" meet, drenched by the night and the rain. Both Isabel and Merle have traveled to the convent in which "their" daughter dwells. The darkness and grain of the film encroaches upon the visibility of the female figures within it, carrying a trace of the processing liquids that mark their relations by signaling a fluidity of shifting constellations of cinematographic elements and deliquescent imagery. Their gestures, clothes, and skin appear to dissolve and emerge from shadows in a movement suggestive of the development of photographic negatives. The air is full of dust that drifts and obfuscates the pale light from the windows. The fluid movements of thousands of particles swirl and pool about the two women, tracing residues of touch in the visual. Prismatically refracted colors trace the tensions of a female subjectivity endlessly drawn through and informed by the dilemma of being mother, daughter, companion, and friend. The air, full of dark shadows, appears heavy and marks the displeasure of their meeting, their suffocation in the presence of each other.

Patterns of light, color, and form are prioritized to destabilize the cinematic determination of woman as image. As Isabel progresses down a corridor, her head turns to gesture her distress. The camera sways uncertainly, as if responsive to the pressures of her body and appears to cause the image to split and then cohere. As the recorded image is refracted through a prism, we see the likeness of her face doubled on the screen through slightly offset traces of light; the form of the secondary image remains less clear. The suddenly visible materiality of the film draws the viewer's attention to its illusionary properties by destabilizing the gaze as the organizing force of onscreen space. The effects of these processes share the visible characteristics of the layering and dissolves that can be found in superimposition, which likewise is not dependent on visual clarity or precise focus.

Fluid (and) Discourse

In *Speculum of the Other Woman,* Irigaray describes the relationship of fluids to the subject of discourse: "The 'subject' identifies himself with/in an almost material consistency that finds everything flowing abhorrent. . . . Not those things in the mother that recall the woman—the flowing things. He cathects these only in a desire to turn them into the self (as same). Every body of water becomes a mirror, every sea, ice."[13] The relationship that is perceived between the image of woman and the solidification of fluids tracks the repression or denial of fluids as the prediscursive ground of philosophy. This freezing and congealing creates a metaphorics of fluids that is external and symmetrical to the (male) subject's solipsistic perception. In this sense, metaphors that congeal fluids into the reflective flat surface of a mirror typify the privileging of the visible in Western philosophical and psychoanalytical discourse. Identified with the cinema screen, the metaphorical flatness of the mirror, in which the subject of discourse identifies himself, is an inappropriate mode for reflecting the diffuse "invisibility" of female sexual organs. Carolyn Burke argues that "man uses woman as a mirror in which he narcissistically seeks his own reflection. Her 'speculum' would permit a different mode of 'specula(riza)tion' curved to the female."[14]

An Irigarayan sense of fluids, which leach and soak through "internal frictions, pressures, movements," de-solidifies and disrupts the philosophical and psychoanalytic subject of the Lacanian mirror stage.[15] Margaret Whitford sees in Irigaray's identification of a female libidinal economy of fluids a move to "initiate the task of revealing and uncovering the female imaginary and bringing it into language."[16] Doane, however, reads Irigaray's association of femininity with the "'real properties of fluids' . . . [as] merely an extension and a mimicking of a patriarchal construction of femininity."[17] Doane's "thematic of liquids" focuses on transitions between sequences effected through match-cuts on images of liquids, such as spillage from a drinking glass, which appear to erode the film's cuts. Doane's thematic accords more to the idealized fluids that Irigaray critiques as part of the suppression of the real properties of fluids. Thus, the sense of fluids that I evoke operates in cinema in relation to the complex interrelations of the elements of light, color, and sound, as they form and exceed the screened image.

An analysis that engages with the physical characteristics of the film, and the residual effects of the photographic in a digital format, does not, however, align female subjectivity with the film text or the body of the film. In her article "This Essentialism Which Is Not One," Naomi Schor writes that to explore fluids as a trace of the maternal body and potential signifying complex through which to theorize the sexual specificity of feminine desire and subjectivity is not an essentialist practice. Schor notes that Irigaray's discourse explores the "fluidity of the feminine" rather than the "femininity of the fluid."[18] That is, she argues that Irigaray's work does not deintellectualize but offers a way grounded in the physical world to theorize issues surrounding femininity so that her work is not one of essentialism but of "radical materialism," offering the physical characteristics of fluids as material for the theorization of a female imaginary.

For theories of subjectivity in film, fluids offer a supplementary paradigm through which to engage with the sexual specificities of female desire. The need here is to theorize difference through a sense of fluids, desire, and the sexual specificities of subjectivity, and through a creative process that does not invoke the division or cut that determines the phallic subject in Lacanian psychoanalysis; it is to discern a trace of the forgotten, of that which is subjugated yet informs the facture and progression of the film. The retention of celluloid and color emulsion as a potential perceptual register variously responsive (active and inactive) to the stimulus of light, liquids, and touch informs the assemblages theorized by Gilles Deleuze and acts as an invitation to affectivity. As a signifying complex for theories of female subjectivity, fluids trace a sense of movement that operates through endlessly shifting configurations of cinematographic elements. For Rebecca Gordon, the making visible of the gendered structures of classical Hollywood cinema in Campion's films at the level of the image, shots, and edits "'shows' the spaces where traditional gender ideology fails, suggesting the places where it has always failed, and thus creating a gap in our film-audience sense of reality."[19] The physical characteristics of fluids are evoked by the interrelations of elemental imagery, camera movement, variations in color and film speed, shifts into close-miking, and the construction of residual sounds to articulate the filmed space.

In *Portrait,* there is a recurring sequence in which Isabel walks directly toward the camera. Through the configuration of movement, sound, bluish color, and distortion, an illusionary space is constructed by the spectator, but it is countered by the closeness of framing and the peripheral darkness of the image. Isabel's image is refracted as she walks, and the two images are partially superimposed; the conventional framing and composition of a portrait blurs in the patterns of light and shadow that form the image and traces a reversal of figure and ground as the undulations of shadow and light that formed an abstract background envelop the image of Isabel. This movement traces a transformation not in matter but in perception and is constituted of the interrelations of light, shadow, color, music, sound, and dialogue, which unfold throughout the film as a "sonorous substance" that "makes the internal rhythm of a scene palpable."[20]

Movement organizes both sound and image, scoring the psychic and somatic processes of subjectivity. Tears seep across the surface of Isabel's skin as we hear her uneven catch of breath, her body shuddering with the carefully subdued sounds of weeping. Isabel's head turns in quiet conversation with herself while each step through the darkness of the corridor is traced by the soft rustle of the thread and weave of her dress as it unfolds, brushing against itself according to her movements. This composite is threaded through with the barely perceptible sounds of the distress that wracks Isabel's body and layered with the resonance of string instruments.

Wojciech Kilar, who composed the film's score, states that the repetition of the music in *Portrait* was formed through the "calls" of two instruments: "First the violins play, then the violas reply. Then lower instruments play first and higher ones, violins, respond."[21] Through this response "an unheard emotion is attained" that describes the sensuous interactions of the film's images as they flow into the music, creating the texture of the film's soundtrack.[22] For Kilar, this musical texture is evoked by and evokes color: "What affects me primarily is the image. That dark color of the images—that this film is rendered in these dark browns and dark greens—this flowed into the character of the music."[23] Informed by the poetic function of Jamesian metaphors of light and shadow, cinematographic color participates in and exceeds the relations of subject and object, figure and ground. The rhythm of the visual and aural participates in the formation of the narrative and signals a trace of the film's material base. *Portrait*'s conjunction of cinematographic color and sound offers a response to Whitford's call for the "formation of a female imaginary" that can be theorized in terms of difference beyond the alienation and division of a Lacanian model of subjectivity.

A Discourse of Color and Fluids

In "The Intertwining—the Chiasm," Maurice Merleau-Ponty theorizes the phenomenon of color as an analogy of the subject's being in and of the visible world. The perception of color is not entirely attributable to light, to the material that reflects, refracts, or absorbs it, nor to the perceiving subject, he argues, but is dependent upon their interrelations. An alteration in density or a textured surface reflects or refracts light; the perception of color and visibility is informed by the material object. In "The Invisible of the Flesh," Luce Irigaray identifies the invisible within Merleau-Ponty's definition of the visible in "The Intertwining—the Chiasm" as a tactile prediscursive ground of subjectivity to draw out the forgotten and suppressed sexual difference in his work.[24] Irigaray traces the shared characteristics of the phenomena of color and fluids: color is not solely attributable to the subject's memories or knowledge, nor to the objects and the world that the subject inhabits, but is a way of being in and of the visible world that for Irigaray carries a trace of a tactile prediscursive relation to the maternal. *Portrait* opens a space in which to theorize the phenomenon of color in relation to fluids and the intertwining of the subject and visible world.

Following Irigaray, Elizabeth Grosz argues that the phenomenon of color shares some of the characteristics of fluids: "In confronting color, the subject is not confronted with a 'pellicle' or atom of being but with a field of differences—differences between colors, shapes, and textures and differences between colors and that which is colored. As Irigaray notes, color here must function as a fluidity; it presumes a metaphorics of the tactile and the feminine."[25] Color is not severed from its material ground or from the (in)visible of the maternal feminine. In *Portrait* color operates as one of the many elements that trace Isabel's subjectivity and desires as she negotiates the perceptible and concealed complexity of the relationships, vagaries of wealth, and ethical dilemmas that surround her. The minutiae of timbre and tone, the spill of light are reminiscent of, and draw attention to, the brushing warmth of air among leaves and of footsteps in the snow.

The movements elicited through the intertwining of variations in color saturation and transparency with the differences in volume, timbre, and clarity draw attention to certain sounds, such as the physicality of breathing within speech, that are associated primarily with Isabel's subjectivity. Rather than suturing the viewer through a succession of point-of-view shots, the viewer is connected to Isabel by the repeated illusion of the film's frame as a surface of refraction rather than reflection. When Isabel suspects that Pansy is in love with Ned Rosier (Christian Bale), whose financial standing is viewed unfavorably by Osmond, Isabel intervenes in Osmond's arrangements for Pansy's marriage, offering her the chance to influence the path her life might take beyond that of exchange between her father and his favored suitor, the wealthy Lord Warburton (Richard E. Grant). When Isabel and Pansy discuss the two conflicting proposals of marriage, Pansy leans close to Isabel's lap, the warmth of the firelight flickering across their skin and filling the air with transient shadows.

Surrounding their discussion are close-ups of each woman—first Isabel, then Pansy—as they move through the room crossing each other's paths. The instability of the fire's flickering sepia light falling across uneven panels of heavy, textured fabric confuses and thus draws attention to the shots' elision of onscreen space. The textural sensuousness is drawn out through the circular, disorienting turn of the camera, resulting in variations in color and intensity. When the effects of the prism are seen, they take on these fluid characteristics, embodying the mottled layers and fluvial form of this conversational space. A residual, ghostlike image of Isabel's face ripples beside her, caught for a moment through the illusionary touch of warmth registering in the film image in catches of color and light. Cinematographic color in particular is susceptible to the fluidity of these movements, allowing details and elements to emerge and dissolve through variations in the activation of a sensitive scheme of emulsion.

The refraction of Isabel's appearance is not only saturated with the sensuous properties of light, color, and warmth but also refuses the simple reversal of a flat mirror reflection. The faint image of Isabel is seen as a replica, adjacent and identical in its movements, rather than the inverse image of a mirror. In this sense Isabel is not objectified by the camera's framing, but the dual image is suggested as a resistance to and engagement with the visible world in all its possibilities. There is no fixed surface to this "mirror"; instead, variations in mottled colors and undulations between figure and ground invoke the relation of viewer and visible world, of sensed and sensible.

En l'air

The muted coloration of many sequences that evoke the sensuous and corporeal facets of Isabel's subjectivity can be traced throughout *The Piano* (Jane Campion, 1993), which was also shot by Dryburgh, as prescient of protagonist Ada McGrath's near-drowning. Campion has spoken of this coloration as evoking a "kind of underwater world."[26] In *Portrait* and *The Piano* this coloration is linked to suffocation and the potential of the environment to overwhelm its inhabitants. Jane Dapkus identifies a chain of images in the

1908 version of James's *Portrait* that is comparable to the liquid imagery of Ada's near-drowning.[27] The final sequence of the novel (and of the film) finds Isabel mourning in the grounds of Gardencourt, where her implacable suitor, Caspar Goodwood (Viggo Mortensen), persists in his attentions. The paragraph Dapkus highlights details Isabel's response to their kiss. The most notable of James's revisions to the 1881 text emphasizes the physical and visual properties of water as metaphors of Isabel's emotional and intellectual expression. James elaborates the sounds that Isabel hears "swimming" in her head and alludes to an indeterminate myth of those who "wrecked and underwater" follow a "train of images as thoughts and reminiscences towards death."[28] As James seeks to evoke the desires of a young woman, he turns to imagery of water and death.

In Campion's adaptation Isabel's moment of complicity and passion in a kiss resonates with threads that spill from the hopes, desires, and apprehensions first encountered through the subjective force of the young women's voice-overs in the film's prologue. Echoing the prologue, dialogue throughout the film touches upon the shifting relationships between the female characters. Aspects of the prologue—particularly fragmentary echoes of its score and its visual effects of black-and-white and slow motion—recur throughout the film to produce a subtle and disquieting effect, prioritizing a discourse of color, refiguring thematic patterns, and shaping the reading of the film's conclusion.

The kiss is one of two possible cumulative points that Campion envisaged for the film's ending.[29] Both scenes were filmed, and the one excluded from the final edit of the film is retained in Jones's published screenplay. The sequence Campion cut shows Isabel returning to Pansy in Rome, whereas James's novel deliberately leaves his heroine *en l'air*, offering to the reader only the suggestion of a "very straight path" back to Rome.[30] Jones's written version of the scene maintains the film's familiar imagery as she describes Isabel reaching out to Pansy, her hands stretching toward her through a pool of light.[31] Once acknowledged as a subtext, this scene informs another possible reading of the film's ending as screened.

The final sequence is structured by three close-ups, which orientate the viewer's attention: one of entangled branches surrounded by mist, one that follows the movements of Isabel's skirt as it flays a dust of ice from the ground, and one of sepia light filtering through the doors of Gardencourt. Each of these three images recalls Deleuze's affection-image, resonating with moments from deep within the film, such as the suffusion of sepia light that can be traced to the conversational space between Pansy and Isabel. Colors and close-ups evoke the illusion of memory, recalling the threads of Isabel's

204

journey and suggesting her ability to drive the narrative as an internal force through her interrelations with various filmic configurations. In these close-ups, subjectivity and embodied consciousness constitute and are constituted by the pressures of fluid movement within the film while also sustaining residual color as the ground of the visible. Not bound by the final image of the film, Isabel Archer, her hand on the latch, hesitates and turns in a movement toward the absent final scene, which carries the threads of the conversational space that unfolded between Pansy, herself, and the film.

This conversational space of gestures and expressions between various layers of the film indicates the potential of fluids in the imagination and formation of a female morphology. The formation of cinematographic meaning through the fluid play of color as the image of something real has psychic and somatic significance for theories of female subjectivity. *Portrait* leads us beyond the potential representation of fluids at the level of the film's image and narrative toward that which can be discerned moving within and in excess of the multiple levels of the film. Through the fluid, Irigaray calls for a transformation in the relation between matter and form that presses upon the surge and dissolve of affect and desire. Transformation effectively contributes to the theory of a fluid ground for film, which offers material for the theorization of a form of sensate subjectivity as a force that can permeate, drive, and disrupt the film's narrative. Fluids as theorized by Irigaray are not actualized as objects but surge between the multiple layers of the film to press upon and transform embodied consciousness as they spill from embodied perception.

Notes

1. Mary Ann Doane, "Woman's Stake: Filming the Female Body," in *Psychoanalytic Criticism: A Reader,* ed. Sue Vice (Cambridge, UK: Polity, 1996), 203.

2. Ibid., 196.

3. Luce Irigaray, "The 'Mechanics' of Fluids," in *This Sex Which Is Not One* [1977], trans. Catherine Porter and Caroline Burke (Ithaca, NY: Cornell University Press, 1996), 106–8.

4. Henry James's *The Portrait of a Lady* was first published in 1881. This article refers primarily to the revised New York edition, published in 1908 with an introduction by James.

5. See Jane Dapkus, "Sloughing off Burdens: Parallel/Antithetical Quests for Self-Actualization in Jane Campion's *The Piano* and Henry James' *The Portrait of a Lady,*" *Literature/Film Quarterly* 25, no. 3 (1997): 177–87; Rebecca M. Gordon, "Portraits Perversely Framed: Jane Campion and Henry James," *Film Quarterly* 56, no. 2 (2002): 14–24; Clair M. Hughes, "The Color of Life: The Significance of

Dress in *The Portrait of a Lady,*" *The Henry James Review* 18, no. 1 (1997): 66–80.

6. Sarah B. Daugherty, "James and the Ethics of Control: Aspiring Architects and Their Floating Creatures," in *Enacting History in Henry James: Narrative Power and Ethics,* ed. Gert Buelens (New York: Cambridge University Press, 1997), 62.

7. Ibid., 69.

8. Geoff Andrew, "The Lady Vanquishes: An Interview with Jane Campion," *Time Out* 1382 (February 12, 1997): 25.

9. Nancy Bentley, "'Conscious Observation of a Lovely Woman': Jane Campion's *Portrait of a Lady,*" in *Henry James Goes to the Movies,* ed. Susan M. Griffin (Lexington: University Press of Kentucky, 2002), 127; Laura Jones, *The Portrait of a Lady* (script including call sheets donated by Roger Ashton Griffiths to the British Film Institute Library, Stephen Street, London, 2006), vi.

10. Ric Gentry, "Painterly Touches," *American Cinematographer* 78, no. 1 (1997): 57.

11. DVD Net review, *The Portrait of a Lady* (Jane Campion, 1996), http://www.dvd.net.au/review.cgi?review_id=634. This review relates to the Region 4 DVD release; the watermarks and distortion are also visible in this sequence on the Universal 2001 Region 2 DVD release.

12. These watermarks do not appear to be visible on the Universal VHS video tape of *The Portrait of a Lady* made for UK distribution.

13. Luce Irigaray, "Volume—Fluidity," in *Speculum of the Other Woman* [1974], trans. Gillian C. Gill (Ithaca, NY: Cornell University Press, 1985), 237.

14. Carolyn Burke, "Introduction to Luce Irigaray's 'When Our Lips Speak Together,'" *Signs* 6, no. 1 (1980): 71.

15. Irigaray, "The 'Mechanics' of Fluids," 109.

16. Margaret Whitford, "Luce Irigaray and the Female Imaginary: Speaking as Woman," *Radical Philosophy* 43 (1986): 3.

17. Mary Ann Doane, *The Desire to Desire: The Woman's Film of the 1940s* (Bloomington: Indiana University Press, 1987), 104.

18. Naomi Schor, "This Essentialism Which Is Not One: Coming to Grips with Irigaray," in *Engaging with Irigaray,* ed. Carolyn Burke, Margaret Whitford, and Naomi Schor (New York: Columbia University Press, 1994), 57–78.

19. Gordon, "Portraits Perversely Framed," 15.

20. Maurice Merleau-Ponty, "Film and the New Psychology," in *Sense and Non-Sense* [1964], trans. H. L. Dreyfus and P. A. Dreyfus (Evanston, IL: Northwestern University Press, 1982), 49.

21. Mark G. So, "Lost Issue Wednesday: Wojciech Kilar Interview," *Film Score Monthly* (July 11, 2001), http://www.filmscoremonthly.com/articles/2001/04_Jul—-Lost_Issue_Wojciech_Kilar_Part_One.asp.

22. Ibid.

23. Kilar also confirms that for him there are certain "psycho-coloristic" connections with certain sounds and with the instruments that produce them and in doing so evokes a relationship that could be described in terms of synaesthesia.

24. Luce Irigaray, "The Invisible of the Flesh: A Reading of Merleau-Ponty, *The Visible and the Invisible,* 'The Intertwining—The Chiasm,'" in *An Ethics of Sexual*

Difference [1984], trans. Caroline Burke and Gillian C. Gill (London: Athlone, 1993), 153–83.

25. Elizabeth Grosz, "Lived Bodies: Phenomenology and the Flesh," in *Volatile Bodies: Toward a Corporeal Feminism* (Bloomington: Indiana University Press, 1994), 104.

26. Mary Cantwell, "Jane Campion's Lunatic Women: Interview" [1993], in *Jane Campion: Interviews,* ed. Virginia Wright Wexman (Jackson: University Press of Mississippi, 1999), 161.

27. Dapkus, "Sloughing off Burdens," 177–87.

28. Henry James, *The Portrait of a Lady* [New York Edition 1908] (London: Penguin, 2003), 635–36.

29. Laura Jones, *The Portrait of a Lady: The Screenplay Based on the Novel by Henry James* (London: Penguin 1997), viii.

30. James, *Portrait,* 640, 636.

31. Jones, *Portrait*, 133–34.

CONTRIBUTORS

KAY ARMATAGE is a professor at the Cinema Studies Institute and the Institute for Women's Studies and Gender Studies, University of Toronto. She is the author of *The Girl from God's Country: Nell Shipman and the Silent Cinema* (University of Toronto Press, 2003) and co-editor of *Gendering the Nation: Canadian Women's Cinema* (University of Toronto Press, 1999). She has made seven films (1975–86) and worked as an international programmer for the Toronto International Film Festival (1982–2004). Her current research is on women's film festivals.

MELINDA BARLOW is an associate professor of film studies at the University of Colorado, Boulder, where she received the Boulder Faculty Assembly Excellence in Teaching Award, the Gold Best Should Teach Award, and the Dorothy Martin Woman Faculty Member Award. Professor Barlow is a film and video historian and art critic who researches the work of independent, living women film- and video-makers and writes about and gives workshops on the art of mentoring women. The editor of *Mary Lucier: Art and Performance* (Johns Hopkins University Press, 2000) and the author of *Lost Objects of Desire: Video Installation, Mary Lucier, and the Romance of History* (forthcoming from the University of Minnesota Press), Professor Barlow is currently working on a book of essays on experimental filmmaker and theater artist Janie Geiser.

VIRGINIA BONNER is an associate professor of film and media studies at Clayton State University in metropolitan Atlanta. She earned her master's degree in art history from the University of Florida and her doctorate in film studies and women's studies from Emory University. She regularly presents papers internationally and for local arts organizations and curates film festivals in the Atlanta area. Her current book manuscript focuses on intersections among avant-garde, feminist, and documentary cinemas—particularly as these modes of filmmaking converge in Left Bank films by Chris Marker, Alain Resnais, and Agnès Varda; she has also published several articles on these filmmakers.

CONTRIBUTORS

MICHELLE CITRON is an award-winning media artist whose work includes the films *Daughter Rite* and *What You Take for Granted . . .* , and the interactive narratives *As American as Apple Pie, Cocktails and Appetizers,* and *Mixed Greens.* She has received grants from the NEA, NEH, and Illinois Arts Council. Her work has been shown at the Museum of Modern Art, the Whitney, the Walker Art Center, the MCA/Chicago, and the American Film Institute, as well as the New Directors, Berlin, London, Edinburgh, SeNef Seoul Net, VAD Festival Internacional de Video I Arts Digital, and Viper film/media festivals. She is the author of the award winning book *Home Movies and Other Necessary Fictions.* She is chair of the Department of Interdisciplinary Arts at Columbia College in Chicago.

CORINN COLUMPAR is an assistant professor of cinema studies and English at the University of Toronto, where she regularly teaches courses on film theory, women's cultural production, various counter-cinematic traditions (especially feminist, Aboriginal, and "independent"), and corporeality and representation. Her work has appeared in a wide variety of anthologies and journals, including *Women's Studies Quarterly, refractory,* and *Quarterly Review of Film and Video.* Her book *Unsettling Sights: The Fourth World on Film* is forthcoming from Southern Illinois University Press.

ALISON HOFFMAN is pursuing her PhD in cinema and media studies at the University of California, Los Angeles. Her dissertation, "Our Bodies, Our Cameras: Women's Experimental Cinema in the U.S. 1963–1976," positions itself at the intersection of women's film and video, the avant-garde, American popular culture of the sixties and seventies, and contemporary (post-)punk feminism. She has published work in anthologies and in periodicals such as *Film Quarterly, PopMatters,* and *Girlfriends Magazine.* She is also an independent film and video curator.

THERESA L. GELLER is the EKI Assistant Professor of Film Studies at Grinnell College. Her dissertation, "Generic Subversions: De-Formations of Character in the Popular Imagination," rethinks film genre in terms of queer and multicultural epistemology. A chapter from her dissertation was recently anthologized in *East Asian Cinemas,* while another chapter, "Queering Hollywood's Tough Chick," appeared in *Frontiers.* Her research on women filmmakers is represented by her contribution to *Senses of Cinema* on Dorothy Arzner and her feminist historiography, "The Personal Cinema of Maya Deren: *Meshes of the Afternoon* and Its Critical Reception in the History of the Avant-Garde," published in *Biography.* Geller's chapter "The Film-Work Does Not Think: Re-Figuring Fantasy for Feminist Film Theory," published in *Gender after Lyotard,* and her essay "The Cinematic Relations of Corporeal Feminism," included in a special issue of *Rhizomes,* represent her ongoing research at the intersections of feminist-queer inquiry and film theory.

CHLOÉ HOPE JOHNSON earned her master's degree in cinema studies at the University of Melbourne, Australia. Her research interests include minority cultures, alternative music scenes, contemporary feminist, critical, and sound theories, and experimental screen studies. She is a contributor to the anthology on women in music *Singing for Themselves: Essays on Women in Popular Music* (Cambridge Scholars Press, 2007).

HOMAY KING is an associate professor in the Department of History of Art and Program in Film Studies at Bryn Mawr College. Her writings have appeared in *Film Quarterly, Camera Obscura, Discourse,* and *The Quarterly Review of Film and Video.* She has published essays on films by Ulrike Ottinger, Michelangelo Antonioni, and Andy Warhol. Her book *Lost in Translation: Orientalism, Projection, and the Enigmatic Signifier* is forthcoming from Duke University Press.

SOPHIE MAYER has taught at the Universities of Toronto, where she received her PhD on feminist film poetics, and Cambridge, where she was a Mellon Postdoctoral Fellow in the Screen Media and Cultures M.Phil. program. She writes for film magazines *Sight and Sound, Vertigo,* and *Little White Lies;* her academic work has appeared or is forthcoming in *Literature/Film Quarterly, reconstruction, Screen, Studies in American Indian Literature,* and *SubStance.* She is the author of *The Cinema of Sally Potter: A Politics of Love* (Wallflower, 2009) and two collections of poetry, *Her Various Scalpels* (Shearsman, 2009) and *The Private Parts of Girls* (Salt, forthcoming).

MICHELLE MEAGHER is an assistant professor of women's studies at the University of Alberta, where she teaches in the area of feminist cultural studies, with emphases on popular culture and visual culture. She is broadly interested in self-representational practices and is currently engaged in a research project that examines how such practices have been taken up by contemporary feminist artists. Her work on Cindy Sherman has appeared in *Women: A Cultural Review, Body and Society,* and *Woman's Art Journal.*

SF SAID has written extensively on cinema for *The Daily Telegraph, Sight and Sound,* and *Vertigo.* His articles include interviews with filmmakers from around the world, major film festival reports, and investigative pieces on emerging trends in cinema. He has served as a program consultant for the Edinburgh International Film Festival and the Institute of Contemporary Arts in London, programming work from countries including Iran, France, China, and Canada. He is the author of the novels *Varjak Paw* (2003) and *The Outlaw Varjak Paw* (2005), which have won many awards, including the BBC Blue Peter Book of the Year for *Outlaw.*

ELIZABETH WATKINS recently completed a British Academy Postdoctoral Fellowship at the University of Leeds, UK, on the significance of color and of the characteristics of the film as material (transparency, saturation, glare, deterioration, and fading) for theories of subjectivity and desire in cinema. She has published in *Parallax* and *Paragraph* and has contributed to collections including *Questions of Colour in Cinema*, edited by Wendy Everett (Peter Lang, 2007), drawing from research on Luce Irigaray and cinema, feminism, and the instabilities of the "film object." She is a visiting research fellow at AHRC Centre CATH at the University of Leeds, and a researcher at the University of Bristol, UK.

Index

abjection, 21, 144

Aboriginal characters, 150, 153–57

abortion, 4–5, 94

aca-fans, 7, 14, 14n13

accented cinema, 153. *See also* postcoloniality

access: to experimental films by women, 24; to media, 12

Acker, Kathy, 1

adaptation, cinematic, 13, 40–43, 196–97, 204

adolescence: and activism, 110, 114, 117–18; and agency, 166, 167, 169, 173; and change, 166, 168; and desire, 149, 167, 181, 197; as excess, 13–14, 181; and filmmaking, 12, 163–65, 168–69, 173–78; and hope, 31, 167, 174, 204; and mass media, 174, 176–77; as outsider status, 173–74, 176, 181; and resistance, 13, 150, 164, 175; and school, 109, 112, 164, 166, 168–69, 174–75, 176; and subcultures, 179; and touch, 30; and voice, 14, 114, 164, 175. *See also* becoming: -grrrl; sexuality: adolescent

Adventures of Kathlyn, The (Francis J. Grandon), 53

adynata, 185

aesthetics. *See* feminist film theory: and aesthetics

affect, 13; in cinema, 22, 62, 196, 200; and the film scholar, 26; as interrelational, 28–31, 149, 153; lack

of, 143–44; as political, 5, 9, 26, 31, 51, 61; produced by artists, 173; and tears, 23, 34, 201; and touch, 26, 27. *See also* digital technology: and affect; 9/11: affective response to; spectatorship: affective; video art: and affect

affection-image, 204

Afghanistan, 12, 164, 165, 167, 168, 170

African women, 107, 109–15

agency, spectatorial: and affect, 172–73, 176, 178; as collaborative, 172; as embodied, 19, 151–52; and community, 124–25, 128, 180–81; and interactivity, 8, 9, 23, 25, 47; and openness, 25, 27, 125; as political, 5, 9, 10–11, 58, 124; producing "viewers," 7, 68; through queering, 176, 178; solicited by film, 83, 120, 122–23, 128, 130, 154; and temporality, 151. *See also* audience; Longinotto, Kim: and spectatorial agency; spectatorship

age, 11, 71, 74, 156, 175. *See also* Varda, Agnès: and aging

Akerman, Chantal, 98–99; *Hotel Monterey,* 98; *Je, tu, il, elle,* 98; *Jeanne Dielman,* 98; *News from Home,* 98; *Toute une Nuit,* 98

Allison, Dorothy, 180

alterity, 185, 186, 187, 192. *See also* difference

Althusser, Louis, 123